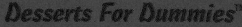

Thinking Ahead As a Dessert Cook

Before tackling a recipe, read it slowly and thoroughly. Do you have all the ingredients necessary? If so, set them out on the counter. If you're missing an ingredient, consider a substitute. Also, if the recipe calls for a piece of kitchen equipment that you don't have, stop before you go too far down the line. Consider whether you can do the job with another tool. In addition:

✔ **Read through all the techniques called for in the recipe, such as folding, whisking, crimping, and so on.** Are you comfortable with them? If not, check out the index in this book and flip to the cited pages to find out how to do these tasks.

✔ **How long will a recipe take to make, including cooking time? Do you have that much time?** Always give yourself more time than the recipe calls for, especially if it's your first time through.

✔ **Look at the recipe a second time and ask yourself: "Does this dessert sound appealing?"** If a recipe captures your interest and gets you salivating just by reading it, chances are you'll do a better job making it.

✔ **Think about whether the dessert is appropriate to follow the main course.** In general (and there are many exceptions), contrasting textures and flavors is the rule; for example, you want light and refreshing desserts after a heavy meal, and vice versa.

✔ **Think seasonally.** Are fresh berries in season? If so, use them. Is it apple season? The fresher the produce, the better.

✔ **Always count how many diners you need to feed before taking on a recipe.** You may need to try a different recipe or increase your proportions. There is nothing worse – or more embarrassing – than coming up short.

✔ **You can double most dessert recipes in this book by simply multiplying each ingredient by two and following the instructions.** If necessary, do your mixing in batches.

✔ **Always check cakes and tarts a few minutes before they're supposed to be done.** You can always put them back in, but ovens don't have a reverse gear.

✔ **Clean up as you go along, both for safety reasons (to minimize bacteria infection) and for organizational reasons (clutter is confusing).** Wash your hands before cooking.

✔ **Have all your most-used tools – whisks, measuring cups, wooden spoons, and so on – within easy reach.**

Happy Dessert Marriages

This . . .	Tastes Great with This . . .
Anise	Raisins or licorice-type desserts; often used alone.
Apple	Cinnamon, lemon, nutmeg, and vanilla; apples do not go well with chocolate.
Apricot	Almonds, a classic combination.
Banana	Chocolate, nutmeg, and caramel.
Cinnamon	Apples, persimmons, cranberries, pears, and other fruits.
Coconut	Chocolate (cookies and cakes), bananas, pineapples, and other tropical desserts.
Coffee	Chocolate, ice cream, and all kinds of nut desserts.
Ginger	Fruits of all kinds and cookies. Be wary of overusing it.
Honey	Lemon, saffron, nuts, and bananas.
Lavender	White chocolate.
Lemon	Almost everything, especially ripe fruits and custards.
Mint	Chocolate (as in chocolate mousse and chocolate sauces), ripe summer fruits like pears and berries, and ice cream.
Nutmeg	Egg custards, nut-based desserts, and vanilla, among many other flavors; another potentially overwhelming flavor.
Orange	Chocolate, mint, and vanilla.
Pineapple	Brown sugar and molasses.
Pumpkin	Chocolate, cinnamon, and nutmeg.
Berry	balsamic vinegar, mint.
Vanilla	Ice creams, tropical fruits, and chocolate, to name a few.

Temperature conversions

°F	°C
250	120
275	135
300	150
325	160
350	175
375	190
400	205
425	220
450	230
475	245

Common Abbreviations

Abbreviation	What It Means
C, c	cup
g	gram
kg	kilogram
L, l	liter
lb	pound
mL, ml	milliliter
oz	ounce
pt	pint
t, tsp	teaspoon
T, TB, Tbl, Tbsp	tablespoon

Food equivalents

3 medium apples or bananas = approximately 1 pound or 500 g

1 ounce baking chocolate = 1 square or 28 g

2 slices bread = 1 cup fresh bread crumbs or 250 mL

1 pound brown sugar = 2 cups packed or 550 mL packed

4 tablespoons butter = ½ stick or 50 to 60 mL

8 tablespoons butter = 1 stick or 125 mL

4 sticks butter = 1 pound or 454 g

1 pound confectioners' sugar = 4½ cups sifted or 1.125 L sifted

1 pound granulated sugar = 2 cups or 500 mL

½ pound hard cheese = approximately 2 cups grated or 500 mL grated

1 cup heavy cream = 2 cups whipped or 500 mL whipped

1 medium lemon = 3 tablespoons juice or 45 mL juice (10 to 15 mL)

1 cup raw converted rice = 4 cups cooked or 1 L cooked

1 pint strawberries = approximately 2 cups sliced or 500 mL sliced

1 pound all-purpose flour = 4 cups sifted or 1 L sifted

5 large whole eggs = 1 cup or 250 mL

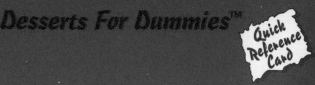

Desserts For Dummies™

Quick Reference Card

BUSINESS AND GENERAL REFERENCE BOOK SERIES FROM IDG

Dessert-Making Timesavers

Follow these timesaving tips:

- Make a double batch of pie dough and keep unused portion in the freezer.

- For easier defrosting, transfer frozen doughs and crusts to the refrigerator the night before.

- Royal icing — 2 cups (8 ounces) confectioners' sugar, 1 egg white, and a few drops of lemon juice stirred together — makes for a quick and easy frosting for cookies or cakes. You can color it with food colorings. Wrapped, it lasts for a month.

- Make fruit purées in season from ripe fruit and store in airtight containers in the freezer (for up to six months).

- For a quick chocolate decoration, scrape the blade of a chef's knife over the surface of a bittersweet chocolate bar to make chocolate curls.

- Make large batches of candied orange and lemon rind. Store in their sugar syrup, refrigerated. They make nice, quick garnishes for desserts of all kinds.

- Lemons and oranges at room temperature yield more juice than cold ones. Also, to make juicing faster and easier, roll them on a countertop while pressing down with your palm.

- Use parchment paper or aluminum foil on cookie sheets to time cleaning up butter.

- Room-temperature egg whites froth up faster than cold ones.

- Add a pinch of cream of tartar to egg whites as they begin to froth for a faster and smoother meringue.

IDG BOOKS WORLDWIDE

...For Dummies: Bestselling Book Series for Beginners

Praise for Desserts For Dummies

"In the world of professional baking, Mr. Yosses is known to teach well, peers and novices alike, with the right mixture of discipline and creativity. With his book *Desserts For Dummies,* this well-known pastry chef, with Mr. Miller's guidance and experience, breaks down the intricacies of baking and pastry into methodical and understandable steps. He takes the fundamental recipes and plays with them to create myriad variations. The chapters on setting up a kitchen and basic work habits are invaluable to anybody that aspires to make wonderful, delicate pastries without leaving the kitchen in a horrific state once its all done.

With this book, Chef Yosses and Mr. Miller will help anyone who is afraid of baking but has always been enchanted by this mysterious and rewarding art."

— Markus Farbinger
Professor and Team Leader for Curriculum and Instruction
in Baking and Pastry Arts
The Culinary Institute of America

"A good chef, like a good writer, knows not only what to put in, but just as important, what to leave out. Bill Yosses and Bryan Miller don't weigh you down with excess facts yet they satisfy your need to know. With their guidance, making desserts is almost as enjoyable as tasting the results."

— William N. Reynolds,
Vice President Continuing Education,
The Culinary Institute of America

Praise for William Yosses

"What an extraordinary pastry chef! I wish he would have been one of my teachers!"

— Dieter Schorner, Chairman, Pastry Arts Program at The French Culinary Institute, Manhattan, NY, and Owner of Café Didier in Georgetown, Washington, D.C.

"The new Bouley Bakery, with its vaulted ceiling, green velvet chairs, and colorful flowers, is the prettiest restaurant I've been in this summer, a cool quiet space I'd be happy to spend time in. . . . The desserts are delicious."

— *The New York Times*

Praise for Bryan Miller

"Everybody in the food business, and a lot who aren't, knows Bryan Miller . . ."

— Jim Quinn, *Town & Country Magazine*

"Miller's lively writing style . . . is one of *The Times'* sparkiest features . . ."

— James Reginato, *W Magazine*

Praise for Cooking For Dummies

"Cooking — like anything — must be fun and should not be taken too seriously. Seasoned with Bryan Miller's hilarious sense of humor, *Cooking For Dummies* helps us do just that."

— Ferdinand Metz, President, The Culinary Institute of America

"The recipes for 'Dummies' are so delicious I felt compelled to eat the book."

— Robert Klein, Actor and Comedian

"Too often cookbooks are sanctimonious, but in *Cooking For Dummies,* the table is a fun place. It will nourish your tummy as well as your humor."

— Jacques Pépin, Chef and Author

™

References for the Rest of Us!™

BUSINESS AND GENERAL REFERENCE BOOK SERIES FROM IDG

Do you find that traditional reference books are overloaded with technical details and advice you'll never use? Do you postpone important life decisions because you just don't want to deal with them? Then our *...For Dummies*™ business and general reference book series is for you.

...For Dummies business and general reference books are written for those frustrated and hard-working souls who know they aren't dumb, but find that the myriad of personal and business issues and the accompanying horror stories make them feel helpless. *...For Dummies* books use a lighthearted approach, a down-to-earth style, and even cartoons and humorous icons to diffuse fears and build confidence. Lighthearted but not lightweight, these books are perfect survival guides to solve your everyday personal and business problems.

> **"More than a publishing phenomenon, 'Dummies' is a sign of the times."**
> — *The New York Times*

> **"...you won't go wrong buying them."**
> — *Walter Mossberg, Wall Street Journal, on IDG's ...For Dummies™ books*

> **"A world of detailed and authoritative information is packed into them..."**
> — *U.S. News and World Report*

Already, millions of satisfied readers agree. They have made *...For Dummies* the #1 introductory level computer book series and a best-selling business book series. They have written asking for more. So, if you're looking for the best and easiest way to learn about business and other general reference topics, look to *...For Dummies* to give you a helping hand.

™

IDG BOOKS
WORLDWIDE

5/97

DESSERTS
FOR
DUMMIES™

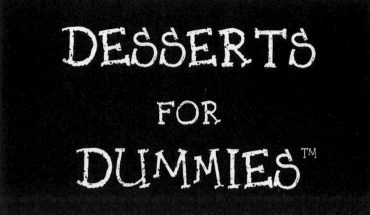

by Bill Yosses
and
Bryan Miller

IDG Books Worldwide, Inc.
An International Data Group Company

Foster City, CA ♦ Chicago, IL ♦ Indianapolis, IN ♦ Southlake, TX

Desserts for Dummies™

Published by
IDG Books Worldwide, Inc.
An International Data Group Company
919 E. Hillsdale Blvd.
Suite 400
Foster City, CA 94404
www.idgbooks.com (IDG Books Worldwide Web site)
www.dummies.com (Dummies Press Web site)

Library of Congress Catalog Card No.: 97-80180

ISBN: 0-7645-5047-0

Printed in the United States of America

10 9 8 7 6 5 4 3 2

1B/QV/RR/ZX/IN

Distributed in the United States by IDG Books Worldwide, Inc.

Distributed by Macmillan Canada for Canada; by Transworld Publishers Limited in the United Kingdom; by IDG Norge Books for Norway; by IDG Sweden Books for Sweden; by Woodslane Pty. Ltd. for Australia; by Woodslane Enterprises Ltd. for New Zealand; by Longman Singapore Publishers Ltd. for Singapore, Malaysia, Thailand, and Indonesia; by Simron Pty. Ltd. for South Africa; by Toppan Company Ltd. for Japan; by Distribuidora Cuspide for Argentina; by Livraria Cultura for Brazil; by Ediciencia S.A. for Ecuador; by Addison-Wesley Publishing Company for Korea; by Ediciones ZETA S.C.R. Ltda. for Peru; by WS Computer Publishing Corporation, Inc., for the Philippines; by Unalis Corporation for Taiwan; by Contemporanea de Ediciones for Venezuela; by Computer Book & Magazine Store for Puerto Rico; by Express Computer Distributors for the Caribbean and West Indies. Authorized Sales Agent: Anthony Rudkin Associates for the Middle East and North Africa.

For general information on IDG Books Worldwide's books in the U.S., please call our Consumer Customer Service department at 800-762-2974. For reseller information, including discounts and premium sales, please call our Reseller Customer Service department at 800-434-3422.

For information on where to purchase IDG Books Worldwide's books outside the U.S., please contact our International Sales department at 415-655-3200 or fax 415-655-3295.

For information on foreign language translations, please contact our Foreign & Subsidiary Rights department at 415-655-3021 or fax 415-655-3281.

For sales inquiries and special prices for bulk quantities, please contact our Sales department at 415-655-3200 or write to the address above.

For information on using IDG Books Worldwide's books in the classroom or for ordering examination copies, please contact our Educational Sales department at 800-434-2086 or fax 817-251-8174.

For press review copies, author interviews, or other publicity information, please contact our Public Relations department at 415-655-3000 or fax 415-655-3299.

For authorization to photocopy items for corporate, personal, or educational use, please contact Copyright Clearance Center, 222 Rosewood Drive, Danvers, MA 01923, or fax 508-750-4470.

About the Authors

Bill Yosses: For ten years, Bill Yosses was the pastry chef at the 4-star (*The New York Times*) Bouley Restaurant in Manhattan. He currently is the pastry chef at Bouley Bakery and teaches dessert-making and baking at The New School for Culinary Arts in Manhattan. He also is a visiting instructor at Greystone, the Napa Valley branch of The Culinary Institute of America (in Hyde Park, NY).

Before that, he trained at a number of top bakeries and restaurants in Paris, including Fauchon, La Maison du Chocolat, and Le Notre Pastry School.

Bryan Miller: Bryan Miller (Rhinebeck, NY) is a former restaurant critic and feature writer for *The New York Times*, who also wrote *Cooking For Dummies* (with Marie Rama), published by IDG Books Worldwide, Inc. He also has written eight other books, including four editions of *The New York Times Guide to Restaurants, The Seafood Cookbook — Classic to Contemporary* (with Pierre Franey), *Cuisine Rapide* (with Pierre Franey), and *A Chef's Tale* (with Rick Flaste).

Miller is the recipient of the James Beard Who's Who Food and Beverage Award, which recognizes outstanding achievement in the field of food and wine.

ABOUT IDG BOOKS WORLDWIDE

Welcome to the world of IDG Books Worldwide.

IDG Books Worldwide, Inc., is a subsidiary of International Data Group, the world's largest publisher of computer-related information and the leading global provider of information services on information technology. IDG was founded more than 25 years ago and now employs more than 8,500 people worldwide. IDG publishes more than 275 computer publications in over 75 countries (see listing below). More than 60 million people read one or more IDG publications each month.

Launched in 1990, IDG Books Worldwide is today the #1 publisher of best-selling computer books in the United States. We are proud to have received eight awards from the Computer Press Association in recognition of editorial excellence and three from *Computer Currents'* First Annual Readers' Choice Awards. Our best-selling *...For Dummies*® series has more than 30 million copies in print with translations in 30 languages. IDG Books Worldwide, through a joint venture with IDG's Hi-Tech Beijing, became the first U.S. publisher to publish a computer book in the People's Republic of China. In record time, IDG Books Worldwide has become the first choice for millions of readers around the world who want to learn how to better manage their businesses.

Our mission is simple: Every one of our books is designed to bring extra value and skill-building instructions to the reader. Our books are written by experts who understand and care about our readers. The knowledge base of our editorial staff comes from years of experience in publishing, education, and journalism — experience we use to produce books for the '90s. In short, we care about books, so we attract the best people. We devote special attention to details such as audience, interior design, use of icons, and illustrations. And because we use an efficient process of authoring, editing, and desktop publishing our books electronically, we can spend more time ensuring superior content and spend less time on the technicalities of making books.

You can count on our commitment to deliver high-quality books at competitive prices on topics you want to read about. At IDG Books Worldwide, we continue in the IDG tradition of delivering quality for more than 25 years. You'll find no better book on a subject than one from IDG Books Worldwide.

IDG BOOKS WORLDWIDE

John Kilcullen
CEO
IDG Books Worldwide, Inc.

Steven Berkowitz
President and Publisher
IDG Books Worldwide, Inc.

Eighth Annual
Computer Press
Awards ≥1992

Ninth Annual
Computer Press
Awards ≥1993

Tenth Annual
Computer Press
Awards ≥1994

Eleventh Annual
Computer Press
Awards ≥1995

IDG Books Worldwide, Inc., is a subsidiary of International Data Group, the world's largest publisher of computer-related information and the leading global provider of information services on information technology. International Data Group publishes over 275 computer publications in over 75 countries. Sixty million people read one or more International Data Group's publications each month. International Data Group's publications include: **ARGENTINA:** Buyer's Guide, Computerworld Argentina, PC World Argentina; **AUSTRALIA:** Australian Macworld, Australian PC World, Australian Reseller News, Computerworld, IT Casebook, Network World, Publish, Webmaster; **AUSTRIA:** Computerwelt Österreich, Networks Austria, PC Tip Austria; **BANGLADESH:** PC World Bangladesh; **BELARUS:** PC World Belarus; **BELGIUM:** Data News; **BRAZIL:** Annuário de Informática, Computerworld, Connections, Macworld, PC Player, PC World, Publish, Reseller News, Supergamepower; **BULGARIA:** Computerworld Bulgaria, Network World Bulgaria, PC & MacWorld Bulgaria; **CANADA:** CIO Canada, Client/Server World, ComputerWorld Canada, InfoWorld Canada, NetworkWorld Canada, WebWorld; **CHILE:** Computerworld Chile, PC World Chile; **COLOMBIA:** Computerworld Colombia, PC World Colombia; **COSTA RICA:** PC World Centro America; **THE CZECH AND SLOVAK REPUBLICS:** Computerworld Czechoslovakia, Macworld Czech Republic, PC World Czechoslovakia; **DENMARK:** Communications World Danmark, Computerworld Danmark, Macworld Danmark, PC World Danmark, Techworld Denmark; **DOMINICAN REPUBLIC:** PC World Republica Dominicana; **ECUADOR:** PC World Ecuador; **EGYPT:** Computerworld Middle East, PC World Middle East; **EL SALVADOR:** PC World Centro America; **FINLAND:** MikroPC, Tietoverkko, Tietoviikko; **FRANCE:** Distributique, Hebdo, Info PC, Le Monde Informatique, Macworld, Reseaux & Telecoms, WebMaster France; **GERMANY:** Computer Partner, Computerwoche, Computerwoche Extra, Computerwoche FOCUS, Global Online, Macwelt, PC Welt; **GREECE:** Amiga Computing, GamePro Greece, Multimedia World; **GUATEMALA:** PC World Centro America; **HONDURAS:** PC World Centro America; **HONG KONG:** Computerworld Hong Kong, PC World Hong Kong, Publish in Asia; **HUNGARY:** ABCD CD-ROM, Computerworld Szamitastechnika, Internetto online Magazine, PC World Hungary, PC-X Magazin Hungary; **ICELAND:** Tolvuheimur PC World Island; **INDIA:** Information Communications World, Information Systems Computerworld, PC World India, Publish in Asia; **INDONESIA:** InfoKomputer PC World, Komputek Computerworld, Publish in Asia; **IRELAND:** ComputerScope, PC Live!; **ISRAEL:** Macworld Israel, People & Computers/Computerworld; **ITALY:** Computerworld Italia, Macworld Italia, Networking Italia, PC World Italia; **JAPAN:** DTP World, Macworld Japan, Nikkei Personal Computing, OS/2 World Japan, SunWorld Japan, Windows NT World, Windows World Japan; **KENYA:** PC World East African; **KOREA:** Hi-Tech Information, Macworld Korea, PC World Korea; **MACEDONIA:** PC World Macedonia; **MALAYSIA:** Computerworld Malaysia, PC World Malaysia, Publish in Asia; **MALTA:** PC World Malta; **MEXICO:** Computerworld Mexico, PC World Mexico; **MYANMAR:** PC World Myanmar; **NETHERLANDS:** Computer! Totaal, LAN Internetworking Magazine, LAN World Buyers Guide, Macworld Netherlands, Net, WebWereld; **NEW ZEALAND:** Absolute Beginners Guide and Plain & Simple Series, Computer Buyer, Computer Industry Directory, Computerworld New Zealand, MTB, Network World, PC World New Zealand; **NICARAGUA:** PC World Centro America; **NORWAY:** Computerworld Norge, CW Rapport, Datamagasinet, Financial Rapport, Kursguide Norge, Macworld Norge, Multimediaworld Norge, PC World Ekspress Norge, PC World Nettverk, PC World Norge, PC World ProduktGuide Norge; **PAKISTAN:** Computerworld Pakistan; **PANAMA:** PC World Panama; **PEOPLE'S REPUBLIC OF CHINA:** China Computer Users, China Computerworld, China InfoWorld, China Telecom World Weekly, Computer & Communication, Electronic Design China, Electronics Today, Electronics Weekly, Game Software, PC World China, Popular Computer Week, Software Weekly, Software World, Telecom World; **PERU:** Computerworld Peru, PC World Profesional Peru, PC World SoHo Peru; **PHILIPPINES:** Click!, Computerworld Philippines, PC World Philippines, Publish in Asia; **POLAND:** Computerworld Poland, Computerworld Special Report Poland, Cyber, Macworld Poland, Networld Poland, PC World Komputer; **PORTUGAL:** Cerebro/PC World, Computerworld/Correio Informático, Dealer World Portugal, Mac*In/PC*In Portugal, Multimedia World; **PUERTO RICO:** PC World Puerto Rico; **ROMANIA:** Computerworld Romania, PC World Romania, Telecom Romania; **RUSSIA:** Computerworld Russia, Mir PK, Publish, Seti; **SINGAPORE:** Computerworld Singapore, PC World Singapore, Publish in Asia; **SLOVENIA:** Monitor; **SOUTH AFRICA:** Computing SA, Network World SA, Software World SA; **SPAIN:** Communicaciones World España, Computerworld España, Dealer World España, Macworld España, PC World España; **SRI LANKA:** Infolink PC World; **SWEDEN:** CAP&Design, Computer Sweden, Corporate Computing Sweden, Internetworld Sweden, it.branschen, Macworld Sweden, MaxiData Sweden, MikroDatorn, Natverk & Kommunikation, PC World Sweden, PCaktiv, Windows World Sweden; **SWITZERLAND:** Computerworld Schweiz, Macworld Schweiz, PCtip; **TAIWAN:** Computerworld Taiwan, Macworld Taiwan, NEW ViSiON/Publish, PC World Taiwan, Windows World Taiwan; **THAILAND:** Publish in Asia, Thai Computerworld; **TURKEY:** Computerworld Turkiye, Macworld Turkiye, Network World Turkiye, PC World Turkiye; **UKRAINE:** Computerworld Kiev, Multimedia World Ukraine, PC World Ukraine; **UNITED KINGDOM:** Acorn User UK, Amiga Action UK, Amiga Computing UK, Apple Talk UK, Computing, Macworld, Parents and Computers UK, PC Advisor, PC Home, PSX Pro, The WEB; **UNITED STATES:** Cable in the Classroom, CIO Magazine, Computerworld, DOS World, Federal Computer Week, GamePro Magazine, InfoWorld, I-Way, Macworld, Network World, PC Games, PC World, Publish, Video Event, THE WEB Magazine, and WebMaster; online webzines: JavaWorld, NetscapeWorld, and SunWorld Online; **URUGUAY:** InfoWorld Uruguay; **VENEZUELA:** Computerworld Venezuela, PC World Venezuela; and **VIETNAM:** PC World Vietnam. 3/24/97

Dedication

This book is dedicated to Jean-Claude Baker and Jean Pierre LeMasson.

Publisher's Acknowledgments

We're proud of this book; please register your comments through our IDG Books Worldwide Online Registration Form located at http://my2cents.dummies.com.

Some of the people who helped bring this book to market include the following:

Acquisitions, Development, and Editorial

Project Editor: Kelly Ewing

Executive Editor: Sarah Kennedy

Copy Editors: Constance Carlisle, Diana R. Conover, Diane L. Giangrossi, Kim Darosett, Joe Jansen, Tina Sims

General Reviewers: Betty Amer, Mia Wheelwright

Editorial Manager: Colleen Rainsberger

Editorial Assistant: Donna Love

Production

Project Coordinator: Debbie Stailey

Layout and Graphics: Angela F. Hunckler, Todd Klemme, Jane E. Martin, Brent Savage, Deirdre Smith, Michael A. Sullivan

Special Art and Photography: Elizabeth Kurtzman, Lou Manna

Proofreaders: Nancy L. Reinhardt, Christine Berman, Kelli Botta, Michelle Croninger, Robert Springer, Janet Withers

Indexer: Lynnzee Elze Spense

Special Help: Stephanie Koutek, Proof Editor

General and Administrative

IDG Books Worldwide, Inc.: John Kilcullen, CEO; Steven Berkowitz, President and Publisher

IDG Books Technology Publishing: Brenda McLaughlin, Senior Vice President and Group Publisher

Dummies Technology Press and Dummies Editorial: Diane Graves Steele, Vice President and Associate Publisher; Mary Bednarek, Acquisitions and Product Development Director; Kristin A. Cocks, Editorial Director

Dummies Trade Press: Kathleen A. Welton, Vice President and Publisher; Kevin Thornton, Acquisitions Manager

IDG Books Production for Dummies Press: Beth Jenkins, Production Director; Cindy L. Phipps, Manager of Project Coordination, Production Proofreading, and Indexing; Kathie S. Schutte, Supervisor of Page Layout; Shelley Lea, Supervisor of Graphics and Design; Debbie J. Gates, Production Systems Specialist; Robert Springer, Supervisor of Proofreading; Debbie Stailey, Special Projects Coordinator; Tony Augsburger, Supervisor of Reprints and Bluelines; Leslie Popplewell, Media Archive Coordinator

Dummies Packaging and Book Design: Patti Crane, Packaging Specialist; Lance Kayser, Packaging Assistant; Kavish + Kavish, Cover Design

◆

The publisher would like to give special thanks to Patrick J. McGovern, without whom this book would not have been possible.

◆

Authors' Acknowledgments

There are many people we would like to thank for their help in putting this massive project together. Foremost are Kelly Ewing, our tireless and endlessly patient project editor, and Sarah Kennedy, who nudged us along the way.

Also, thanks to Gina Fox of Rhinebeck, NY, an Olympian home baker who generously passed along tips that were used in this book. Also thanks to Cesare Casella, who cooked fabulous Tuscan meals for us when we were too fatigued to stand straight after days of dessert-making. In addition, we owe a great debt to Kris Ensminger, who intrepidly assisted us in preparing desserts for the photographs in this book. Also, thanks to our illustrator, Elizabeth Kurtzman.

We also owe a big thanks to Mark Reiter, our agent at International Management Group, for helping make it happen.

And thanks to our exceptional photographer, Lou Manna, the man who never met a dessert he didn't like.

Contents at a Glance

Cartoons at a Glance

By Rich Tennant

page 201

page 7

page 229

page 321

page 297

page 107

page 47

page 151

Fax: 508-546-7747 • E-mail: the5wave@tiac.net

Recipes at a Glance

Cakes

Cookies

Crêpes and Blinis

Custards and Puddings

Frostings, Glazes, Sauces, and Other Toppings

Fruits

Granités, Sorbets, and Ice Creams

Ladyfingers

Lowfat Desserts

Meringues

Miscellaneous Desserts

Mousses

Parfaits and Frozen Soufflés

Pies and Tarts

Puff Pastry, Cream Puffs, and Eclairs

Table of Contents

• •

Introduction

· ·

*I*f you're the type who gets slightly nervous when sautéing a veal chop, chances are you cringe in terror at the prospect of making a soufflé. When someone suggests that you do so, you suddenly remember some critical household chore that needs attending, like simonizing the driveway. Why is this? How can perfectly competent home cooks get so unraveled at something as innocent and harmless as a dessert?

Understanding dessert cookery is like taking an automobile repair course — you need to understand the principles that make the whole thing work before you fiddle with the parts. When it comes to desserts, you need to understand things such as the role of egg yolks in batters and custards, egg whites as a leavening agent, the delicate chemistry of doughs, and much more.

Desserts For Dummies explains all of these principles and much more so that you can approach any dessert recipe with the knowledge to make it work. In addition — just like the automobile repair course — you discover what you need to do the job. And in what we might call the lifestyle section, Part VI, we anticipate real-life situations and offer help on cooking for a mob, making holiday desserts, making great lowfat desserts, and more.

About This Book

Because some desserts require a modicum of precision, in measuring and cooking, don't expect to always hit a home run the first time. If your cookie bottoms resemble the aftermath of a forest fire and your cake can double as a Frisbee, don't fret — give the cake to the kids. Then analyze the mistake and start again. Look at how many times Thomas Jefferson reworked the Declaration of Independence before getting it to the table.

Desserts For Dummies is more than a laundry list of recipes. It walks you through the techniques of different desserts step by step, telling you what to look for, like textures and colors, as the recipe progresses. That way, you can often make a quick mid-course correction if something goes awry. Moreover, if you understand the techniques of dessert-making, you can eventually branch out on your own, adding different flavors or garnishes as you go along.

Each type of dessert in this book — egg-based custards, cakes, ice creams, and so on — carries with it specific rules that must be followed. That's why we emphasize techniques throughout the book. After all, a cook with a good grasp of techniques — whether it's pastry rolling or cake decorating — is a happy cook.

Conventions Used in This Book

A few notes about the ingredients before you begin:

- ✔ All milk is whole unless otherwise specified.

- ✔ All eggs are large.

- ✔ All butter is unsalted so that you can control the salt in a recipe yourself. Margarine is not a suitable substitute for butter, especially in pie crust.

- ✔ All dry ingredients are measured level — that is, filled to the top and scraped even with a straight object.

- ✔ All salt is common table salt unless otherwise specified.

- ✔ All-purpose flour is assumed unless otherwise specified. Although some recipes are best with cake flour, you can substitute all-purpose flour.

- ✔ All fruits are ripe but not overly soft unless otherwise specified.

- ✔ All lemon juice is freshly squeezed and strained.

- ✔ Zest of lemon refers to grated lemon zest (just the yellow skin) unless otherwise specified. (Lemon zest is sometimes cut into thin strips.)

- ✔ When nutmeg is called for, it should be freshly grated.

- ✔ We prefer that you use fresh vanilla beans, although we do list vanilla extract as an alternate ingredient. When mixing the vanilla bean with other ingredients, be sure to remove it before serving.

  Also, when we say add the vanilla throughout the recipes, we're referring to either the vanilla bean or the vanilla extract. If we want you to add only one or the other in that step, we refer to the full name — for example, add the vanilla bean.

And keep in mind . . .

- ✔ Techniques that apply to most or all kinds of dessert cookery (whisking and folding, for example) are described outside of specific recipes and in Appendix A.

- ✔ We assume that you have the following basic tools: mixing bowls, whisks, spatulas, wooden spoons, measuring cups (dry and liquid), measuring spoons, and cookie sheets. Additional tools required are listed at the top of each recipe.

✔ Preparation time includes the time it takes to make the recipe from beginning to end (excluding the time listed in Cooking time).

✔ When we say electric mixer, we're referring to both a kitchen mixer and a handheld mixer.

✔ All temperatures are in Fahrenheit. To convert to Celsius, use this formula: Celsius = (°F–32) × ⁵/₉.

✔ Before you start cooking, read through the recipe thoroughly. Determine (1) whether you really want to do it, (2) whether you have all the necessary equipment, and (3) whether you have all the necessary ingredients. You should have all ingredients and equipment organized on the counter (with any necessary preparation such as chopping or sifting done in advance).

✔ Know your pots and pans and their exact measurements so that you're not running around at the last moment.

✔ Know your oven temperature. It's not critical that the temperature precisely matches the heat indicated on the dial, only that you're always aware of the exact temperature. (Use a good oven thermometer.)

✔ Clean up as you go along. This makes for less of a chore later and also helps you stay organized while cooking.

✔ These recipes are designed to be doubled or more. Just multiply all ingredients (unless otherwise stated).

A note about measurements: Any professional baker will tell you that measuring dessert ingredients by weighing (in ounces and pounds) is the most exact and reliable method. The next best measurement is level cups. We list both types of measurements in the recipes so that you have a choice. We also give metric equivalents in Appendix B.

Foolish Assumptions

You may wonder why this book is called *Desserts For Dummies*. The title is not meant to be insulting. Rather, it reflects our approach to cooking. Our operating assumption is that you've never prepared a homemade dessert in your life, and we start with the most elemental information. This way, no one is left asking questions. From there we show you more advanced techniques step by step — again, answering every question along the way.

The term *dummy* may imply that everything in this book is utterly simple. In fact, we get quite sophisticated, with recipes for puff pastry, elegant meringue cakes, and much more. But we take small steps along the way so that no one gets lost.

How This Book Is Organized

The goal of *Desserts For Dummies* is to get you up and whisking as soon as possible. After all, that's the fun part. First, however, we quickly run you around the track of must-do's so that your cooking can be as seamless and satisfying as possible. After that, the book is organized so that you can go right to your area of interest — cakes, sorbets, or soufflés, for example — and start from there. The major sections, or parts, are organized according to the broad category of desserts they include: flour-based desserts, egg-based desserts, cakes, and so on.

Part I: Getting Started

This get-ready section starts with a discussion of basic kitchen equipment for dessert-making. You don't need any esoteric or expensive machines to make the recipes in this book. A stand-up electric kitchen mixer is invaluable, to be sure, but you can get along quite well with an inexpensive handheld mixer to start. Some sort of ice cream machine is needed to emulsify and freeze ice cream, and they range in price from under $40 for little hand-cranking models (and they work quite well!) to $250 or more for refrigerated units. Aside from those, the tools are rather basic and relatively inexpensive — you probably have a lot of them already.

We also talk about setting up your kitchen for dessert-making — again, with economy and limited space in mind. We also discuss ovens and broilers because baking is such a precise art.

Part II: Flour Power: Pie Doughs, Tarts, and Puff Pastries

In this part, you roll up your sleeves and begin. Part II covers what we call flour-based desserts — that is, pies, tarts, and puff pastry. Appropriate fillings go with each type of desserts. Puff pastry, perhaps the scariest of all tasks to the novice, is described in minute, step-by-step detail. We also toss crêpes and blinis into this part because they're flour-based as well.

Part III: Egging You On

In this part, we cover egg-based desserts like custards, puddings, and meringues. We start off telling you more about eggs than you ever wanted to know and then move on to the simplest of egg desserts, the custard. We then cover all-American puddings and soufflés.

Part IV: A Real Cake Walk

This part is devoted to cakes, a giant category that also involves cake fillings and icings. As you can see in Part IV, cakes come in many guises and names, which is part of the wonder of them, and we push all of them across the table at you.

Part V: Good Cold Things

Ice cream bases are the focus of this part. We show you how to achieve the most concentrated flavors and the smoothest textures, as well as how to store your cold creations. We also describe fruit sorbets of all sorts, as well as the incredibly easy and delicious granités.

Part VI: Special Desserts for Special Occasions

In this part, we address special occasions: desserts to make for large holiday gatherings, big blasts, or when your Little Leaguer shouts to the dugout and six rows of the bleachers, "Victory party at my house!" We also offer an array of delicious lowfat desserts.

Part VII: The Part of Tens

We also organize this technique-oriented book around the way people live. Obviously, many home cooks today do not have time to come home from work and whip up a black forest cake while the kids are dueling like Robin Hood with sharp metal kitchen skewers. So in this part, we offer ten desserts that you can prepare in half an hour — no kidding. And because so much of a dessert's appeal is visual, Chapter 18 demonstrates various ways to make any dessert look as if it came out of a professional kitchen.

Part VIII: Appendixes

This part gives you a glossary of common dessert lingo. We also give you handy measurement and conversion tables. And because some of the recommended kitchen equipment and specialty foods may not be available everywhere, we include a directory of mail-order sources.

Icons Used in This Book

In the margin throughout this book, you see cute little icons that cause text to stand out. Well, we didn't add these icons just to make the pages pretty. The following list is a guide to what each icon means.

This chef's toque, a symbol of culinary authority, alerts you to the type of inside advice a kitchen professional can give.

This symbol warns you when a particular technique requires extra vigilance to succeed or when a potential accident may result in injury.

We show you so many techniques along the way in this book. Some, however, fall into the category of must-know because they cut across all areas in dessert-making. This icon marks those techniques.

We try to anticipate potential problems with all recipes — too much evaporation in a pot, too much sugar added to the meringue — and this icon offers mid-course solutions.

Chocoholics may want to search for recipes that contain various kinds of chocolate. This icon makes the search easy.

With children getting more involved in the kitchen these days, we decided to underscore recipes that they can participate in with their parents.

Desserts are 50 percent visual titillation. This icon points to desserts that are particularly spectacular looking. It also highlights tips for making your desserts look stunning.

Part I
Getting Started

The 5th Wave   By Rich Tennant

"SEE HOW I'M GETTING FIRM PEAKS? THIS IS HOW YOU WANT YOUR WHIPPED CREAM PIES."

In this part . . .

Making desserts is sort of like snow skiing — if you don't have the proper equipment, you're sure to take a fall. That's why the first part of this book talks about the supplies necessary to succeed without flying off of a mogul. You don't have to spend a fortune — indeed, many home cooks already have most or all the items we discuss — but you do need to be organized and know which equipment and ingredients work best with which job.

And because so much baking involves precise oven temperature, we go into detail regarding ovens and broilers. It's no big deal if your oven is off by 10°or more — as long as you're aware of it and compensate.

Finally, we discuss your kitchen, however humble it may be. Organization, not size, is the key.

Chapter 1

On Your Mark, Get Set . . . Whisk!

Many accomplished home cooks would no sooner bake a fruit tart than paddle a canoe backwards to Tierra del Fuego. What's so scary about making desserts, anyway? If you want something to get scared about, look at some commercial desserts, which can have a shelf life longer than the life of a bowling ball. And check out the ingredients, full of names with 13 syllables, most ending with the word *glutinum*.

Actually, after you discover a few simple techniques, desserts are no more threatening than any other kind of cooking. In fact, they can be more fun because you can make a huge mess along the way. What's more, desserts, especially soufflés and cakes, look great coming out of an oven.

And, just to make sure that you experience all the positives, we spend this chapter outlining the principles of making great desserts, from being precise to having an eye for presentation.

Thinking like a Sweet Chef

Making desserts requires all the skills and sensibilities, plus more, of any good cook. For one, the ingredients can be somewhat fragile and unforgiving at times. And the techniques used in making desserts require a great degree of precision. Another challenge is the way desserts are served; they usually stand alone on the plate, with no easy opportunities for camouflage. Desserts make an entrance like the belle of the ball, with everybody watching — and her dress had better be perfect.

Here are some reminders to inscribe on your apron:

✔ **Take measurements seriously:** After you tap the measuring cup on the counter, the contents should not go above or below the rim.

✔ **Weighing is serious business:** Get an accurate scale and use it. The best ones have a large, removable bowl that holds 4 cups (16 ounces) flour or more. Digital scales are popular, and they're fairly accurate. In general, which type you get doesn't matter as long as it is accurate (try it in the store, if you can) and can hold the quantities of ingredients you need. Measuring in batches because your scale bowl is too small is a nuisance. Don't forget to set your scale to zero with the bowl on top.

✔ **Think about presentation:** Desserts are 50 percent visual stimulation. Always think of little ways to garnish them or to give them a little pizzazz. (See Chapter 18.)

✔ **Desserts always follow a meal:** You cannot plan desserts in a vacuum. First consider the type of dishes served before your dessert and then think how the dessert can punctuate them. Cheesecake after fondue or pizza should be an indictable offense. (See the sidebar "What's for dessert?" for more advice.)

What's for dessert?

In this sidebar, we give you some casual and very arbitrary suggestions on the types of desserts that go well with different types of meals. Of course, the first rule is that the lighter the meal, the more substantial the dessert can be. In contrast, a meal with a rich sauce might call for something cleansing, like sorbet or ice cream. It also goes without saying that the accompaniments to main dishes also help determine the appropriate dessert.

✔ **Beef stew:** Avoid chocolate. Try a light fruit dessert (see Chapter 17) or a meringue dessert (see Chapter 8).

✔ **Grilled fish with vinaigrette-style sauce:** A light main course like this goes well with a rich and full-flavored chocolate mousse (see Chapter 19), chocolate cake (see Chapter 9), or a dacquoise (see Chapter 8).

✔ **Sautéed fish with egg-based sauce:** Because eggs are in hollandaise sauce, avoid egg-based desserts. Go with a crunchy textured dessert like a tart (see Chapter 3) or a baked meringue (see Chapter 8).

✔ **Seafood casserole:** This soft and liquid dish can call for any of the sponge cake recipes (see Chapter 9) in this book or a classic fruit tart (see Chapter 3).

✔ **Roasted pork or lamb:** Meat is relatively heavy, so you should go with something refreshing like a lemon-lime charlotte (see Chapter 10) or a lowfat dessert like fruit soup or poached pears (see Chapter 19).

✔ **Steak:** This all-American meal, despite being substantial, traditionally goes with a hefty dessert like a pie (see Chapter 3), a puff pastry dessert like a napoleon (see Chapter 4), or a frozen parfait (see Chapter 13).

✔ **Pasta carbonara:** Considering all the butter and cream in a carbonara sauce, you can go with something light and cleansing like a granité (see Chapter 12), maybe served with a slice of pound cake (see Chapter 16).

✔ **Pasta with white clam sauce:** This lighter, full-flavored pasta calls for something like fresh fruit with zabaglione, which has lots of wine flavor, or crème brûlée (see Chapter 7).

✔ **Pasta with grilled vegetables:** Follow this healthful, lowfat meal with something relatively lowfat and tasty, like lemon angel food cake (see Chapter 17).

✔ **Lasagna:** This is a creamy and heavy dish, so you don't want to follow it with a creamy dessert. Try homemade sorbets (see Chapter 12) or marinated strawberries (see Chapter 19) with Anise Drop Cookies (see Chapter 16).

✔ **Hamburgers/hot dogs:** This homey American dish calls for a homey American dessert like brownies (see Chapter 20) or chocolate chip cookies (see Chapter 16).

✔ **Roasted chicken or roasted turkey:** These are relatively lean main courses, so a rich dessert, like bread pudding or Indian pudding, goes well (see Chapter 7).

✔ **Omelet:** Egg-based desserts are out. A ripe fruit dish works well.

✔ **Peanut butter and jelly:** Once again, this most American of repasts, which is sweet and rich, calls for something minimally sweet and simple. Try lemon meringue pie (see Chapter 8) or any type of cookie (see Chapter 16).

✔ **Although precise recipes are important in dessert-making, you don't always have to unquestioningly adhere to them.** If you want to experiment with a flavor here or there or use a different garnish, go for it.

✔ **Always consider the particular tastes — or specific food allergies, such as to nuts — before embarking on a big dessert.**

✔ **Pick desserts that are appropriate to the number of guests.** You may not want to spend the end of the meal in the kitchen with elaborate garnishing and flambéing.

✔ **Be thrifty.** Never throw out excess ingredients that you can use in other ways. (See the "Using leftover ingredients creatively" section, later in this chapter.)

✔ **You can double virtually all the recipes in this book by simply multiplying each ingredient by two and following the instructions:** If necessary, do your mixing in batches.

However, if you want to cut a recipe in half, you must consider the size of your kitchen mixer (if you have one). Most stand-alone kitchen mixers need a minimum of two egg whites in the bowl to work properly. Hand mixers can handle very small quantities.

The pleasures of precision

Some dessert-phobics have confessed that sweets are scary to make because they have such a small margin of error, compared to regular food. Most desserts, unlike some main courses, require strict attention to measurement as well as cooking time. That's why organization is so critical before you jump into a recipe. If you have everything ready to go and have noted the techniques encountered in the recipe, the challenge suddenly becomes minimal. You can gain great satisfaction in, say, assembling all the ingredients for a soufflé and then seeing it puff up like a peacock in the oven.

To be sure, many desserts are less forgiving visually as well, which is another reason why precision is so important. Desserts are a solo act, flubs and all, with no mashed potatoes to hide behind. But a dessert cook can employ many tricks to perform cosmetic surgery on a tart's broken crust or a scorched custard. (See the section "Performing Cosmetic Surgery on Desserts," later in this chapter.)

How to read a dessert recipe

Before tackling a recipe, take a good look at it. If you start to chuckle when you get to the part that says, "Now take your Cambodian Lilac Stamen and blend it with the Valencian orange flour. . . .", you may want to consider a more homespun recipe. Or, if the recipe calls for a piece of kitchen equipment that you don't have, stop before you get to those steps and consider alternative techniques.

Following are tips for reading recipes:

- ✔ **Start by reading all the ingredients — a well-written recipe lists the ingredients in the order in which they're used.** Make sure that you have all the ingredients. Also make sure that you *like* all the ingredients.

- ✔ **Look at the recipe a second time and say to yourself, "Does this dessert sound appealing?"** Just because the recipe is in a book doesn't mean that you'll like it. If a recipe captures your interest and gets you salivating just by reading it, chances are you'll do a great job making it.

A really big cheese in the dessert world

Over the centuries and on both sides of the Atlantic, many chefs have influenced the desserts that we enjoy today. Following is a brief history of a giant among dessert chefs.

Carême (1784-1833) — Marie-Antoine Carême, whom friends called Antonin (we don't know why), has been hailed as "The Cook of Kings and the King of Cooks." He started cooking at age 15 in a modest Paris restaurant. But soon he proved to be so talented and punctual at work that he found an easier job at a famous pastry shop on the rue Vivienne. As the story goes, King Louis XVIII ("The Eclair Regent") had quite the sweet tooth and soon became addicted to young Carême's glazed doughnuts as well as his little butter cookie figurines — most popular were those shaped like Marie Antoinette (with or without a head — 2 francs).

Carême was so smart and so efficient that he actually found time to take drawing lessons while his cookies were baking. In the early 19th century, only rich people at the court purchased art. So young Carême drew mostly pictures of kings and queens posing next to horses or standing around all dressed up in their castles. He then got the idea to put these drawings on cakes, using a pastry bag and "royal" icing. Louis XVIII was so enamored of these cakes that he invited Carême to the palace to bake.

Encouraged by the king, Carême started building cake castles, cake horses, and even cake countries. He went to England and did the same there. Then he went to see Czar Alexander (known as "The Profiterole King") in Saint Petersburg. Carême is said to have made more money in those endeavors than any pastry chef in New York City today, even accounting for inflation.

When Carême was in his 40s, he started a book about all of this, but he died before he got to the horse part. Nonetheless, pastry chefs today think he was one wild and crazy guy. You can see Carême's picture in a lot of dessert books.

- ✔ **Mentally run through all the techniques called for in the recipe, like folding, whisking, crimping, and so on.** Are you comfortable with them? If not, check out the index in this book and flip to the cited pages to find out how to do these tasks. Don't try to learn a technique while you're in the middle of a recipe.

- ✔ **Consider the time required to complete the recipe.** Always give yourself more time than the recipe calls for, especially if it's your first time through.

- ✔ **Always consider how many guests you need to feed before taking on a recipe.** You may decide to try a different recipe or increase your proportions. There is nothing worse — or more embarrassing — than having ten guests and eight slices of tart.

Organizing your ingredients

You wouldn't attempt the Boston Marathon without first securely tying your shoes, and you wouldn't sail in the America's Cup race without battening down the hatches and all that stuff. Similarly, you shouldn't just shamble into the kitchen and start tossing together a plum tart with hazelnut crust.

Well, you could, in theory. But you would spend so much time lurching around the kitchen looking for this ingredient and that piece of kitchen equipment — while the crust is burning in the oven — that you may never try making a dessert again. It seems too obvious, but preparation is 50 percent of all cooking — maybe 60 percent when making desserts.

All your ingredients and equipment needed for the recipe should be on the counter within easy reach. That way, all you have to do is think about the recipe and any other potential disasters that are lurking around the house.

The Bare Necessities: A Pantry List for Desserts

What do you always need in the pantry to be ready to whip up a dessert? Have the following items on hand, and chances are you'll always be prepared.

- ✔ **Baking powder:** A chemical leavener consisting of baking soda and acid. When mixed with a liquid and heated, baking powder produces carbon dioxide gas that makes batter rise. You can use two types of baking powder:

  - • **Single-acting baking powder:** Requires only liquid (such as combining dry and wet ingredients) to activate. You should use this baking powder only if baking takes place immediately after mixing the batter. Within half an hour, this baking powder loses its leavening power.

  - • **Double-acting baking powder:** Releases gas in two stages and enables batters to stand for a period of time without losing their leavening power immediately. This effect is helpful if you have to stagger your baking time. Check the freshness date because baking powder can lose its effectiveness if left on the shelf for a year or more. To test, mix 1 teaspoon baking powder with $1/3$ cup (3 ounces) water. If it fizzes, it's good.

    All recipes in this book call for double-acting baking powder. The most prevalent commercially available brands include Royal and Calumet. Aluminum-free Rumford is sold in health stores.

✔ **Baking soda:** A leavening agent for many baked goods and batters, especially those that contain an acidic ingredient like vinegar or buttermilk. You also can use it in a refrigerator (with lid open) to absorb odors. Change the box every six months.

✔ **Brown sugar:** Use brown sugar in recipes that call for a caramelized sugar flavor. Store in a canister with a tight-fitting lid. Brown sugar comes either packed or pourable, sometimes called *brownulated*. Have both types on hand.

✔ **Butter:** Always have plenty of butter on hand for making pie crust, batters, sauces, and so on. Buy unsalted, or sweet, butter so that you can control the amount of salt in a recipe. Butter has a shelf life of a month or more in the refrigerator; you can store excess butter in the freezer for up to a year.

✔ **Chocolate:** Have 8-ounce bars of bittersweet and semisweet chocolate on hand for all kinds of recipes, from mousses to cookie batter. Milk chocolate melts at a lower temperature than other chocolates, so store it in a cool place.

Store all chocolate in a cool, dry place (not the refrigerator), tightly wrapped. Chocolate also comes in chip form. (For more on chocolate, see Chapter 20.)

✔ **Cinnamon:** A spice frequently used in cookies and puddings. Keep the powdered form in an airtight jar.

✔ **Cornstarch:** A thickening agent (100 percent refined starch) sometimes used in place of flour — for example, when making pastry cream or ladyfingers.

✔ **Corn syrup:** An all-around sweet syrup, sometimes flavored with vanilla, for batters of all kinds.

✔ **Cream (heavy cream or whipping cream):** A cream that generally has a 36 to 40 percent butterfat content, which allows it to whip up into a solid. The high percentage of fat gives it a rich texture and flavor that is desirable in many desserts.

✔ **Cream of tartar:** A by-product of wine-making, it's also known as potassium acid tartare. You can use cream of tartar in tandem with baking soda to leaven baked goods. As a stabilizer, you can use it to improve the quality of whipped egg whites — producing smaller air bubbles — and to give meringues fuller body.

✔ **Eggs:** Use medium to large eggs, as fresh as possible. Raw eggs are good for about four weeks beyond their packing date. (See Chapter 6.)

✔ **Flour (all-purpose):** For all kinds of baking and batters. Store in an airtight glass or plastic container, away from sunlight.

✔ **Flour (cake):** The preferred flour for light-textured cakes and other desserts with a light, soft crust. Cake flour is made from wheat with a soft, smooth texture and pure white color. Use cake flour for cakes and doughs because it yields a flakier consistency. It's generally available at supermarkets. If you don't find it with the other flours, check the cake mix section. Be sure to buy plain cake flour, not the self-rising kind, which already contains added leavening and salt. Store in an airtight glass or plastic container, away from sunlight.

- **Gelatin:** A colorless, odorless, and sugarless powder (not to be confused with Jell-O, which is the trademarked name for a flavored gelatin-based dessert). You can use gelatin in cake fillings and to stabilize whipped creams. Gelatin needs to soften in cool water for five minutes before using — it dissolves in water and becomes a thickening agent. Gelatin continues to thicken a mixture over a 24-hour period.

- **Honey:** For sweetening certain batters and other mixtures.

- **Jams and preserves:** It's always a good idea to have several fruit jams or preserves on hand for glazing tarts and certain pie crusts. Apricot, orange, plum, and cherry are good choices.

- **Lemons:** You can use the juice and skin (zest) of lemons all the time in every kind of dessert. Lemons should be firm, not mushy, and the skins should be bright and unblemished.

- **Liqueurs:** Some recipes, such as soufflés, pies, and dessert sauces, call for optional liqueurs like a splash of rum, Grand Marnier, Kirsch (cherry liqueur), or other flavored alcohol.

- **Milk:** Use whole milk, as fresh as possible, unless skimmed milk is called for.

- **Nonstick spray:** It's not something to eat, but worth knowing about anyway. Pam is the best-known brand. Nonstick vegetable spray works well to prevent batters and other foods from sticking to a pan or baking sheet.

- **Nutmeg:** Whole nutmeg is far superior to the powdered variety. Scrape whole nutmeg on a grater — but be careful, it's very potent. Keep it in an airtight jar. You can use nutmeg to season puddings, pies, and sauces.

- **Nuts:** Store walnuts, pecans, pistachios, hazelnuts, almonds, and other nuts (whole or peeled) in airtight containers.

- **Sugar:** Use white granulated sugar as an all-around sweetener. Use confectioners' sugar for fine textures and for whipped cream.

- **Vanilla bean:** The best vanilla beans are cured by a natural sun-drying process that intensifies their flavor. Most flavor is in the powdery inner seeds — that's why we ask you to split them lengthwise. The flavors imparted are stronger when the bean is *infused* — allowed to *steep* (sit in a hot liquid to extract flavor, like a tea bag) — in a hot liquid, such as milk.

You can buy good fresh vanilla beans from mail-order outlets (see Appendix C). Such vanilla beans are more fragrant and powerful than the kind you find on the spice rack at the supermarket. Many vanilla extracts are very good, too. Vanilla extract, sold in bottles, doesn't have the flavor intensity of beans, but it's convenient to use in many recipes.

✔ **Vegetable shortening:** Used primarily for pie dough, to give it a flaky crust. Get solid, white all-vegetable shortening, like Crisco.

Storing extra ingredients

You can recycle or store many ingredients in dessert-making, if they're not used up the first time around. Even when the quantity of an ingredient seems too little to save — say, two egg whites — store it anyway; you can add them to fresh ingredients the next time. (See the following section for tips on how to use extra ingredients.) Following are some tips for storing your extra ingredients:

✔ **Freeze leftover egg yolks:** Add 1 tablespoon sugar per cup of yolks to prevent them from becoming rock solid when frozen. You can store egg yolks for three to four weeks in an airtight plastic container or storage bag.

✔ **Freeze egg whites in ice-cube trays:** The egg whites should last about a month or more if kept frozen. Thaw at room temperature.

✔ **Store chocolate in plastic wrap and keep it in a cool place (but not in the refrigerator or freezer):** If you keep the chocolate between 55° and 70°, it should last two months or more. Don't worry if the chocolate develops a little white bloom on top — it's harmless and melts away when heated.

✔ **Store cakes and cookies in plastic wrap and then freeze.** Well-wrapped cakes can last a month. Defrosting cakes and puff pastry while they're still in the wrapping retains some of the moisture. For cookie dough, it's better to roll the uncooked dough into a cylinder, wrap it in plastic, and then freeze. Then just remove the dough from the freezer, remove the wrap, slice into cookie shapes with a serrated knife, and bake.

✔ **Cover puff pastry in plastic wrap and then freeze.** Tightly covered puff pastry lasts for three to four weeks in the freezer.

✔ **Cover raw pie crust in plastic wrap and then freeze.** Pie crust lasts up to two weeks in the freezer.

✔ **Keep in mind that batters and soft doughs don't freeze well.** Firm, drier doughs freeze well for up to a month.

✔ **If you freeze pie or tart dough, roll it out before you freeze it.** The dough freezes quicker that way and is much easier to work with when thawed.

Using leftover ingredients creatively

At one time or another, you'll find yourself with a leftover ingredient, whether it's whipped cream or melted chocolate. There is a limit to what your dog can eat or what your freezer can hold, so here are some suggestions for immediate use:

- **Buttercream frosting:** Use to frost cookies.

- **Cake batter:** Pour into greased muffin tins and bake.

- **Cake icing:** Decorate cookies or brownies.

- **Caramel:** Make butterscotch: Melt the caramel in a pan and add an equal amount of heavy cream. Stir until combined and use as a dessert sauce. You can store this sauce in the refrigerator for two weeks or more.

- **Chocolate (melted):** Line a small loaf pan with plastic wrap and sprinkle over it chopped nuts of your choice; pour the melted chocolate over the nuts and let set in a cool place. When firm, you'll have your own chocolate bar. Store at room temperature in plastic wrap.

- **Chocolate mousse:** If you're making chocolate mousse for a cake filling and have some left over, scoop it into a martini glass and eat it all yourself — unless you have enough to share.

- **Egg yolks:** Because egg yolks don't freeze as well as egg whites (yolks get very gummy), use them as soon as possible. Make a sabayon sauce (see Chapter 19) and serve with fresh fruit or cake.

- **Ice cream base:** Do not store ice cream base because it can go bad quickly. Use it all at once.

- **Ladyfingers:** Make a variation of tiramisu by dipping ladyfingers in coffee, spreading confectioners' sugar over them, and serving them with ice cream or flavored yogurt. Or make little sandwiches and dust with cocoa.

- **Meringue:** This doesn't last long unless you bake it. Pipe out into strips and bake in a 275° oven for about 1 hour. You can use these crunchy sticks to decorate cakes and ice creams.

- **Pie filling:** Serve with ice cream or cakes.

- **Sugar syrup:** This holds well in an airtight container at room temperature. Use it to sweeten ice tea and other cold drinks.

- **Whipped cream:** Store, covered, and re-whip it if it breaks down — it'll come back.

Forming Perfect Flavor Marriages

There are few concrete rules in dessert-making, but certain flavors traditionally go well with certain ingredients. Refer to Table 1-1 until you feel confident branching out on your own.

Table 1-1	Happy Dessert Marriages: Common Dessert Flavors and Things That Enhance Them
This Flavor . . .	*Tastes Great with This . . .*
Anise	Raisins or licorice-type desserts; often used alone.
Apples	Cinnamon, lemon, nutmeg, and vanilla; apples don't go well with chocolate.
Apricot	Almonds, a classic combination.
Banana	Chocolate, nutmeg, and caramel.
Cinnamon	Apples, persimmons, cranberries, pears, and other fruits.
Coconut	Chocolate (cookies and cakes), bananas, pineapples, and other tropical desserts.
Coffee	Chocolate, ice cream, and all kinds of nut desserts.
Ginger	Be wary over overusing it; goes with fruits of all kinds and cookies.
Honey	Lemon, saffron, nuts, and bananas.
Lavender	Goes well with white chocolate and vanilla ice cream.
Lemon	Almost everything can be enhanced by lemon. Especially welcome with ripe fruits and custards.
Mint	Chocolate (as in chocolate mousse and chocolate sauces); ripe summer fruits like pears and berries; and ice cream.
Nutmeg	Another potentially overwhelming flavor. Marries well with egg custards, nut-based desserts, and vanilla, among many other flavors.
Orange	Chocolate, mint, and vanilla.
Pineapple	Brown sugar and molasses.
Pumpkin	Chocolate, cinnamon, and nutmeg.
Raspberry	Mint, hazelnuts, and custards.
Rosemary	Pine nuts, vanilla ice cream (as an ingredient), and apples.
Strawberries	Chocolate (especially coated in chocolate), balsamic vinegar, and mint.
Vanilla	Ice creams, tropical fruits, and chocolate, to name a few.

Performing Cosmetic Surgery on Desserts

Remember that nobody is perfect. Even professionals find that, for whatever reason, their desserts sometimes come out looking as if they took the first cannonball at Fort Sumter. Don't be afraid to perform cosmetic surgery before serving these dishes. Your little black medical bag should be filled with whipped cream, confectioners' sugar, ice cream, mint leaves, sliced fruit, and anything else that can repair things that have gone wrong. Here are some examples:

- **Cake (burned on bottom):** Cut off the burned part with a serrated knife. Be careful to do so evenly so that the cake is not lopsided. A burned bottom usually doesn't affect the flavor of the rest of the cake.

- **Cake (lopsided):** Build up the frosting on the low side of the cake's surface so that it appears to be more even.

- **Cake (holes in side):** Sometimes a cake sticks to the side of the pan, and the cake comes out with holes or indentations on the side. Before covering these problem areas with frosting, try picking cake remnants from the pan and reassembling and reattaching them to the sides of the cake.

- **Soufflé (collapsed):** Remove the contents of the soufflé mold carefully and place them on a serving dish. Serve artfully with fruit compote, ice cream, or jam. Fallen soufflés are very chic these days in restaurants. (See Chapter 11.)

- **Pies (parts of the edge fall off):** Use jam to glue the broken pieces back on.

- **Sponge cake (breaks coming out of pan):** Use broken pieces to make English trifle (see Chapter 11) or an improvised strawberry shortcake (see Chapter 10).

- **Meringue:** High humidity can make meringue gummy textured. (You can tell after you bake the meringue; if it's soft to the touch after sitting out for 30 minutes, it will be gummy.) If this happens, place the meringue back in a 275° oven for 30 minutes to dry it out and make it crisp again. The meringue should hold up this time.

One cardinal rule of professional dessert chefs is to never underestimate the redemptive power of confectioners' sugar. You should also keep in mind the cosmetic qualities of whipped cream and ice cream.

Protecting Your Precious Creations (And Fingers)

Dessert-making carries all the normal potential kitchen hazards, plus a few peculiar ones. Following are tips to make sure that you don't become a victim.

- ✔ **Whenever you're using a large knife to chop chunks of chocolate, chop nuts, or chop any other hard ingredient, use two hands.** One should be on the handle, and the other should be on top of the blade (toward the tip). To avoid having the tip gouge your hand, put a folded towel or potholder between your hand and the blade.

- ✔ **If you're a '60s fan, take off your dangling beads before cooking.** They can get in the way and cause accidents. In fact, take off any loose jewelry and avoid loose-hanging clothing or hair that can get caught in a machine.

- ✔ **Wipe up spills and clean pots as you go along.** This habit is more hygienic as well as more efficient. Leaving spills, especially of dairy products, is an invitation to bacteria. Be especially vigilant if you work over a porous wood counter, where bacteria can lodge in the tiny cracks.

- ✔ **Don't let eggs, cream, milk, and other perishables sit out on the counter.** Warm dairy products (75° or more) can spoil quickly — they also are prone to contamination by bacteria.

- ✔ **Always keep egg yolks covered and cold and heat them only when ready.** Yolks are the major source of the salmonella bacteria — egg whites are virtually all water and are relatively safe. Thus, whole eggs should be kept cold until used, too.

- ✔ **It goes without saying, but wash your hands thoroughly before any kind of cooking.** Your hands carry bacteria from all over the house, or worse, from outside the house. Unsanitary hands — or hands with open sores or cuts — are a major source of food contamination.

- ✔ **Always return kitchen tools to the place you found them.** There's nothing worse than racing around the room looking for a potholder as your cake burns. Most kitchen accidents occur when people are rushing.

Chapter 2
Kitchen Setup and Equipment

• •

In This Chapter

▶ Tools for mixing and whisking

▶ The basic baker: Equipment for all situations

▶ Those special tools that are never around when you need them

▶ Big guns for special purposes

• •

*Y*ou don't need a warehouse of fancy kitchen equipment to make great desserts, but you do need a basic store of quality utensils to make the job efficient and pleasurable. In this chapter, we share with you the secrets of setting up your kitchen and acquiring the most essential cooking equipment.

Setting Up Your Kitchen

You may not have a whole lot to say about the overall design of your kitchen if it's already in place, but you can do things to make it more efficient and pleasant to work in. For example, additional lighting can make a big difference. If it's inconvenient (or too expensive) to have extra, permanent lighting installed, investigate portable lights that screw on or clip onto different surfaces. Also, don't clutter precious counterspace with machines, cookbooks, hubcaps, wine bottles, and the like. Dessert-making, in particular, requires a lot of workspace.

When setting up your kitchen, here are a few points to keep in mind:

✔ **Counter height:** To minimize chiropractic bills, work on a counter that allows your back to be straight and your shoulders square. When bending forward, always return to an upright position. Don't lean on the counter when you work.

- **Exhaust:** Good fan ventilation eliminates smoke and excess heat. If you don't have a fan, try to achieve cross-ventilation with windows.

- **Floor:** Dessert-making can be messy. Your floor surface should be easy to clean and, ideally, not slippery when wet. (Ceramic tiles can be quite slippery; try linoleum, certain tiles, and tight-grooved wood instead.) Rubber-soled shoes are the most comfortable and safest in the kitchen.

- **Utensils:** The kitchen tools that you use most frequently — whisks, knives, spatulas, spoons — ideally should be within arm's reach of your major work surface. If you don't have much counterspace, consider hanging these utensils on pegs. Likewise, storage choices should be made with frequency of use in mind.

- **Lighting:** Adequate lighting is a given. Think about portable clip-on lights if necessary. If you don't want strong lighting in the kitchen when you're not working, consider dimmer switches.

- **Ovens:** Anyone who cooks much knows how much of a nuisance it can be to bend over constantly to look into a low oven. Many people have no choice in the matter, but if you're in the market for a new oven, consider an eye-level wall unit. This height makes monitoring cakes and other baked goods easier. With eye-level ovens, however, be extra careful about spurts and splashes that could hit you in the face.

  Also, a glass-fronted oven with an internal light is a good choice for bakers.

- **Refrigerator:** This should be several steps from your workspace. Also — and few people think of this — it's a good idea to check the temperature of a refrigerator from time to time. Any outdoor thermometer will do. The ideal refrigerator temperature is between 36° and 38°.

What kind of oven is right for you?

The decision regarding electric or gas ovens is largely a toss-up. Both ovens can do the job, and both can be accurate. More important than the source of heat, however, is the inside metal surface of the oven that radiates heat.

Knowing the temperature of your oven is critical. To discover your oven temperature, we recommend an oven thermometer to keep track of the actual temperature, regardless of what the oven thermostat says.

A *convection oven* circulates hot air while cooking. The advantage of the convection oven (a luxury, not a necessity, for a home cook) is speed and even baking. Your cakes cook faster and brown evenly, but turning your baking sheet around halfway through the baking time (when baking with a regular oven) works well, too.

✔ **Sink:** Dessert-making creates a lot of dirty utensils, so having a double sink is handy. (Stainless steel is best.) Don't let the sink pile up to the ceiling before cleaning — certain doughs and batters turn to cement after a few hours.

✔ **Temperature/humidity:** The ideal temperature for dessert-making is 70°. At this temperature, butter and pie dough remain intact and don't melt. Chocolate holds its texture nicely. Also, this temperature is cool enough that cream and dairy products don't spoil as quickly.

As for humidity, you can't do much about it except run the air-conditioner. Humidity (and altitude) affects bread-making more than dessert-making.

Kitchen Tools

To make desserts properly, you need some special equipment that's not as common to other types of cooking. We've broken down the equipment you need into categories for easy reference.

Mixing musts

Much of dessert-making involves tossing stuff into a bowl and mixing it up so that it becomes something else. Sometimes you can mix with a handheld whisk or large spoon, but other chores, like making meringue or certain cake batters, are best done with mechanical help. Here's a rundown of the basic mixing tools to consider as you progress along the baking highway.

✔ **Electric blender:** The electric blender is far more utilitarian than many home cooks realize. Because its blade rotates so much faster than that of a food processor, it's better for reconstituting (emulsifying) dessert sauces, especially those sauces that contain eggs. The blender is also a perfect vehicle for making quick fresh fruit sauce (put in some fresh strawberries, a little sugar, and maybe some Grand Marnier, for example). Moreover, you don't need 32 speeds on your blender. You can do well with just three. Prices range from about $50 to $150.

✔ **Electric handheld mixer:** This little machine can save a lot of time when you're whipping egg whites, simple batters, and the like. (See Figure 2-1.)This mixer is also portable, which is convenient. A hand-held mixer is relatively inexpensive (under $30) and is widely available.

hand mixer

Figure 2-1:
An electric
handheld
mixer.

Remember that you have to move the handheld mixer all around when using it — leaving it on one spot won't fully whip cream or egg whites. And because you don't feel the texture, or thickness, of food with an electric mixer the same way you do with a handheld whisk, stop occasionally to determine the texture.

✔ **Food processor:** Many families today have food processors, but not all know how to use them properly for dessert-making. Many food processors come with a whisk attachment that can approximate the whipping action of an electric mixer. They're most valuable for making pie and tart dough. Food processors range in price from about $100 to $250, depending on size.

✔ **Kitchen mixer:** Although we try to keep expenses down regarding machines, a good kitchen mixer, like the well-known KitchenAid, is an invaluable tool for the home dessert maker. You'll find yourself turning to a kitchen mixer continually — for mixing batters, making pasty dough, whisking, making dessert breads, kneading, and more. Kitchen mixers are also good for making soft batters, such as some chocolate mixtures. If you invest in a kitchen mixer, get one with a bowl that has a 3-quart capacity or more. This size can handle most home chores. Kitchen mixers cost anywhere from $250 and up.

A handheld electric mixer can perform most of the chores of a big kitchen mixer. The only exception might be very thick doughs that might be too dense for a little hand mixer. It's really just a matter of convenience.

If you use a large kitchen mixer with a removable bowl, take this precaution to avoid getting covered in flour. Before blending in the bowl of a kitchen mixer, lower the work bowl all the way down so that the paddle barely touches the flour. Start the machine on slow and gradually raise the bowl to working height — this process prevents the flour from flying out of the bowl when you start the mixer.

If you buy a kitchen mixer, such as a KitchenAid, make sure that you get one with enameled paddles and mixer attachments. (The aluminum ones can discolor some egg-based pastries like pâte à choux.)

✔ **Pastry blender:** This handy device has a handle and a U-shaped working end made of six wires (the wires are connected to either end of the handle). You use a pastry blender primarily to break up room-temperature butter into little nuggets, which is the ideal size for blending into flour to make pie dough. You also can use a pastry blender to combine butter with flour. It costs around $10.

✔ **Whisks:** In this book, we probably use a whisk more than any single kitchen tool. (See Figure 2-2.) To get started, have several types of whisks for the various chores you'll be performing. Get stainless steel whisks that have comfortable handles (try them in the store) and smoothly welded connections so that food cannot lodge anywhere. Whisks cost from $5 to $10 each.

Figure 2-2:
A whisk.

The basic sauce whisk has nine sturdy looped wires and is used to mix, blend, emulsify, and aerate. This whisk is good for warm custards or liquid dessert sauces.

The balloon whisk, so named for its shape, is more flexible than the basic sauce whisk and is designed to introduce air into cream and egg whites (so that they fluff up) and into liquids that you want to aerate. Get two sizes — say, one 10 inches long and one 15 inches or so long.

✔ **Wooden spoons:** You can never have too many wooden spoons. You can use spoons for all kinds of cooking, not just dessert-making. Get lots of wooden spoons, in all sizes — 12 to 14-inch spoons are particularly useful for stirring thick batters. Just make sure that they're strong and well made. Good wooden spoons cost up to $5 each.

ESSENTIAL SKILL

Whisking: The dessert cook's aerobics

The purpose of a whisk, whether it's a conventional whisk or a fatter, rounded balloon whisk, is to incorporate air into cream, egg whites, or whatever ingredient you're mixing. Here is the proper way to whisk:

1. Dip the working end of the whisk into the liquid at one side of the bowl. Quickly move the whisk across the bottom of the bowl while you gradually lift it out of the liquid, taking some of the liquid with it.

This step is where the air is introduced.

2. Continue this motion, perhaps tilting the bowl toward you at about 45°, to bring most of the liquid to one side. Keep stroking the whisk and lifting the liquid to incorporate more air, until the liquid reaches the desired consistency.

Useful utensils

Making desserts calls for all kinds of little chores — before you get to the mixing and cooking stage. The following common tools help you do all these tasks.

✔ **Bowl scraper:** This scraper is nothing more than a semi-flexible piece of plastic that allows you to scrape all the batter out of a bowl much more efficiently, and neatly, than using a spoon. (See Figure 2-3.) About $3.

Figure 2-3:
A bowl
scraper.

✔ **Duck press:** Oops! Wrong book — forget that we mention it.

✔ **Grater:** You can use a simple stainless steel kitchen grater almost daily. (See Figure 2-4.) Use the smallest holes for grating lemon zest, which is used frequently in desserts. About $4.

✔ **Knives:** Dessert-making requires three basic knives: a small paring knife (2 to 4-inch-long blade), a serrated knife (generally with a 4-inch blade or longer), and a chef's knife (10- to 12-inch blade). (See Figure 2-5.) As with any knives, always run them over a steel every time you use them to bring back the edge. Knives that are used at home need professional sharpening only once a year, especially if you always use a sharpening steel (see the following sidebar).

Figure 2-4: A grater.

Using a knife steel

1. Hold the steel firmly in one hand at a slight angle away from you and grasp the knife in the other hand.

2. Hold the knife blade at about a 30° angle against the tip of the steel.

3. With a smooth, even stroke, run the blade down the steel shaft, stopping near the protective handle; repeat on the other side of the steel.

4. To test whether your knife is sharp, hold a piece of writing paper and swipe the edge gently with the knife.

A sharp knife will cut through cleanly; a dull knife will tear the paper.

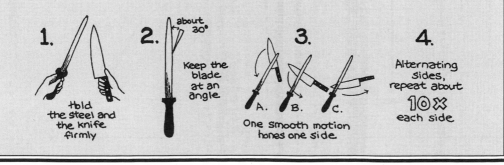

How to use a Sharpening Steel

1. Hold the steel and the knife firmly

2. about 30° Keep the blade at an angle

3. A. B. C. One smooth motion hones one side.

4. Alternating sides, repeat about 10X each side

Figure 2-5:
Essential
dessert-
making
knifes.

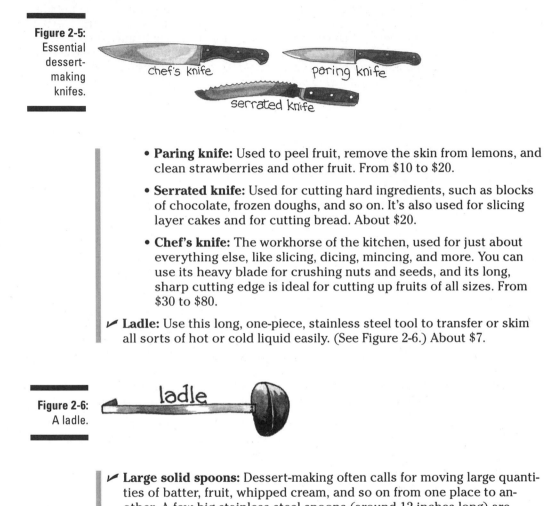

- **Paring knife:** Used to peel fruit, remove the skin from lemons, and clean strawberries and other fruit. From $10 to $20.

- **Serrated knife:** Used for cutting hard ingredients, such as blocks of chocolate, frozen doughs, and so on. It's also used for slicing layer cakes and for cutting bread. About $20.

- **Chef's knife:** The workhorse of the kitchen, used for just about everything else, like slicing, dicing, mincing, and more. You can use its heavy blade for crushing nuts and seeds, and its long, sharp cutting edge is ideal for cutting up fruits of all sizes. From $30 to $80.

✔ **Ladle:** Use this long, one-piece, stainless steel tool to transfer or skim all sorts of hot or cold liquid easily. (See Figure 2-6.) About $7.

Figure 2-6:
A ladle.

✔ **Large solid spoons:** Dessert-making often calls for moving large quantities of batter, fruit, whipped cream, and so on from one place to another. A few big stainless steel spoons (around 12 inches long) are always useful for that. About $5.

✔ **Offset spatula:** This long, narrow spatula with a stepped handle is a real asset to dessert makers because it can easily slide under cookies and other flat cakes. (See Figure 2-7.) It's also good for spreading icings and batters. Get one that has a 10 to 12-inch stainless steel blade. About $6.

Figure 2-7:
An offset
spatula.

✔ **Narrow spatula:** The long, narrow, round-tipped blade is ideal for removing crêpes and blinis from a pan. About $6.

✔ **Perforated spoons:** These spoons are used to lift fruit from its marinade or cooking liquid or to lift any food out of a liquid when you want the liquid left behind. (See Figure 2-8.) Get several perforated spoons in different sizes. About $5.

Figure 2-8:
Perforated
spoons.

✔ **Rolling pin:** Rolling pins come in a confounding array of sizes and shapes. We recommend one that comes with handles that rotate on ball bearings. From $10 to $20.

✔ **Rubber spatulas:** Another workhorse of the dessert cook, rubber-tipped spatulas are invaluable for mixing, folding egg whites, scraping bowls, and more. (See Figure 2-9.) The better spatulas are made of heat-resistant synthetic so that they aren't disfigured when exposed to a hot pan. Get a bunch of them in different sizes. About $5.

Figure 2-9:
A rubber
spatula.

✔ **Sifter:** Many times you're asked to sift flour before adding it to a recipe. The reason is that flour sitting in a bag tends to lump, which can make your batter lumpy. The rotating rods of a sifter break up these lumps and allow the flour to fall through the tiny mesh holes (see Figure 2-10). This way, your flour is evenly textured and easier to measure. You can also use a sifter for confectioners' sugar to eliminate lumps. About $10.

Figure 2-10:
A sifter.

✔ **Wire strainers:** You can use a good all-around wire strainer for countless tasks, like straining flour, crushed nuts, and sauces. Get one about 9½ x 10 inches across the top. Good large strainers cost about $20.

Super bowls

Ask any cook, and he or she will tell you that you can never have enough bowls. Stacking stainless steel bowls, in particular, are invaluable. Buying several in each size for starters is a good idea. Many home cooks have glass mixing bowls and ceramic bowls. These are fine, but they're more fragile than stainless steel.

✔ **Copper egg-white bowl:** Copper has a unique effect on egg whites. Because of a particular chemical reaction (see Chapter 6), whipped egg whites come out higher and more stable when whipped in a copper bowl. If you get one, buy a copper bowl that's at least 12 inches across the top and thick enough to take a beating over the years without losing its shape. It can cost $20 to $30 or more.

✔ **Mixing bowls (stainless steel):** We've yet to meet a home cook who has enough stainless steel mixing bowls. You can use them almost every day, and not just for dessert-making. Get several bowls in sizes ranging from 1 to 3 quarts or larger, depending on your needs. They nest easily for storing. Depending on size, they cost from about $8 to $20.

✔ **Trifle bowl:** Glass or Plexiglas is great for serving the classic English Trifle (see Chapter 11) or other layered desserts like custards (see Chapter 7). A classic trifle bowl is deep, rather wide-bottomed and has near-vertical sides. (See Figure 2-11.) Because a trifle bowl is clear, you can see the layering on the sides. Get the 3-quart or 4-quart size. Prices vary widely depending on material and workmanship, from $20 up.

Figure 2-11:
A trifle
bowl.

Extra equipment

Just when you thought you were set up, here are some other odds and ends that will come in handy no matter what kinds of desserts you make.

✔ **Oven thermometers:** No two ovens are exactly alike, and in baking, precision is all-important. Invest in a quality oven thermometer. Get one that's sturdy — we like stainless steel with a thick, clear thermometer — accurate, and easy to clean. Quality thermometers run $25 to $50.

✔ **Oven timers:** Oven timers come in every shape and size. What type you get doesn't matter, as long as it has an easy-to-read face, works reliably, and is loud enough so that you can hear it from another room. Prices vary widely, from $10 to $50 or more.

✔ **Pastry wheel:** These wheels are invaluable in helping you evenly trim all sorts of pie doughs and pastry. (See Figure 2-12.) The 4-inch steel wheel is run over the pastry and a little bit in from the edge — using a pastry wheel is much easier and neater than using a knife. A pastry wheel also comes with jagged edges to create various designs. About $15.

Figure 2-12:
A pastry
cutting
wheel.

Measuring up

So many desserts require precise measurements, and when it comes to baking, there's little room for variation. For that reason, quality measuring tool are critical. Avoid cheap little plastic cups because the handles invariably break off. Stainless steel is better in the long run.

- ✔ **Dry measuring cups:** Investing in a nesting set of stainless steel measuring cups is best (plastic handles invariably break). Get a set that ranges from $^1/_4$ cup to 1 cup in capacity with long, sturdy handles for easy scooping. A four-set of stainless steel cups costs roughly $20.

- ✔ **Liquid measuring cups:** Glass containers are the best for liquid measures because you can see precisely how much you're putting in them. Get several 1 cup containers and several containers that hold 2 cups, and at least one 1 quart measure. You'll need them. They run about $3 to $8 depending on size.

- ✔ **Measuring spoons:** Don't skimp on something as important as measuring spoons, which bakers use all the time. Get a good set of stainless steel spoons, from 1 tablespoon to $^1/_4$ teaspoon, that you can hang right near the working counter. A good set costs about $15.

- ✔ **Scale:** Because so many kitchen scales are on the market today, from inexpensive plastic spring-loaded versions to high-tech digital types, recommending any one kind is hard. Above all, get a scale that's accurate — you can even ask to test it in the store. And for dessert-making, get a scale that can hold 3 or 4 cups of flour at one time so that you're not constantly reloading. They cost from $25 to $75.

Baking tools

Baking has a whole lexicon and equipment battery to itself. You don't have to run out and get all these things, though. First, think about the type of baking that you want to try right now. Then get the tools necessary for it. If you continue down that road, you'll eventually have mostly all of these things — two of each in some cases.

- ✔ **Baking ring:** This simple, stainless steel device is placed atop a baking sheet and then filled with batter, creating the effect of a cake pan. You use this ring for eggy batters, like custard-based tarts. The ring form promotes quick setting. It usually measures about $^3/_4$ inches high. About $10.

- ✔ **Baking sheet:** Having two sturdy baking sheets is important because they come in handy for all sorts of tasks, like making pastries and buns, functioning as a base for cake molds, and much more. Good baking sheets have slightly angled edges about $^1/_2$ inch high to hold any butter or juice that may ooze out of the pastries. Improved technology has made nonstick baking sheets a smart buy. They're slightly more expensive than plain aluminum — consider one or two of each. Standard size is 16 x 12 inches; round sheets come in diameters of 8 inches, 12 inches, and up to 20 inches or more. Always know your oven dimensions before buying large sheets. Baking sheets run from $10 to $20.

✔ **Cake cooling racks:** You can improvise cooling racks in many ways. But having a good cooling rack on hand is wise to make sure that all your good work doesn't collapse because of uneven cooling. (See Figure 2-13.) Professional bakers have different shaped racks for different cakes, but the home baker can do just fine with one rectangular wire rack 16 to 20 inches or larger. The important thing is that air gets under the cake so that it cools from all sides. About $10.

Figure 2-13:
A cake cooling rack.

✔ **Cake ring:** You can use this 9-inch wide stainless steel ring, shown in Figure 2-14, to make all sorts of light cakes, eggy tarts, and tortes. It can serve as a mold for frozen cakes. (The cakes can be constructed within the ring, demolded, and frozen.) It runs about $15.

Figure 2-14:
A cake ring.

✔ **Cake strips:** You use these widely available strips of aluminum-coated fabric when you want to keep your cake from forming a dome in the center, which tends to happen when the cake cooks unevenly. Soak the strips in water and wrap them around the outside of the cake pan, just before baking. This process slows the heat that reaches the perimeter and cooks the cake more evenly. About $6 for a pack of 3.

✔ **Cookie cutters:** The best are made of stainless steel, and they come in every conceivable shape. About $10 per set.

✔ **Cookie sheet:** These flat sheets, with rims only at the two narrower ends for ease of grasping, are designed so that heat reaches the batter evenly. Aluminum is the most common material, but make sure that it's thick (more than two pounds weight is how the industry classifies them) so that it doesn't warp. Stainless steel is easier to clean but not as heat efficient, and nonstick aluminum is a good option. About $10.

✔ **Crème brûlée dish:** These narrow, low-sided porcelain dishes with fluted edges, which make an authentic-looking crème brûlée, create a custard with a wide surface for broiling. (See Figure 2-15.) You can also make crème brûlée in all kinds of similar-shaped dishes or ramekins. The real things can cost from $5 to $15 apiece.

Figure 2-15:
A crème
brûlée dish.

✔ **Crêpe pan:** This long-handled pan, with a roughly 7-inch-wide bottom, has been used for centuries in France. (See Figure 2-16.) Usually made in black steel, these pans need to be well-greased and well-dried after cleaning. Nonstick crêpe pans are widely available, but they tend to leave a shiny skin on the surface of the crepe rather than a nice earthy and textured look.

Figure 2-16:
A crêpe
pan.

✔ **Custard cups:** As opposed to vertical-sided soufflé dishes, porcelain or ceramic custard cups are bowl-shaped and designed to gently conduct the heat of a bain-marie to the egg mixture inside. (See Figure 2-17.) Most custard cups are 8 ounces, for individual servings. About $5 each.

Figure 2-17:
A custard
cup.

✔ **Double boiler (bain-marie):** We use this boiler frequently in our recipes as a way to prepare egg sauces without having them curdle from overheating. (See Figure 2-18.) A double boiler is simply a bowl with a rounded bottom (preferably metal in order to transfer heat more efficiently) for easy whisking, set into a slightly larger pot holding hot or simmering water — because boiling water can get no hotter than 212°, the sauce can never exceed that temperature. About $20.

Figure 2-18:
A double
boiler.

✔ **Génoise pan:** We talk a lot about the basic génoise cake, or sponge cake, in this book. (See Chapter 9.) It's really one of the foundations of cake-making. For this reason, it's a good investment to get a *génoise pan,* a slope-sided (1¹/₂ inches high) round aluminum pan that is designed to produce a firm, semidense, and evenly cooked cake. About $12.

✔ **Jelly roll pan:** This wide, shallow, rectangular pan is designed to hold liquid batters and also to make airy cakes like a jelly roll. (See Figure 2-19.) You also can use it as an all-around baking or roasting sheet. It usually comes in aluminum and is lined with parchment paper to make cake removal easier. About $15.

Figure 2-19:
A jelly roll
pan.

✔ **Muffin tins:** These standard, inexpensive tins have 12 flared compart-ments (nonstick works very well). The wide tops and narrow bottoms create fast and even rising. About $5.

✔ **Parchment paper:** Parchment paper is thick, sturdy paper that's burn-resistant. Always have this around whenever you want to prevent foods from sticking to a baking sheet in the oven, especially macaroons, meringues, and certain kinds of muffins and cakes. About $5 a roll.

✔ **Pie plate:** This is another must-have item in a baker's kitchen. Usually 8 to 11 inches wide and made of aluminum, they're incredibly versatile. The flat rim helps prevent overflow during baking, but it's still a good idea to place pie plates over a baking sheet to avoid spills in the oven. Glass pie plates are popular, too, but if you buy only one kind, get the more sturdy aluminum. About $2 each.

✔ **Pot de crème:** This specialty porcelain pot comes with a lid and is designed to hold the ultra-rich chocolate dessert called pot-de-crème (see Chapter 7), which is a chocolate-flavored custard. (See Figure 2-20.) Sizes vary. Around 8 ounces makes a generous single serving. About $5 each.

Figure 2-20: Pot de crème.

✔ **Round cake pan:** The key to a good cake is evenly heated batter, and the design of this basic round cake pan does just that. Usually made of inexpensive aluminum, they're round with straight sides to promote uniform rising and have little outward turned lips. About $10.

✔ **Soufflé dishes:** Straight-sided, porcelain dishes like these are perfect for maximizing the rising effects of egg whites. (See Figure 2-21.) They come in sizes ranging from individual servings to several quarts. About $5 each.

Figure 2-21: A soufflé dish.

✔ **Springform pan:** This contraption may be intimidating to novice bakers, but just think of it as a cake pan with a cummerbund. (See Figure 2-22.) The expandable, clipped sides and detachable base are designed for cakes that, because of their composition, can be a nightmare to *demold* (or remove) from normal cake pans. These kinds of cakes include cheesecake, certain honey or molasses type cakes, fruit-filled cakes, and so on. Get a nonstick springform pan, which, when unclipped, leaves your cake perfectly smooth-sided. The best all-around size is 12 inches in diameter. About $12 each.

Figure 2-22:
A springform pan.

✔ **Tart mold:** Every baker needs a steel tart mold or ring measuring about 10 to 14 inches in diameter and 1/2 inch high for making all sorts of tarts. (See Figure 2-23.) Black steel holds heat evenly and promotes puffed crusts and nice browning. About $10.

Figure 2-23:
A tart mold and ring.

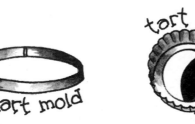

✔ **Tube pan (angel food pan):** Also commonly called an angel food pan, this 4 1/2 -inch-high pan with a hollow tube in the middle is ideal for light, high-rising cakes such as angel food. (See Figure 2-24.) The pan is inverted to allow the cake to cool and demold easily. The most common size has a 9-cup capacity. About $15.

Figure 2-24:
Angel food pans.

Working with fruit

A paring knife (see the section "Useful utensils," earlier in this chapter) is the most useful tool for peeling, pitting, stemming, and cleaning fruit. Some other specialty tools come into action as well.

- ✔ **Cherry pitter:** It looks suspiciously like a painful dental tool, but this device is designed to remove pits from cherries. If you make a dessert that includes cherries, a cherry pitter is a real timesaver. About $12.

- ✔ **Citrus juicer (reamer):** The inexpensive citrus juicer should be near your work counter at all times because so many recipes call for lemon juice. (See Figure 2-25.) About $4.

Figure 2-25:
A citrus juicer (reamer).

- ✔ **Citrus stripper:** This tool has a little protrusion that peels away one neat strip of citrus zest. (See Figure 2-26.) It also works on cucumbers, beets, carrots, and other firm vegetables. About $5.

Figure 2-26:
A citrus stripper.

- ✔ **Citrus zester:** This tool has five little holes at the end for peeling threads of lemon zest (also limes and oranges). (See Figure 2-27.) It also works on firm vegetables, like carrots and beets. You can deep-fry the skins of vegetables and serve them as garnish. About $5.

Figure 2-27:
A citrus
zester.

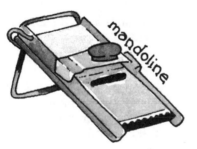

✔ **Mandoline:** This tool has nothing to do with ethnic music. The French mandoline is a device that slices, *juliennes* (cuts thin strips on a bias), and waffle-cuts fruits and vegetables. The food item is placed in a little compartment and held in place by a handle. You run the food over an adjustable blade. (See Figure 2-28.) A mandoline is great for apple tarts and any dessert that requires precise cutting. The stainless steel version is durable, but quite expensive: $150 or more.

A plastic Japanese-made version does a credible job as well (under $40). In both cases, be extremely cautious when running foods over these sharp blades.

Figure 2-28:
A
mandoline.

Miscellaneous items

Some of the following items are the kinds of things you see in cookware stores and say, "What in the world is that?" Yes, some are esoteric, and you can live without them. Others are more fundamental.

✔ **Candy thermometer:** This special thermometer, sometimes encased in a protective stainless steel cage, measures the heat of sugar syrup. (See Figure 2-29.) Temperatures in candy-making are critical, and a good thermometer is essential. Good ones made for professional use have a bright yellow background, which makes it easy to read the mercury, and clips to hold them to the pot. You can get a perfectly good one at most supermarkets for about $5.

Figure 2-29:
A candy
thermometer.

✔ **Chocolate thermometer:** If you plan to make a lot of chocolate candies and other desserts, this would be a worthwhile investment. As we explain in Chapter 20, chocolate must go through several stages of heating and melting in order to achieve a nice glossy sheen. A long (12 inches) thin chocolate thermometer (registering from 60° to 120°) helps measure this. Get one that is easy to read — some have tiny print that is impossible! About $15.

✔ **Ice cream scoop:** The scoop is just what it says. It's for scooping out ice creams and sorbets. So why do you need a scoop when a big spoon can do the job? Mostly for cosmetic reasons: If you're serving a homemade sorbet or ice cream, it's nice to present it attractively.

Such scoops come in many shapes and sizes. The average home cook does well with the nonmechanical insulated aluminum scoop. A fluid inside the scoop heats up under hot tap water or boiling water (use a potholder if you get it very hot). You can find ice creams scoops in various sizes.

✔ **Nutmeg grater:** You can't compare freshly grated nutmeg with pow-dered nutmeg in a jar. The whole nutmeg has much more flavor. This inexpensive little device allows you to control the amount of nutmeg added. Just run it up and down against the teeth on the flat surface and watch the amount of nutmeg that falls below. You also can use the part of a kitchen grater with small, rough-edged holes. About $5.

✔ **Tongs:** Dessert-making often requires picking up hot things. Simple and inexpensive stainless steel tongs (see Figure 2-30) are just the item.

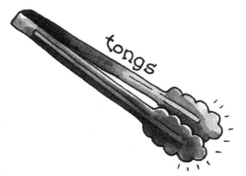

Figure 2-30:
Tongs.

Luxury machines

The term luxury in this section's heading may be misleading, because if you make ice cream, you need a machine of some sort. The refrigerated models could be considered luxury items because they require no manual labor. Some people we know prefer to make ice cream with hand-crank devices that use rock salt for cooling because those folks can judge the texture better than they can by looking in an electric machine. You certainly get a workout that way.

✔ **Hand-crank ice cream machine:** This machine has an aluminum barrel in the center that's surrounded by ice and salt in a wooden bucket. The ice cream base is placed in the aluminum barrel, and you churn up ice cream in as little as 20 minutes. It comes in both electric and hand-cranked models. Some of these models also have a refrigeration unit.

✔ **Single-quart crank ice cream machine:** This little plastic model has an aluminum liner that holds brine solution. The liner is placed in the freezer for 8 hours before the ice cream base is poured into it. By cranking for 10 minutes or so, you can make a quart (there's a $1^1/_2$-quart model, too) of very nicely textured, well-aerated ice cream. This model is perfect for those who have little time to make ice cream the traditional way. It's also good for making sorbets and for churning frozen drinks. About $30.

✔ **Electric refrigerated ice cream machine:** A refrigerated ice cream machine does it all for you — that's why one costs from $250 and up. All you have to be concerned with is making a good ice cream base.

✔ **Juicers:** Many dessert recipes, especially sorbets and granités, call for all kinds of fruit juice and even some vegetable juices. (See Figure 2-31.) A good electric juicer, which strains out all pulp and gives you pure juice, is handy to have around. Juicers vary widely in price, from around $75 to several hundred dollars, but they can save lots of time and effort.

Figure 2-31:
An electric
fruit juicer.

Pastry pluses

If you plan to experiment with dessert pastries, here are a few handy
items to know about.

- **Marble slab:** If you work a lot with tart and pie dough, you may want to
  get a thick marble slab ($^3/_4$ inch or more is best so that it retains its
  coolness and won't move around as you work on it). The cool surface
  of marble prevents butter from melting when you're working it into
  certain doughs. Many cooks like to have marble slabs built into their
  countertops. (Marble slabs aren't cutting boards — if you cut on them,
  you dull your knives quickly. You should have a separate wood or
  synthetic cutting board.) From $50 to $150 and up.

- **Pastry bags and tips:** A pastry bag is usually made of coated nylon. (See
  Figure 2-32.) For all-around use, we recommend a 14-inch to 16-inch bag.
  (See Chapter 4 for instructions on using it.) We also recommend a #5 or
  #6 tip (that's about the size of your little finger). Also, get a *star tip* if you
  want to get fancy. That's a tip with v-cuts to make a striped line of
  frosting. Of course, you can find hundreds more tips and experiment.
  Depending on the tip you insert, you can use pastry bags to make
  meringue domes, icing flowers, and decorative dessert pastries.

Figure 2-32:
A pastry
bag and
tips.

✔ **Pastry brush:** You can use wooden-handled brushes with tight natural bristles (preferable to stiffer nylon) to apply butter and other fats to all sorts of pastries. (See Figure 2-33.) Get them with bristles at least 4 inches long.

Figure 2-33:
A pastry brush.

Part II
Flour Power: Pie Doughs, Tarts, and Puff Pastries

The 5th Wave   By Rich Tennant

"AFTER WALT RETIRED FROM THE NAVY HE TOOK UP BAKING. THAT'S WHY ALL HIS ECLAIRS LOOK LIKE SUBMARINES."

In this part . . .

In Part II, we reach into the flour bin, get dusty, and start making some classic American pies. The first thing you need to find out, however, is how to make a great pie crust — the greatest-tasting apple filling inside leaden crust never won any ribbons. Like everything else in dessert-making, great pie crust requires attention to small details, and a little patience.

Then we move on to French tarts, fruit strips, and the like. Tart doughs are sweeter, made with almond flour or other flours, and easier to work with than pie dough. You can see the unique characteristics of each and why they work best with specific recipes.

In this vein, we make an elegant raspberry tart coated with a fresh raspberry glaze, an apricot tart, a pineapple tart and the classic Linzertorte from Austria.

Chapter 3

Pies and Tarts

In this chapter, we investigate the delicious possibilities of pies and tarts. The major difference between the two is the pastry that holds them. In American-style pies, the pastry is made with flour, water, fat (butter or vegetable shortening), and salt. Tart dough usually contains ground almonds and has a crunchy texture.

Another major distinction between the two doughs is appearance. Pies are deeper and usually have a top crust. Tarts are shallower and usually don't have a top crust.

It's worth the time to master the Basic American Pie Dough and the French Tart Dough — pâte sablé. These doughs let you whip together a beautiful fruit pie or tart when the produce is in season or put together a festive dessert, like banana cream pie, for a party.

In this chapter, we start with American pie dough and how to make it. Then we give you all kinds of fillings for sensational pies.

The tart section begins with a discussion of tart doughs. We then give recipes for some of the world's most popular tarts.

Know Your Dough

Before tackling pies and tarts, you should take a little time to understand the basics of each dough.

For American pie doughs, the goal is to achieve a light texture and slightly puffed and golden-brown appearance. This look occurs when the fat in the dough (butter or shortening) separates the starch granules and causes the dough to puff up just a little. You need to roll pie dough quickly so that the butter and shortening does not warm up too much and liquify. Also, you should roll pie dough as lightly and as gently as possible — working it too much or too forcefully makes it tough.

On the other hand, French tart dough should be slightly dry in texture, and the nut flavor should meld with the rich butter flavor, creating a beautiful combination.

General tips for pie and tart doughs:

- ✔ **Always work with cold (not rock hard) butter.** When the dough goes in the oven, it should have little chunks of butter (or shortening) throughout. Those chunks lift the dough and make it light and flaky.

- ✔ **You don't need to sift the flour that you use for pie and tart dough.**

- ✔ **Consider doubling the dough recipe and freezing the remaining dough for later use.** Roll out the leftover dough first (this makes it easier to defrost) and cover tightly in plastic wrap. Frozen dough will be good for at least a month.

- ✔ **After you make a pie dough, refrigerate it until needed.** Dough is actually better after it rests for two hours or more in the refrigerator — but not much more than that. (See Figure 3-1.)

Refrigerating Pie Dough

Figure 3-1:
Refrigerating
pie dough.

Place the dough on plastic wrap and roll out to a 2" thick, rough oval. Fold wrap over the dough and chill!

✔ **Remember that the more you mix or roll dough, the tighter it gets — and the tighter it gets, the tougher it gets.** That's why we remind you to mix just enough to blend the ingredients, and no more.

✔ **Chill the dough before you roll it because it will be slightly sticky and warm from the mixing.** By chilling the dough, the shortening has a chance to solidify, making the dough easier to work with.

✔ **When we say *lightly flour a counter* before rolling out dough, we mean *lightly*.** If you use too much flour as you're working the dough, the ratio of flour to fat changes, and you can wind up with a hubcap rather than a pie shell.

✔ **American-style pie crusts are best when light golden-brown and a little bit rough textured from the morsels of fat melting.** The crust should not be absolutely smooth. French-style crusts also are better when golden-brown.

✔ **The greatest enemy of pie and tart doughs is excess moisture.** If your fruits leak too much moisture during the cooking process, you have a soggy crust. To avoid a soggy crust, you may want to cook your fruit — usually berries, peaches, and other juicy fruits — with a little cornstarch. For example, a pound of peaches takes about $1/3$ cup ($1 1/2$ ounces) cornstarch and $1/3$ cup (2 ounces) sugar for a pie. Cook until the juices come out and start to thicken with the cornstarch.

Pie trivia

Here's a little food for thought while waiting for your pie or tart to cook.

1. **Which American actors or comedians are most associated with pie-throwing?**

2. **In the late 16th century, puckish Italian gourmets sometimes startled guests by serving a giant pie that held live animals. What type of animals were they?**

3. **What popular song of the early 1970s celebrated this special type of dessert? Who sang it?**

4. **Pie has a homonym, spelled this way: *pi*. What in the world does that mean?**

5. **What 1964 movie originally had a brawling pie fight at the end — but it was cut out by the director because the actors lost their professional composure and had too good a time doing it?**

6. **What kind of pie did Marlon Brando order in the diner scene of *The Wild Ones*?**

7. **The Three Stooges made 190 comedies for Columbia Pictures. How many contained bona fide pie fights?**

Answers: 1. *The Three Stooges,* Soupy Sales. 2. Birds. 3. "American Pie," Don McLean. 4. The ratio of the circumference of a circle to its diameter, or, more simply put: 3.1415926. 5. *Dr. Strangelove,* directed by Stanley Kubrick. 6. Apple pie. 7. Five.

Making Pie Dough

When one thinks of the old-fashioned American farmhouse pies, it's usually those Norman Rockwell, golden, dome-shaped delights. This lovely, puffed and golden crust is achieved by blending the right amount of butter and vegetable shortening (you can use lard rather than shortening, but it's harder to find). In the following recipes, we use all-vegetable shortening like Crisco. You may want to experiment by substituting some butter for the shortening and see the difference. Some cooks prefer a blend of shortening and butter 70 to 30 percent or even 50-50 — butter adds flavor to the crust.

To make a really great pie crust, you need to understand what this blend of simple ingredients is all about. Pie doughs, like people, have different densities, different elasticities, and sundry different qualities. Making pie doughs may sound daunting, but the good news is that you can tackle this topic one dough at a time and enjoy some terrific homemade pies along the way.

Great moments in pie-throwing

Pie-throwing — that is, tossing a pie in someone's face — is an all-American tradition. (Did you ever see Francois Mitterand get nailed by a pie?) Cream pies hit politicians, comedians, actors, and public speakers of all types. This action of benign (but sloppy) aggression probably says something about the American psyche, but we can't figure out what. In today's hard-edged, aggressive world, pie-throwing seems more quaint than threatening. And it's always funny. Here are some highlights in the history of this unsanctioned sport:

✔ 1974: Seabee Leon L. Louie was court-martialed for throwing a chocolate pie at Warrant Officer Timothy Curtin. At the trial, comedian Soupy Sales testified on behalf of the defendant that pie-throwing was a way of relieving tension "without hurting anyone." The jury disagreed, reducing Louie to second class seaman, restricting him to the base for six months, and fining him $400. The Navy said that this was the first court-martial ever involving pie-throwing.

✔ 1981: William F. Buckley Jr., speaking at a Young Republicans forum at the University of Arizona, in Tucson, found himself at the other end of a flying coconut cream pie. The attack was believed to have been carried out by a dessert-tossing gang known as the Oddfather. The gang supposedly executed pie-throwing contracts for $5 each.

Having removed most of the coconut-flecked custard from his face, Mr. Buckley remarked: "They went to all the trouble of throwing the pie and didn't stay around to see the reaction."

Pie quotes of the decade

Richard (Otto) Filsinger, a blackjack and baccarat croupier at Harrah's Atlantic City Casino, has won every pie-eating contest that he's entered since 1988 — including the big annual charity event to benefit the cancer unit at Shore Memorial Hospital in Somers Point, NJ.

According to *The New York Times,* Associated Press, and the *Guinness Book of World Records,* Filsinger said of a competitor's sportsmanship: "He was shaking some of the pie off of his face instead of eating it," the 6-foot-1, 250-pound Filsinger remarked after a grueling contest (which he won). "The rules are you have to eat the entire pie, without using your hands. If any of the pie falls on the table, or on the sand, you have to eat that, too. I didn't see much of his pie going into his mouth, but when I have my face in a pie, I don't see much of anything."

And on the winning attitude: "One year, one casino threw cherries into the blueberries, and that was disgusting because I don't like cherries," Mr. Filsinger said. "But I ate the pie anyway, and I won. And sometimes they put on a crumb crust, which requires a different strategic approach. But I don't let it stop me. Nothing can stop me."

American-style pie dough is nothing more than flour, fat (butter or lard), water, and salt — some cooks add an egg, but we prefer the texture without egg. The main difference among American pie doughs is the type and amount of fat in them. When making this type of dough, butter or lard is cut into little pieces and partially mixed with flour — you want to have tiny nuggets of butter or lard throughout the dough. These nuggets melt while baking and give the crust its wonderful flaky quality. This flaky process occurs because the fat morsels expand as they melt and create tiny air pockets in the dough.

Basic American Pie Dough

This American pie dough recipe calls for ice water mixed with the flour. When a recipe calls for ice water, make sure that you measure only the water, without the ice cubes, or your measurements will be off.

We recommend a blend of delicate cake flour and all-purpose flour for this pie dough because it blends better with the shortening. Often we call for cake flour alone. Cake flour, which is available in most supermarkets, is a low-gluten flour that is excellent for many types of baking because it's exceptionally light.

Tools: *Electric mixer (optional), plastic wrap, 9-inch pie plate, rolling pin*

Preparation time: *10 minutes (plus 2 hours refrigeration)*

Baking time: *None*

Yield: *Dough for 1 pie in a 9-inch pie plate*

1¼ cups (10 ounces) shortening	*1 teaspoon salt*
2 cups (8 ounces) cake flour	*1 cup (8 ounces) ice water*
2 cups (8 ounces) flour	*½ inch pat of butter, for greasing the pie dish*

Pie Dough

1 With a knife, cut the shortening into nickle-size pieces and place in a large bowl. Add the flour and mix only enough to combine, or coat, the shortening nuggets with flour.

2 Add the salt and, while continuing to mix, drizzle in the ice water — blend just until the dough comes together or starts to look like a thick paste. Remove from the bowl and place on a flat surface that is dusted with flour. With your hands, pat down the dough into a rough rectangle about 1 inch thick. Cover in plastic wrap and refrigerate for 2 hours. (The shortening needs to chill and solidify, which makes the dough easier to roll out and work with.)

Rolling out the dough and laying it in the pie pan

1 Using your fingers, spread the butter back and forth over the pie plate until well covered.

2 Remove the dough from the refrigerator and place it on a lightly floured flat surface. Cut the dough in half and place half into the refrigerator. Using a rolling pin, roll out half of the dough into circle that is a little bigger than the circumference of the pie plate — that is, roughly an 11-inch circle for a 9-inch pie plate. Dust the dough and the counter frequently to prevent sticking — but use very little flour each time.

3 To lift the dough, place a rolling pin close to 1 edge of the pie plate. Lift about 3 inches of the edge of the dough up onto the rolling pin. Slowly roll the pin towards you while lifting the dough.

4 To lay the dough over a buttered pie plate: Gently place the rolling pin over one edge of the pie plate and unroll the dough over the entire plate. Then lift the edges of the dough so that gravity lowers it into the bottom of the plate. With your fingers, press the dough into the corners of the plate. The dough should cover the sides, leaving about an inch or two of overlap on the edge.

5 After adding the filling, remove the other half of the dough from the refrigerator, roll it thin, and cover the pie. Squeeze the edges of the dough together and crimp to form a fluted edge.

TOQUE TIP

Pie dough and gluten

Gluten is the protein that when mixed with water becomes elastic. In proper proportions, it gives dough or bread its individual texture — too much gluten or too much working or kneading makes it rubbery. In a pie dough, very little gluten is desired because you want a dough that is flaky and falls apart, not one that has a resilient texture like some breads.

Choosing Your Pie Filling

After you make a pie crust, you need something to put in it. Fresh fruits are a simple and delicious option, and you can vary the flavors as you like with cinnamon, vanilla, mint, nutmeg, flavored liqueurs, and more.

Several classic American pies call for a custard base and cream topping rather than a top crust. They include banana cream pie and every kid's favorite, chocolate cream pie.

Frequently, fruits and vegetables are briefly boiled in water to remove their acidity before adding them to a dish. *Blanching* simply means to immerse in rapidly boiling water for 30 seconds and then drain in a colander.

Mom's Apple Pie

Here's a classic American apple pie made the way Mom did it — even if it wasn't your mom! If your crust is light and golden, you can't go wrong with this one. (For the best crust, prepare the Basic American Pie Dough recipe, earlier in this chapter.)

Tools: *Rolling pin, 9-inch pie pan, pastry brush*

Preparation time: *45 minutes (not including pie crust)*

Baking time: *40 minutes*

Yield: *6 to 8 servings*

(continued)

¹/₂ cup (2 ounces) cornstarch

¹/₂ cup (3 ounces) sugar

2 teaspoons cinnamon

10 Granny Smith or Golden Delicious apples, cored, peeled and each sliced into 12 even wedges

juice from 1 lemon (2 tablespoons)

1 pie dough for a 9-inch pie pan

1 egg

1 tablespoon water

¹/₄ teaspoon salt

1 Preheat oven to 375°.

2 In a small bowl, mix together the cornstarch, sugar, and cinnamon.

3 In a large bowl, combine the apples and lemon juice. Sprinkle the sugar mixture over the apples. Toss the apples to coat well. Let sit to marinate while you assemble the crust.

4 Meanwhile, roll out the pie dough and place half of the dough in the pie pan. (See the Basic American Pie Dough recipe, earlier in this chapter, for detailed instructions.)

5 Transfer the apples and any juices in the bowl to the pie crust. With a wooden spoon or your hand, arrange the apples evenly around the edges, forming a slight mound in the middle. (This process makes the pie look better when it cooks — it will have a dome in the center rather than an indentation.)

6 Cover with other piece of dough. Brush the dough with egg wash (whisked egg, water, and salt). Using a knife, make three 1-inch cuts in the top of the dough to allow steam to escape during baking. Bake for about 40 minutes, until the crust is golden-brown.

Plum Pie

Plums have a lot of juice, which can make a pie crust soggy. That's why we add cornstarch to this recipe — cornstarch soaks up the plum juice and turns it into a sweet, fruity paste.

For best results, use the Basic American Pie Dough recipe, earlier in this chapter. You can also prepare this pie without the top crust, creating a Plum Tart (which you can see in the color photo section of this book).

Try substituting apricots or nectarines (which have a similar texture to plums) in this recipe. Check out the color section of this book for a look at the Nectarine Pie variation of this recipe.

Tools: *Rolling pin, 9-inch pie pan, pastry brush*

Preparation time: *45 minutes (not including the crust)*

Baking time: *40 minutes*

Yield: *6 to 8 servings*

$^1/_2$ cup (2 ounces) cornstarch	*1 pie dough for a 9-inch pie pan*
$^1/_2$ cup (3 ounces) sugar	*1 egg*
15 ripe plums, pitted, skins left on	*1 tablespoon water*
juice from 1 lemon (2 tablespoons)	*$^1/_4$ teaspoon salt*

1 Preheat oven to 375°.

2 In a small bowl, mix together the cornstarch and sugar.

3 In a large bowl, combine the plums and lemon juice. Sprinkle the sugar mixture over the plums. Toss the plums to coat well. Let sit to marinate the plums while you assemble the crust.

4 Meanwhile, roll out the pie dough and place half in the pie pan. (See the Basic American Pie Dough recipe, earlier in this chapter, for detailed instructions.)

5 Transfer the plums and just a little bit of the plum juices to the pie crust. With a wooden spoon or your hand, arrange the plums evenly around the edges.

6 Cover with other piece of dough. Brush the dough with egg wash (whisked egg, water, and salt). Using a knife, make three 1-inch cuts in the top of the dough to allow steam to escape during baking. Bake for about 40 minutes, until the crust is golden-brown. (This pie can be baked without a top crust, if preferred.)

Sour Cherry Pie

For this recipe, we break our orthodox commitment to freshness and call for canned sour cherries. Why? Well, in this case, they work well because sour cherries are canned at the peak of ripeness and have a nice tart-sweet flavor. Using canned cherries also saves you the time of pitting 2 pounds of cherries, which may not be as ripe. If you want, use 2 pounds of pitted sour cherries in the recipe and follow the same instructions.

For the best pie dough, prepare the Basic American Pie Dough recipe, earlier in this chapter.

(continued)

Tools: *Rolling pin, 9-inch pie pan, pastry brush*

Preparation time: *45 minutes (not including pie crust)*

Baking time: *40 minutes*

Yield: *6 to 8 servings*

¹/₂ cup (2 ounces) cornstarch	*1 pie dough for a 9-inch pie pan*
¹/₂ cup (3 ounces) sugar	*1 egg*
two 12-ounce cans sour cherries in juices, drained	*1 tablespoon water*
	¹/₄ teaspoon salt
juice from 1 lemon (2 tablespoons)	

1 Preheat oven to 375°.

2 In a small bowl, mix together the cornstarch and sugar.

3 Place the cherries in a large bowl. Add the lemon juice and sprinkle the sugar mixture over the cherries. Toss to coat well. Let sit to marinate while you assemble the crust.

4 Meanwhile, roll out the pie dough and place half in the pie pan. (See the Basic American Pie Dough recipe, earlier in this chapter, for detailed instuctions.)

5 Transfer the cherries to the pie crust. With a wooden spoon or your hand, arrange the cherries evenly around the edges, forming a slight mound in the middle. (This makes the pie look better when it cooks — it will have a dome in the center rather than an indentation.)

6 Cover with the other piece of dough. Brush the dough with egg wash (whisked egg, water, and salt). With a knife, make three 1-inch slashes in the top of the pie so that steam can escape during cooking. Bake for about 40 minutes, until the crust is golden-brown.

Rhubarb Pie

This summer pie is a special treat, blending the tart-sweet flavor of fresh rhubarb with the puffed, golden pie crust. Be sure to remove the leaves from the rhubarb stalk because the leaves can be toxic. (See the Basic American Pie Dough recipe, earlier in this chapter.)

Tools: *Large pot, medium pot*

Preparation time: *1 hour (not including pie crust)*

Baking time: *45 minutes*

Yield: *6 to 8 servings*

17 cups (136 ounces) water	1 pie dough
2 pounds (20 stalks) fresh rhubarb, washed and cut into 2-inch segments	1 egg
	1 tablespoon water
1 cup (6 ounces) sugar	$^1/_4$ teaspoon salt
$^1/_2$ cup (2 ounces) cornstarch	

1 Preheat oven to 400°.

2 Bring 16 cups (128 ounces) water to a boil in a large pot. Blanch the rhubarb 30 seconds and then drain. (Dropping it briefly in boiling water reduces its acidity and makes it easier to work with.)

3 In a medium pot, bring 1 cup (8 ounces) water to a boil. In a bowl, mix the sugar and cornstarch together and pour into the boiling water. Add the blanched rhubarb, stirring gently — not too brusquely, or the rhubarb will shred. When this mixture thickens, pour it into a wide bowl to cool.

4 When the mixture is thoroughly cool, pour it into the pie crust. Place the top crust on the pie. Brush the dough with egg wash (whisked egg, water, and salt). Bake for 45 minutes, until the crust is golden-brown.

Banana Cream Pie

Talk about a party pie. Everybody loves a banana cream pie. This custardy version with a whipped cream topping requires a crust that's precooked so that the custard doesn't seep in and make it soggy. Precooking makes the crust hard and impervious. Once the crust is baked, you can set it aside at room temperature, covered with plastic wrap, for a day. For the best results, use the Basic American Pie Dough recipe, earlier in this chapter.

If you don't want to use a pastry bag, you can use a rubber spatula to spread the whipped cream mixture over the pie.

Tools: *Rolling pin, 9-inch pie pan, parchment paper, weights, medium pot, electric mixer (optional), bowl, plastic wrap, pastry bag with #5 star tip (optional)*

Preparation time: *40 minutes (not including pie crust)*

(continued)

Baking time: *35 minutes*

Yield: *6 to 8 servings*

1 pie dough for a 9-inch pie pan (bottom crust only)

2¼ cups (18 ounces) milk

½ cup (3 ounces) sugar

2 ripe bananas

¼ cup (1 ounce) cornstarch

Pie Dough

3 eggs

2 egg yolks

1 vanilla bean, split lengthwise, or 1 teaspoon vanilla extract

⅓ envelope powdered gelatin

2 cups (16 ounces) heavy cream, very cold

⅓ cup (1½ ounces) confectioners' sugar

Pie Dough

1 Preheat oven to 375°.

2 Roll out the bottom half of the pie dough into an 11-inch circle. Place it in the pie pan. With a fork, prick the bottom of the dough all over.

3 Cut a sheet of parchment paper to fit inside the pie dough. Place weights over the paper to hold down the dough (otherwise, the pie dough could rise up like a balloon). You can use navy beans, rice, or even a pie plate or fry pan that fits inside the dough.

4 Bake for 25 minutes. Remove the weights and parchment paper and continue to bake for another 10 minutes. (This process makes the pie dough brown and crispy.) Remove the dough and allow it to cool as you make the banana cream filling.

Filling

1 In a medium pot, bring 2 cups (16 ounces) milk and the sugar to a boil.

2 Meanwhile, in a bowl, mash 1 banana with a fork. Add the cornstarch, eggs, egg yolks, and vanilla.

3 Whisk the banana mixture while gradually pouring in the hot milk. The mixture will be liquid at this point.

4 Pour this mixture back into the pot used for the milk. Over medium heat, continue whisking even more until the mixture thickens to a thick pudding consistency — about 3 minutes. Remove from heat and transfer to a bowl. Cover with plastic wrap and refrigerate for about 15 minutes.

5 Slice the remaining banana and place the pieces around the bottom of the pie shell. Remove the vanilla bean from the cooled banana mixture. Pour the cooled banana mixture over the banana slices. (The mixture should be cool but not so cold that it sets and becomes solid — if it does, just whisk to make it smooth and soft.) Refrigerate while you make the topping.

Pie Topping

1 Pour $^1/_4$ cup (2 ounces) milk into a pot and sprinkle the gelatin over it. Let sit at room temperature so that the gelatin moistens.

2 In a bowl, combine the heavy cream and confectioners' sugar. Whip the cream until it reaches soft peaks.

3 Warm (but don't boil) the milk-gelatin mixture to melt the gelatin, stirring. When the gelatin has melted (sand-like grains of gelatin are no longer visible), remove from heat.

4 Whisk the cream more while drizzling in the gelatin mixture. Whisk until the cream forms stiff peaks.

5 Place the whipped cream in a pastry bag with a #5 star tip (or use a rubber spatula).

6 By squirting out small, equal-size amounts at a time, cover the pie filling with little star patterns of whipped cream. Refrigerate. Serve the pie well chilled.

Chocolate Cream Pie

This all-time classic has many variations, especially for the chocolate filling. Some recipes call for a thick and rich base, like chocolate pudding. Others have a lighter, almost frothy base. This version falls somewhere in between, having a lovely chocolate-vanilla base and a puffy whipped cream topping. For the best results, use the Basic American Pie Dough recipe, earlier in this chapter.

Tools: *Medium pot, plastic wrap, electric mixer (optional), pastry bag with #5 star tip*

Preparation time: *40 minutes (not including pie crust)*

Cooking time: *None*

Yield: *6 to 8 servings*

1 vanilla bean, split lengthwise, or 1 teaspoon vanilla extract

2 $^1/_4$ cups (18 ounces) milk

$^1/_3$ cup (1$^1/_2$ ounces) confectioners' sugar

3 tablespoons cocoa powder

2 tablespoons cornstarch

3 eggs

2 egg yolks

2 ounces bittersweet chocolate, chopped

1 prebaked 9-inch pie crust

$^1/_3$ envelope powdered gelatin

2 cups (16 ounces) heavy cream, very cold

$^1/_2$ cup (3 ounces) sugar

(continued)

Filling

1 In a medium pot, bring the vanilla, 2 cups (16 ounces) milk, and confectioners' sugar to a boil. Remove the vanilla bean. Remove from heat.

2 In a large mixing bowl, combine the cocoa, cornstarch, eggs, and egg yolks.

3 While whisking the mixture, gradually pour in the hot milk. It should reach a loose pudding consistency.

4 Pour this mixture into the pot that was used for the milk. Over medium heat, continue whisking until the mixture thickens even more to a thick pudding consistency — about 3 minutes. Add the chopped chocolate and stir until fully mixed. Transfer to a bowl, cover with plastic wrap, and refrigerate for about 15 minutes — not too much longer or else the filling will solidify. (If it does, just whisk it until smooth.)

5 Pour the cooled mixture into the pie shell. Refrigerate while you make the topping.

Topping

1 Pour the remaining milk into a pot and sprinkle the gelatin over it.

2 In a bowl, combine the heavy cream and sugar. Whip the cream until it reaches soft peaks.

3 Warm (but do not boil) the milk-gelatin mixture to melt the gelatin, stirring. When the gelatin has melted (sand-like grains of gelatin are no longer visible), remove from heat.

4 Whisk the cream more while drizzling in the gelatin mixture. Whisk until the cream forms stiff peaks.

5 Place the whipped cream in a pastry bag that has a #5 star tip (or use a rubber spatula).

6 By squirting out small amounts at a time, cover the pie filling with little star patterns of the whipped cream mixture. Serve the pie well chilled.

French Tart Doughs

French cooks prefer very smooth dough mixtures that are blended with ground almonds or other nuts to make them crunchy.

A tart is essentially an open-topped dessert with a nutty crust. It's made in a tart pan (also called tart mold or ring), which has low sides (sometimes fluted — see equipment in Chapter 2). In addition, French tart doughs often are lined with a baked thin custard (so it's firm, not liquid).

Madame de Sablé

In researching these doughs, we came across the name of Madame de Sablé, who lived in the 17th century and, evidently, was one of France's early gourmets and gourmands. (She may well be the person who invented the famous almond-flavored tart crust described in this section.)

All we know about Madame de Sablé comes from a local writer of the time who noted: "Since she has become devoutly religious, she is fonder of good food than anyone else in the world; she maintains that there is no one who has such discriminating taste as herself. She is always inventing some clever new trick."

Although most American pie doughs are meant to be filled while the dough is raw and then everything cooked together, many French tarts have pre-cooked crusts. This process gives the crust a toasty, nutty flavor. A fresh fruit mixture — sometimes raw, sometimes cooked — is then added.

No matter what kind of dough you make, remember not to overmix or overwork the dough — the more you work the dough, the more elastic and tough it gets. If you overmix the dough by mistake, try painting it green and using it a Frisbee.

Basic French tart dough

A popular French tart dough is pâte sablé, which is made with slivered almonds that are churned up in a food processor until reaching the consistency of rough flour. Pâte sablé is the most luxurious of all tart doughs — rich and buttery, sweet and nutty. This dough is great for berry tarts.

French Tart Dough

If you want to try making pâte sablé, check out this recipe (see photo).

Tools: *Electric mixer (optional), food processor (optional), plastic wrap, rolling pin, tart ring, scissors*

Preparation time: *35 minutes (plus 1 to 2 hours refrigeration)*

Baking time: *None*

Yield: *Enough for one 9-inch tart*

(continued)

³/₄ cup (6 ounces or 1¹/₂ sticks) butter, cut into dime-size pieces, cold

¹/₂ cup (2 ounces) plus 1 tablespoon confectioners' sugar

2 cups (8 ounces) cake flour

2 eggs

pinch of salt

zest of 1 orange

¹/₂ cup (2 ounces) whole blanched almonds

¹/₂-inch pat of butter, for greasing the cookie sheet

1 Place the butter and ¹/₂ cup (2 ounces) confectioners' sugar in a bowl. Blend with an electric mixer (preferable) or wooden spoon until soft.

2 Pour half of the flour over the butter. While mixing, add the eggs. Then, while still mixing, add remaining flour, salt, and orange zest. Keep mixing until thoroughly blended (about 1 minute) — but no more, or you'll make the pastry tough.

3 In a bowl or food processor, place the almonds and 1 tablespoon confectioners' sugar. Process until powdery. (If you don't have a food processor, chop the almonds as finely as you can with a large knife.) Add the almond-sugar mixture to the dough mixture and mix about 30 seconds or until well-incorporated.

4 Scoop the dough onto a sheet of plastic wrap. Lightly flour your hands and press the dough into a rough oval no more than 1 inch thick. (This process helps the dough cool faster and roll out easier.) Cover the dough with another sheet of plastic wrap and refrigerate for 1 to 2 hours.

5 To roll out the dough: When the dough is cool, remove from the plastic wrap and place on a lightly floured board. Sprinkle the top of the dough with flour.

6 Use a rolling pin to gently roll out the dough, working from the center toward the edges. Maintain equal pressure on both ends of the rolling pin to assure even thickness. Roll the dough out into a round about ¹/₄ inch thick and about 13 inches in diameter. (This size gives you enough to overlap the tart ring.) If you want a quick way to measure the thickness, ¹/₄ inch is about the thickness of 50 pages of a book.

7 Place the tart ring over a cookie sheet (butter the part of the cookie sheet that is covered with the tart ring). Now you're ready to pick up the tart dough.

8 Place the rolling pin on one edge of the dough. Lift the edge of the dough onto the rolling pin. Then roll back the rolling pin to pick up all the dough — it's sort of like rolling up a carpet with a giant rolling pin inside. Then you roll the dough back out over the tart ring.

9 Lift the edge of the tart dough that is hanging over the edge of the ring so that gravity lowers the center dough into the bottom of the plate. With your fingers, press the dough into the corners of the ring. The lip of the ring should have about an inch or two overlap.

10 Using scissors, cut off the ragged edges of the overhanging dough. Use your fingers to crimp the dough on the lip of the ring into fluted or crimped edges all around.

11 Store in the refrigerator up to 3 days or in the freezer up to 2 weeks until ready to use.

Tart crusts are generally lined with almond cream, and then baked to cook the almond cream and make it firm. Then the fresh fruit is placed on top.

Raspberry Tart

French Tart Dough (see recipe earlier in this chapter) usually has a layer of almond cream or coconut cream over the bottom, with fresh fruit. You can make this tart with blackberries, huckleberries, blueberries, or strawberries (halved) and use their respective jams for glaze (see photo).

Tools: *Food processor, 9-inch tart ring, small pot, pastry brush*

Preparation time: *15 minutes (not including French Tart Dough)*

Baking time: *40 minutes*

Yield: *Enough for one 9-inch tart*

¹/₂ cup (2 ounces) blanched whole almonds

1 tablespoon confectioners' sugar

¹/₂ cup (4 ounces or 1 stick) butter, quartered, room temperature

¹/₂ cup (3 ounces) sugar

2 eggs

9-inch French Tart Dough in a tart ring

¹/₂ cup (4 ounces) seedless raspberry jam

4 cups (32 ounces) fresh raspberries

Almond Cream

1 Preheat oven to 400°.

2 Place the almonds and confectioners' sugar in a food processor and process for about 5 minutes or until the mixture is powdery.

3 Place the butter in a bowl. Begin mixing and add the sugar. Mix together until smooth and then add the almond-sugar mixture. When the mixture is smooth, add the eggs. Continue to mix, scraping down the bowl occasionally, until smooth — about 5 to 7 minutes total. (If mixing by hand, mix about twice that time.) Keep cool.

(continued)

4 Using the back of a spoon, spread the almond cream over the base of the tart shell to about ¼-inch thickness. Smooth the cream with the back of a spoon. (Push the almond cream about halfway up the edge of the tart ring.)

5 Bake for 40 minutes or until golden-brown. Remove to a rack to cool (about 20 minutes).

Assembly

1 Spread all but 2 tablespoons of the raspberry jam on top of the tart shell. Arrange fresh raspberries over the jam in concentric circles.

2 For the glaze, warm the remaining raspberry jam in a pot. Using a pastry brush, dab jam atop each raspberry.

Austrian-German-Style Tarts

So far, we've made tarts and pies with basic flour and butter doughs. Another type of dough worth knowing about is the Austrian-German, which is based primarily on nuts, thus having a much more crumbly texture. This type of dough is exceedingly easy for home cooks because it doesn't require rolling. You just blend the ingredients, mold them, and lay them in the tart pan.

Almond paste is commonly used in all kinds of baking, especially Austrian and German. Almond paste is made of crushed almonds sweetened with sugar and flavored with almond extract. You can find it in any baking specialty store or by mail-order (see Appendix C).

If your almond paste forms lumps and is watery when mixing it with eggs, it's because you've added the eggs too quickly. Pour out as much liquid as you can and start again, adding liquid little by little.

Linzertorte

The best known dessert using Austrian-German doughs is the Linzertorte, which is associated with Linz, Austria. It's basically a tart made with an almond crust and a fruit preserve filling (see photo). It has a latticework crust — that is, strips of dough are laid across the top in a checkerboard fashion, leaving some of the raspberry jam exposed.

Tools: *Electric mixer (optional), tart mold, pastry bag with #5 tip (round or star)*

Preparation time: *20 minutes*

Baking time: *40 minutes*

Yield: *6 to 8 servings*

1 cup (7 ounces) packed brown sugar

^{1}/$_2$ cup (2 ounces) almond paste

2 eggs, cold

^{1}/$_2$ cup (4 ounces or 1 stick) butter, room temperature

^{1}/$_2$ cup (4 ounces) vegetable shortening, such as Crisco

1^1/$_4$ cups (7 ounces) flour

pinch of salt

1 teaspoon ground cinnamon

2 teaspoons baking powder

^{1}/$_3$ cup (1^1/$_2$ ounces) cake flour

1^1/$_2$ cups (12 ounces) raspberry preserves

^{1}/$_2$ cup (4 ounces) apricot preserves

1 Preheat oven to 400°.

2 With a electric mixer or wooden spoon, combine the brown sugar and almond paste. Mix until the mixture breaks down into small pieces.

3 While mixing, add 1 egg and mix until the mixture becomes smooth and creamy. When you see the mixture forming on the side of the bowl, stop and scrape it down.

4 Add the butter and shortening while mixing. Continue to mix until all lumps are dissolved.

5 Add the flour, salt, cinnamon, baking powder, and the remaining egg. Mix until incorporated.

6 Add the cake flour. Scrape down the bowl once. Continue to mix until smooth.

7 Using a wooden spoon, spread about ^{3}/$_4$ of the dough mixture over the bottom of the tart pan. Use the spoon to smooth the dough mixture over the tart. The mixture should slope upward toward the sides of the tart mold. The dough should be about ^{1}/$_2$ inch thick.

(continued)

8 In a bowl, combine the raspberry preserves and the apricot preserves. Stir to blend. Use a wooden spoon to spread the preserves evenly over the tart dough. Apply more preserves to the outside edges of the tart bottom than to the center.

9 Spoon the remaining dough into a pastry bag with a #5 (or smaller) round or star-shaped tip. Squeeze out parallel strips of dough over the top of the tart.

Repeat this process again at 45° angles to form diamond shapes on the top of the tart. Leave some of the preserves exposed.

10 Squeeze some dough around the rim of the tart. Crimp the dough with your fingers to form a decorative pattern — the particular pattern is not vital, but just be consistent all the way around the rim of the tart.

11 Bake for about 40 minutes or until the crust is golden-brown.

Tip: Notice that we add eggs to the almond paste mixture one at a time. This process prevents the mixture from breaking apart and getting lumps from too much liquid hitting the batter at once.

Chapter 4

All Puffed Up: Puff Pastry, Cream Puffs, and Eclairs

In This Chapter

▶ The wondrous chemistry of puff pastry

▶ How to wow the crowd with puffed desserts

▶ Pâte à choux: The pastry with a hole in the middle

▶ Petting the pastry swan

▶ The ultimate cream puffs and killer eclairs

For many home cooks, the notion of making puff pastry is about as alien as disassembling a transmission. But when you break down the process into easy-to-follow steps, as we have in this chapter, you see that this elegant and versatile pastry is within the reach of any home cook.

Puff pastry is essentially many layers, or *leaves,* of a flour and water dough, blended with butter. The dough is rolled out and then folded over repeatedly to create pastry layers within. In the heat of an oven, the butter melts, separating the leaves of pastry. The water in the dough turns to steam and causes the puffing and separating. Puff pastry can expand to three or four times its original thickness. There are various methods for making puff pastry, including some shortcut methods, but in this chapter, we show you how to make the classic French puff pastry, which is by far the best.

Puff pastry is used in desserts like napoleons, tarts, fruit strips, decorative bite-sized pastries, and more.

After you make a terrific puff pastry, you may want to try making a pâte à choux (prounced *Pot-ah-Shoe*) — it will be a cinch in comparison. Pâte à choux is the pastry used for cream puffs and eclairs. It is a smooth, soft, and eggy dough that can be squeezed out of a pastry bag and into all kinds of decorative shapes. In this chapter, we show you how to make little decorative pastry swans that enhance any dessert when you really want to blow your guests away. You can also spoon pâte à choux onto a baking sheet — in the oven, the dough puffs up into a ball and becomes hard and golden on the outside, hollow and eggy inside. You can fill the hole with all kinds of sweet ingredients like whipped cream and pastry cream.

Getting Psyched about Puff Pastry

Puff pastry is the most utilitarian — and elegant — of all dessert pastries. It is ethereally light, rich with butter, and has an extraordinary layered texture that crumbles in the mouth into a thousand little savory pieces — we're getting excited just writing about it! Puff pastry also looks great, especially when glazed with egg wash (whole eggs and water whipped with a fork) so that it looks golden and shiny.

And there's more. You can wrap puff pastry around cooked or marinated fruit (a fabulous combination), slather it with custards and mousses, dust it with sugar and ground nuts, and make all kinds of cool-looking *petits fours* (bite-size dessert tidbits). Because puff pastry has a flexible yet sturdy texture, it doesn't fall apart when you bend and twist it to encase foods or custards. Many chefs encase fish, meat, and vegetables in puff pastry, too. And, puff pastry is the basis for the famous French croissant.

As versatile and wonderful as puff pastry is, it does have limitations. The following are things you can't do with puff pastry:

- Wrap brussel sprouts in it to trick your kids into eating them
- Make toys
- Write a letter on it
- Rent a hotel room
- Get cash from an ATM machine

Puff pastry, above all, is about butter. Don't worry, puff pastry is not something you eat every day. Finding out how to incorporate butter into a flour pastry is what this chapter is all about.

The birth of puff pastry

Around the campfire at pastry chef summer camp, old timers like to recount the story of the invention of the puff pastry. It seems that long ago a commis (one of the underlings in the kitchen hierarchy) was told by his chef to make some dessert pastry. The young commis had his mind on other things that day — namely a comely young lass down at the butcher shop in town. He was so distracted and anxious to visit the butcher shop that he forgot to put butter in his dough mix. When he realized this hours later, he panicked, thinking about the chef's response when he found out.

The commis decided to try blending some butter into the already firm dough. He did this by adding butter little by little, folding the dough over each time, and pressing it into the dough. When this unorthodox and unusual pastry was baked, something bizarre happened: It puffed up and up, forming thin layers like sheets of paper.

The chef was so excited upon seeing this incredible creation that he asked the commis to show him how to replicate his brilliant invention. (By the way, the young lass married the blacksmith.)

Mastering the art of foolproof puff pastry

Following are tips to keep in mind when you begin working with puff pastry dough. Just for the record, the term for incorporating butter into a puff pastry doughs is *roll-in*. Toss this term around whenever you meet a pastry chef.

✔ **When rolling out puff pastry, try this little trick to stretch the dough.** You should have a work table or counter with a blunt edge (not sharp enough to cut the dough). As you roll out the dough, you hang half of it over the edge as you work. In doing this, half of the dough dangles off the table, stretching because of gravity — actually, you enhance gravity by pulling on the dough a little to stretch it more. (See Figure 4-1.)

Now, we have to be honest with you. The first time you try this, the chances of the overhanging dough falling on the floor are about 110 percent. Just pick it up (make sure that your kitchen floor is very clean!) and put it back on the counter. Start again. You'll get the hang of it.

✔ **The butter should always be cold when you start.** Butter softens as you mash it with your hands until it forms a smooth paste with no holes. You must start with cold butter; if you start with room temperature butter, by the time you mash it, the butter is nearly melting.

Figure 4-1:
Rolling out
puff pastry.

Hang the dough over the edge half way as you roll... ...using gravity to stretch it!

- ✔ **As you work the puff pastry dough, be sure to maintain a fairly symmetrical square shape.** This way, when you fold the dough, it retains an even shape, which is easier to work with and yields a symmetrical dough that is easier to subdivide for various uses.

- ✔ **While rolling out the puff pastry dough, dust it (and the counter) frequently with flour so that the dough doesn't stick.** But be very sparing with the flour, using just enough to dust, but not more. You don't want extra flour working its way into the dough because excess flour can dry out the dough.

- ✔ **Keep track of your folds.** Puff pastry is folded and refrigerated six times. With all of this repeated folding and refrigerating, it's easy to lose count of how many folds you have made. To remind yourself, make indentations in the top of the dough with your fingertips — one for the first turn, two for the next, and so on.

- ✔ **As you fold the dough, make sure that it's even all over — that is, without parts that are thicker than others.** This technique yields an attractive puff pastry that doesn't look like a bulging car tire about to blow out.

- ✔ **After you roll out the puff pastry to make a particular recipe, let it rest in the refrigerator for about 30 minutes before proceeding.** If you don't, the puff pastry shrinks dramatically during cooking, making your beautiful napoleon look like a refrigerator magnet.

Before you take on any recipe — but especially one (such as puff pastry) that requires concentration and lots of elbow grease — be sure to have all the required tools on hand as well as all the ingredients.

Here are two more reminders before you start:

- ✔ **Puff pastry freezes well for up to a month, but before you freeze it, roll it out into about $1/2$ inch thickness (roughly 12 x 12 inches).** Rolling out the dough before freezing makes it easier to defrost and to work with later.

- ✔ **What if, while you're rolling the puff pastry, butter squishes out the side of the dough?** Pat a little flour over the spot to form a little bandage.

Classic Puff Pastry

This is the time-tested recipe for puff pastry (see photo). There are quicker versions, such as one that requires only two turns (or folds) of the dough rather than six, but the result is not close to the version here. (If you're going to tackle it, you may as well go for the real thing — see Figure 4-2.)

Tools: *Electric mixer (optional), chef's knife, plastic wrap, rolling pin*

Preparation time: *3 hours*

Baking time: *None*

Yield: *20 servings*

$2^1/_2$ *cups (20 ounces or 5 sticks) butter, cold*

4 cups (16 ounces) flour

2 teaspoons salt

1 cup (8 ounces) water, very cold

1 Place $^1/_2$ cup (4 ounces) butter, cut into small pieces, in a bowl and soften it (or dust your hands with flour and soften it in a bowl).

2 Add all the flour and salt at once and mix. After a minute or so, start gradually adding the cold water while mixing. (If possible, have someone else drizzle the water in while you're working the dough.) Continue mixing until the dough comes together in a loose ball; this process takes about 3 minutes. If you're doing this by hand, you must mash everything in a bowl and add the cold water gradually, blending with floured hands, until it's a firm paste — about 15 minutes. If the dough is still too dry while mixing, add 1 or 2 more tablespoons of water.

3 Place the dough on a lightly floured surface and work it into a ball with your hand. With a chef's knife, slice an X in the top of the dough.

Cover the dough with plastic wrap and refrigerate for at least 2 hours. (If you have the time, you can refrigerate the dough for 24 hours — in fact, the dough is better that way because it becomes more supple and easier to work with.)

4 Complete a *roll-in*. Remove the remaining butter and dough ball from the refrigerator (so that both ingredients will be the same temperature when you roll the dough later). Place the cold butter on a floured surface and then whack it repeatedly with a rolling pin to soften. After the butter is soft, work it more with your hand, punching it a little bit. The butter should reach a putty consistency and contain no lumps. Shape the butter ino a 5 × 9-inch rectangle.

5 Place the dough ball, cut side up, on a floured surface. With a rolling pin, roll out the dough along the four triangles to form flaps on the outside of the rolled dough. Roll out the flaps so that they are 6 to 8 inches long. Also, a slight mound should form in the center of the dough; this extra thickness prevents the butter from squeezing out the bottom when you roll the dough.

(continued)

6 Use a spatula to pick up the butter rectangle from the counter. Place the rectangle of butter atop the mound in the dough. Arrange the butter so that the edges point to the flat side of the dough. Keeping the dough as square as possible at all times during this process is important. Dust off any excess flour from the dough continually.

7 Fold the right flap over the butter. Don't allow any air bubbles into the dough. Next, fold the left flap over the top. Press firmly all around. Then do the same with the top flap and lastly, the bottom flap. Make sure that you dust off all flour as you fold. Press the whole dough gently to firm it up and eliminate air bubbles. Turn over the dough and place the folded side down.

8 Start rolling out the dough, first rolling from the center of the dough to the edge farthest away from you. Roll the top, then the bottom, and then the sides until the dough is about 2 feet long and about 8 inches wide. Using both hands, work your way under the dough to cradle it on your forearms. Flip the dough. Continue rolling out the dough while rotating it, always keeping the dough edges square. (Very lightly flour the pastry every time you flip it. You should have a thin sheet about 3 times as long as the original square.)

9 Look at the dough and, in your mind, divide it into thirds. Grabbing the 8-inch edge farthest from you, fold two-thirds of the way down the dough. Pat it down gently. Grab the edge closest to you and lift to place it evenly over the top. Make sure that you keep the edges square. Congratulations — this is called your first turn.

10 Repeat the process. (If, during this process, the dough gets elastic feeling because it's being worked too much, refrigerate the dough for an hour and then do the second turn.) After you've finished the second turn, press two fingers into the top of the dough to indicate how many turns you've completed. (It's amazing how easily you can forget.)

11 Refrigerate the dough after every 2 turns and let it rest for an hour. Complete a total of 6 turns. Puff pastry can be frozen, if well wrapped, for 2 weeks.

Puff Pastry Fruit Strips

One of the easiest desserts — one that you can vary endlessly — uses fruits that are firm and not overly juicy, such as blueberries and blackberries. The fruits should hold together and not leak all over. We like plums, apricots, figs, and strawberries.

If you keep puff pastry on hand (see the Classic Puff Pastry recipe), these beautiful fruit strips are easy to make at the last minute. For the almond cream base, try the recipe in Chapter 3. Or, for an easier version, replace the almond cream with plum preserves.

Tools: *Rolling pin, pizza cutter or paring knife, pastry brush, sieve, ruler*

Preparation time: *30 minutes (not including puff pastry or almond cream)*

Baking time: *45 minutes*

Yield: *8 to 10 servings*

Classic Puff Pastry, measuring 6 x 3 inches

1 egg yolk, beaten

1 cup (8 ounces) almond cream or plum preserves

1 slice day-old bread, cut up into bread crumbs in a food processor (or minced with a knife)

10 plums, pits removed, quartered, and sliced into roughly ¼-inch crescents

confectioners' sugar for garnish

1 Preheat oven to 375°.

2 Roll out the dough into a 14 x 6-inch rectangle. (See Figure 4-3.) Use a pizza cutter (which works best) or a paring knife to remove the ragged edges from the dough and make a clean rectangle. Cut off 1-inch strips from the outside edges of the pastry rectangle. Using the pastry brush and the beaten egg yolk, glue the strips to the rectangle's perimeter to form a border all around.

3 Using the pastry brush and remaining egg yolk, paint the puff pastry rectangle with egg yolk.

4 Refrigerate the dough while preparing the almond cream (see the Raspberry Tart recipe in Chapter 3) and fruits.

5 When the almond cream is ready, remove the dough from the refrigerator and prick the center of the pastry rectangle with a fork. (Otherwise, the pastry puffs up too high in the oven.)

6 With a wooden spoon, lay about 4 tablespoons of almond cream (or plum preserves) in the center of the pastry. Spread it evenly with a spatula or the back of the spoon.

7 Sprinkle the bread crumbs over the almond cream — the crumbs absorb excess juice from the plums as they cook.

8 Arrange the sliced plums over the tart in a decorative fashion. Stick each slice of plum a little bit into the almond cream (or plum preserves).

9 Use a sieve to sprinkle the tart generously with confectioners' sugar.

10 Bake for 45 minutes or until the pastry is golden-brown.

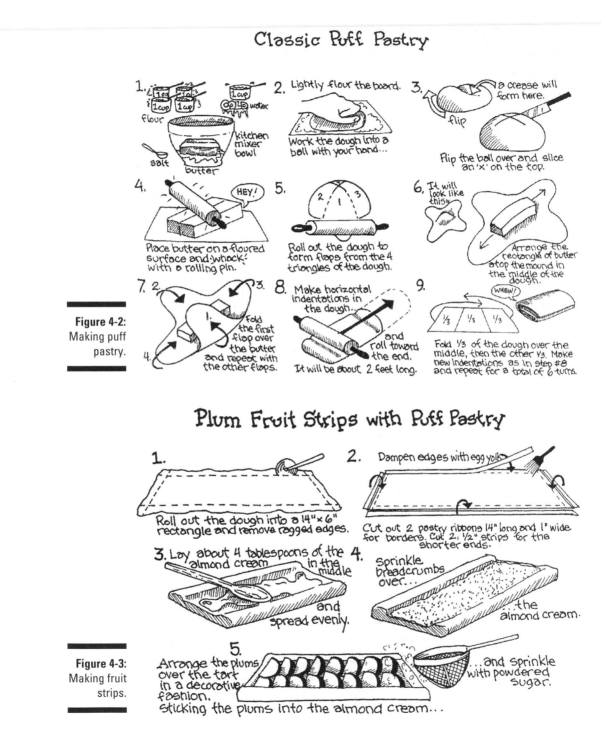

Figure 4-2:
Making puff
pastry.

Figure 4-3:
Making fruit
strips.

Pears in Puff Pastry

The traditional way to make pears in puff pastry is to encase the entire fruit and then serve it with a sauce. In recent years, chefs have modified the recipe to accommodate lighter preferences. In this version, we lay a strip of pastry around the pear in a decorative pattern, leaving some of the pear exposed. You can serve it with vanilla ice cream or any kind of fruit sorbet. (See Chapter 12.) This recipe also works very well with apples, but make sure that you use Granny Smith apples — others are too soft and turn too brown in the oven.

Tools: *Rolling pin, pizza cutter or paring knife, yardstick or ruler, aluminum foil, sieve*

Preparation time: *25 minutes (not including the puff pastry)*

Baking time: *40 minutes*

Yield: *4 servings*

strip of puff pastry, 3 x 8 x 1 inch thick

1 egg yolk

4 ripe fresh pears (Bosc, Anjou, or Bartlett pears are the best)

$1/2$ teaspoon ground ginger

1 teaspoon cinnamon

$1/2$ teaspoon freshly ground nutmeg (20 fast scrapes over a grater)

2 or 3 shakes paprika

1 teaspoon fennel seed (optional)

3 tablespoons confectioners' sugar

1 Preheat oven to 375°.

2 Roll out the puff pastry to $1/8$ inch thickness, measuring at least 14 x 4 inches. (See Figure 4-4.)

3 Using a pizza cutter or paring knife and a yardstick or ruler, evenly trim ragged edges from the dough, leaving a neat rectangle. Cut part of the dough lengthwise into about 8 strips measuring $1/4$ inch wide and 14 inches long. Refrigerate.

4 Beat the egg yolk in a bowl. Peel the pears as cleanly as possible. (See the sidebar "Peeling decorative pears.")

5 Immediately after peeling the pears, dip them all over in the egg wash to prevent discoloration.

6 In bowl, combine the ginger, cinnamon, nutmeg, paprika, and fennel seed. Sift the confectioners' sugar over and stir.

7 Distribute the spice mixture over a plate. Dredge the puff pastry strips in the spices.

(continued)

8 Take 1 pastry strip and spiral it over 1 of the pears from top to bottom. (See Figure 4-4.) Repeat with remaining pears.

9 Cut the remaining puff pastry (which should measure 2 x 14 inches) into four ¹/₂-inch x 14-inch strips. Twist the remaining strips into loose corkscrew shapes.

10 Place the corkscrew strips on a separate baking sheet and bake for 15 minutes. Place the pears on another baking sheet that is lined with a double-folded sheet of aluminum foil. Bake for 40 minutes.

11 When you remove the pears from the oven, sift confectioners' sugar generously over them. Do the same to the corkscrew strips. First place the pears under a broiler for about 20 seconds or until the sugar glazes and starts to smoke. (Move the sheet pan around under the broiler to glaze evenly.)

12 On a separate sheet pan, broil the corkscrew strips until they glaze. The corkscrew strips should be balanced artistically against the pears when served.

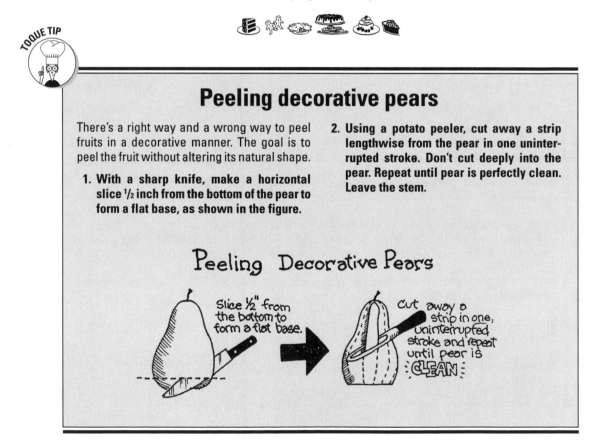

Peeling decorative pears

There's a right way and a wrong way to peel fruits in a decorative manner. The goal is to peel the fruit without altering its natural shape.

1. **With a sharp knife, make a horizontal slice ¹/₂ inch from the bottom of the pear to form a flat base, as shown in the figure.**

2. **Using a potato peeler, cut away a strip lengthwise from the pear in one uninterrupted stroke. Don't cut deeply into the pear. Repeat until pear is perfectly clean. Leave the stem.**

Peeling Decorative Pears

Slice ½" from the bottom to form a flat base.

Cut away a strip in one, uninterrupted stroke and repeat until pear is CLEAN

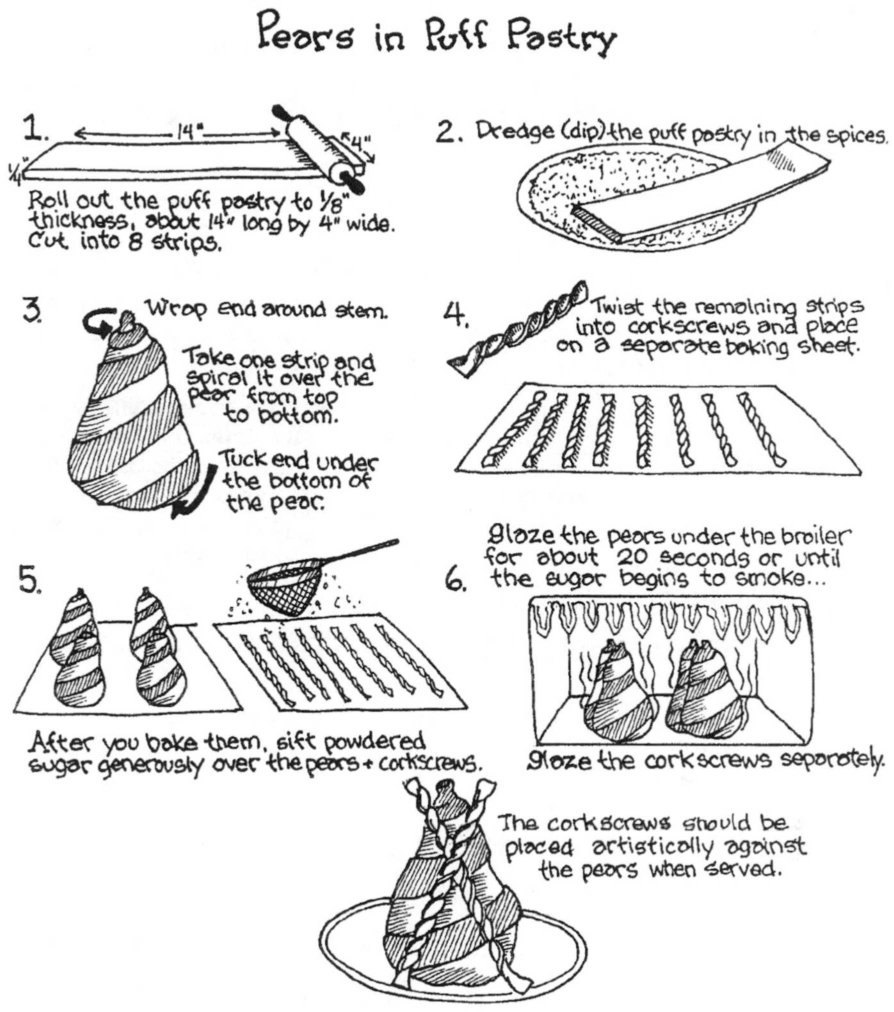

Pears in Puff Pastry

1. Roll out the puff pastry to 1/8" thickness, about 14" long by 4" wide. Cut into 8 strips.

2. Dredge (dip) the puff pastry in the spices.

3. Wrap end around stem.
   Take one strip and spiral it over the pear from top to bottom.
   Tuck end under the bottom of the pear.

4. Twist the remaining strips into corkscrews and place on a separate baking sheet.

5. After you bake them, sift powdered sugar generously over the pears + corkscrews.

6. Glaze the pears under the broiler for about 20 seconds or until the sugar begins to smoke...
   Glaze the corkscrews separately.

The corkscrews should be placed artistically against the pears when served.

Figure 4-4:
Pears in
Puff Pastry.

Napoleons

Napoleons are the towering, crunchy, luxurious condominiums of the dessert world. Made from layers of puff pastry, napoleons are usually coated with a light sugar glaze or a dusting of confectioners' sugar.

In the old days, chefs used to glaze the top of the pastry with a sugar mixture and then draw chocolate gridiron stripes across it. All that extra sugar, however, can be too much for today's tastes. We prefer a lighter glaze, as you see in the following recipe — thin and brittle, adding to the textural appeal of the dessert. Other than that, a napoleon is just sheets of puff pastry held together by a mortar of pastry cream.

Working with pastry cream

For the best pastry cream:

✔ If you're not using the pastry cream right away, cover it with plastic wrap to prevent a skin from forming on top and refrigerate it. Make sure that the plastic wrap touches the surface of the pastry cream in the bowl, preventing air from reaching it. Otherwise, the skin forms.

✔ If you want to use the pastry cream after it's been refrigerated overnight, whip it well with a thin wire whisk to bring back the fluffy texture.

✔ If you scorch the pastry cream as you're cooking it, remove all the good pastry cream from the pot and leave the scorched part in the pot. Scorching, unlike burning, does not ruin the whole sauce.

✔ If your pastry cream gets too dry or concentrated after sitting awhile, add a tablespoon or two of whipped cream and whisk well.

✔ If the eggs curdle while you're cooking the batter, continue cooking and whisk faster until the batter thickens. Transfer to a mixing bowl or an electric mixer. Mix for two minutes. The mixture should become smooth again.

Following are tips on working with napoleons:

✔ Serve napoleons within several hours of being made.

✔ As you're laying pastry cream on the pastry sheets, place raspberries or halved strawberries on the side of the pastry so that you can see them when you assemble the dessert.

Who discovered vanilla?

It's often said that Marco Polo, the original gourmet shopper, brought back the vanilla bean from the Far East. He didn't. The vanilla bean is native to greater Central America and was discovered by the Spanish conquistadors in the 16th century. We qualify the word discovered because indigenous Indians had been using vanilla to flavor drinks and food for hundreds of years. According to historical accounts, when vanilla was introduced to Spain, its first use was to flavor drinks.

Today, vanilla comes from Central America, Madagascar, Mexico, Guinea, Mauritius, the Seychelles, and Tahiti (this is purportedly the best, with a more assertive aroma and more complex flavor). The vanilla pod grows on a vine that can reach more than 300 feet. Real vanilla flavor, which comes from the scrapings of the inner pod (and the pod itself immersed in hot liquid), is significantly better than vanilla extract in a bottle. For a subtle but pure vanilla flavor in custards and pastry creams, place a whole unsliced pod into the milk as it is heating and take it out at the last minute.

Napoleon with Strawberries

In this recipe, we use a lighter filling of part pastry cream and part whipped cream. The basic vanilla pastry cream is the filling for profiteroles, eclairs, puff pastries, napoleons, and much, much more. It's nothing more than a sweetened combination of milk, eggs, and sugar thickened with cornstarch (because it yields a smoother consistency).

When the pastry cream is done, you can flavor it with rum, Grand Marnier, or a liqueur of your choice. For chocolate-flavored pastry cream, mince about 2 ounces of bittersweet chocolate, sprinkle it into the hot pastry cream, and stir.

For this recipe, you need to make the Classic Puff Pastry, found earlier in this chapter.

Tools: *Medium pot, electric mixer (optional), plastic wrap*

Preparation time: *1 hour 30 minutes (not including Classic Puff Pastry)*

Baking time: *40 minutes*

Cooking time: *10 minutes*

Yield: *12 servings*

2 cups (16 ounces) milk	*2 tablespoons confectioners' sugar*
1 vanilla bean, cut lengthwise, or 1 teaspoon vanilla extract	*1 teaspoon vanilla extract*
1/2 cup (3 ounces) sugar	*flour, for dusting rolling surface*
1/4 cup (1 ounce) cornstarch	*puff pastry, measuring 8 x 6 inches*
4 egg yolks	*confectioners' sugar, for dusting pastry*
2 cups (16 ounces) heavy cream, very cold	*1 tablespoon grated orange zest, or 1 tablespoon Grand Marnier*
	2 cups (16 ounces) strawberries, stems removed, and sliced and washed (optional)

Vanilla Pastry Cream

1 In a medium pot, combine the milk and the vanilla bean or 1 teaspoon vanilla extract. Bring to a boil.

2 Meanwhile, in a separate bowl, blend the sugar and cornstarch, add the egg yolks, and then whisk to combine.

3 When the milk has boiled, drizzle it over the egg mixture while whisking rapidly. Return the mixture to the milk pot and return it to a boil. Remove from heat. Pour into a mixing bowl, let cool for 15 minutes covered with plastic wrap, and refrigerate until used.

(continued)

Whipped Cream

In a mixing bowl, combine the heavy cream, confectioners' sugar, and second teaspoon of vanilla extract. Whip until stiff peaks form. Refrigerate until ready to use.

Napoleon

1 Preheat the oven to 400°.

2 On a lightly floured surface, roll out the pastry to 15 x 15 inches. Cut into 3 equal rectangles. (See Figure 4-5.)

3 Place the dough on a sheet pan or cookie sheet and bake for 5 minutes — you don't need to butter the pan because the dough has plenty of butter in it.

4 After the strips begin to puff, take another baking sheet or a cooling rack and place it on top of the strips to prevent them from puffing up any more.

5 Bake for about 40 minutes or until the pastry is golden-brown.

6 Flip the 3 pastry strips over and liberally sift confectioners' sugar over them. Place the strips under the broiler for 30 to 40 seconds or until the sugar melts into a glaze. Remove from oven, place on a flat cookie sheet or a large platter, and let cool.

Filling

1 Whisk or mix the refrigerated pastry cream until the filling is very smooth. (It gets rubbery in the refrigerator.)

2 When the pastry cream is softened, whisk $1/3$ of the whipped cream into the pastry cream. Add the remaining whipped cream with a spatula. Add the orange zest or Grand Marnier (or liqueur of choice).

Assembly

1 Place 1 of the rectangles on a flat surface and place $1/2$ of the pastry cream mixture on top of it. Place $1/2$ of the strawberries slices on top. (See Figure 4-6.)

2 Place the second layer of puff pastry over the filling and place the remaining pastry cream and sliced strawberries on top. Cover with the third rectangle and refrigerate.

Baking a Napoleon

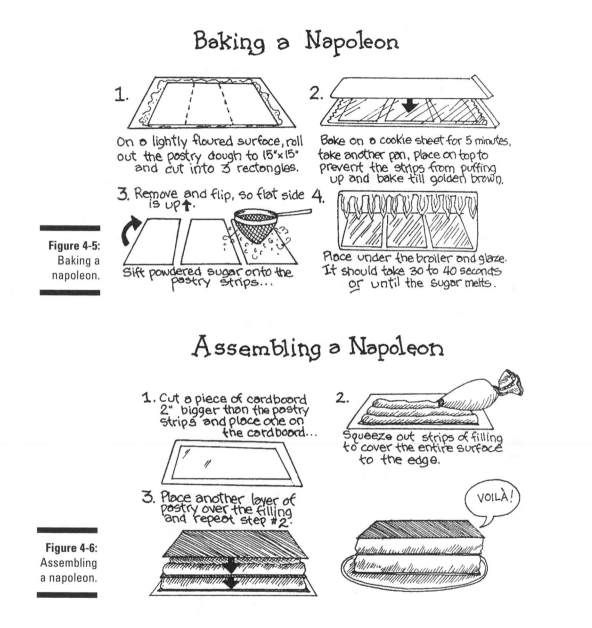

1. On a lightly floured surface, roll out the pastry dough to 15"x15" and cut into 3 rectangles.

2. Bake on a cookie sheet for 5 minutes, take another pan, place on top to prevent the strips from puffing up and bake till golden brown.

3. Remove and flip, so flat side is up↑. Sift powdered sugar onto the pastry strips...

4. Place under the broiler and glaze. It should take 30 to 40 seconds or until the sugar melts.

Figure 4-5: Baking a napoleon.

Assembling a Napoleon

1. Cut a piece of cardboard 2" bigger than the pastry strips and place one on the cardboard...

2. Squeeze out strips of filling to cover the entire surface to the edge.

3. Place another layer of pastry over the filling and repeat step #2.

VOILÀ!

Figure 4-6: Assembling a napoleon.

What Exactly Is Pâte à Choux?

Pronounced pot-ah-shoe, pâte à choux is a workhorse of the pastry world, a rich, eggy dough that puffs up when cooked. You use pâte à choux primarily for eclairs, but if you use your imagination, it can be the foundation of all sorts of desserts.

You can make pâte à choux by hand, mixing with a wooden spoon, but it's tough to do — the dough gets so thick and dense at the end that you may need a barbell instructor to help you finish it. An electric mixer saves a lot of grunt work.

Pâte à choux is different from other doughs: When it bakes, a hole is created in the center, which is a convenient place to pump in various fillings. This hole is ideal for piping in fillings for eclairs and the like. The empty center is caused by steam escaping from the batter as the heat reaches the center of the dough that you've shaped and placed on a baking sheet. For this reason, we recommend allowing the pâte à choux to cook thoroughly. The outside should reach a rich, dark, golden-brown color. If the pastry has too much white around the edges, it will be mushy inside.

When you make pâte à choux, keep the following tips in mind:

- When you take the baked pâte à choux out of the oven, it should be thoroughly dry to the touch and the color of toasted hazelnuts all over.
- The dryer the pastry mixture becomes as a result of stirring in the pot, the more puffed and golden the pâte à choux will be.

Basic Pâte à Choux for Eclairs

This pastry, when baked in strips, puffs up and has a long cavity in the center that you can fill with all sorts of flavored creams.

If you want to make this pastry richer, use all milk and no water. For a lighter texture, use all water. We prefer the middle ground.

Tools: *Heavy-bottomed saucepan, electric mixer (optional), pastry bag with #6 tip, parchment paper,*

Preparation time: *20 minutes*

Baking time: *30 to 40 minutes, depending on size of the dough*

Yield: *Enough for 16 medium eclairs*

¹/₂ cup (4 ounces) milk

¹/₂ cup (4 ounces) water

¹/₄ teaspoon salt

1 tablespoon sugar

1 teaspoon vanilla extract

¹/₂ cup (4 ounces or 1 stick) butter

1 cup (4 ounces) cake flour, sifted

5 eggs

¹/₂-inch pat of butter, for greasing parchment paper

1 Preheat oven to 400°.

2 Combine the milk, water, salt, sugar, vanilla extract, and butter in the saucepan. Bring to a boil.

3 Add the flour all at once, stirring. Reduce to medium heat. Continue stirring the dough around the bottom of the pot. Keep moving the dough around to prevent browning. Stir for about 5 minutes and then remove from heat. It should look like a thick paste — a hot and wet pie dough.

4 Place the dough in a metal bowl. Mix on low for a minute or until the mixture cools (or beat by hand with a thick wooden spoon). Add the eggs one at a time while mixing, allowing each egg to incorporate before you add the next one. (This process takes about a minute of mixing.)

5 After all the eggs are incorporated, keep mixing until the dough is cool. The dough should be shiny, smooth, and thick enough to stick to a spatula, but loose enough to be piped out of a pastry bag.

6 Cut a piece of parchment paper to fit your baking sheet. Place the parchment paper on the baking sheet and grease it with the butter.

7 Carefully fill the pastry bag with the dough, forcing it down toward the open end with the tip. Hold the bag by the tip and place it on the surface of the buttered parchment paper. Hold the bag at a 45° angle and squeeze evenly while drawing the bag toward you slowly but smoothly.

This process will make strips 2 inches wide and 4 inches long. Bake them for 35 minutes until golden-brown. Cool for 15 minutes.

8 Fill the eclairs with the flavored pastry cream.

Profiteroles

These festive ice cream puffs will satisfy your every childhood fantasy. You can smother profiteroles *(pro-feet-air-rolls)* in melted chocolate (and top with whipped cream), dust with confectioners' sugar, or garnish with other sauces, like vanilla or butterscotch. Chocolate, however, is the traditional version.

Preparing a pastry bag

When you buy a pastry bag, it usually comes with a very narrow cone-shaped end — too small to use, really. Before you modify that hole, determine the smallest pastry tip that you plan to use with the bag. Cut the end of the bag with scissors, just wide enough to hold your smallest tip without it falling through. The bag now works for all equipment used in this book.

If you cut the hole in the pastry bag too wide, you can salvage the bag by putting a bigger tip in the bag first and then placing any smaller tip inside of that.

Follow these steps for preparing the pastry bag:

Cut the end of the pastry bag, just enough to hold your smallest tip, without falling through.

1. **Once the tip you want is firmly inserted in the pastry bag, place one hand all the way down into the bag. Use the other hand to fold about 2 to 3 inches of the bag outward back over itself. Remove your hand from inside the bag.**

2. **Using a spatula or large spoon, fill the narrow end of the bag as close to the tip as possible.**

   The purpose of this tight packing is to eliminate air pockets.

3. **When the bag is three-fourths full, twist it counterclockwise, if you're right-handed, or clockwise, if you're left-handed.**

Whatever you do, this movement should be made with your whole arm, because the result will be smoother and the surface will be more even than if you use your wrist for the movement.

This great-looking dessert is little more than a pâte à choux that is halved, garnished with ice cream, and covered with a quick chocolate sauce.

Profiteroles with Hot Chocolate Fudge Sauce

Everybody loves this chocolate-smothered creation, especially kids (see photo). You really have to assemble this dish at the last minute. Some restaurants fill the pastries with ice cream and freeze them until used. Don't try that — the pastry invariably is soggy when it warms up.

For a refreshing lowfat version of profiteroles, halve the pastries horizontally. Fill half with the sorbet of your choice. Place the other half on top and garnish with a fresh fruit purée.

For this recipe, you use the Basic Pâte à Choux for Eclairs recipe and the Vanilla Pastry Cream from the Napoleon with Strawberries recipe, both earlier in this chapter.

Tools: *Parchment paper, pastry brush, chopstick or pencil, pastry bag and #6 to 8 tips, 2 pots, strainer*

Preparation time: *1 hour (not including Basic Pâte à Choux for Eclairs or Vanilla Pastry Cream)*

Baking time: *1 hour*

Yield: *About 20 profiteroles*

3 cups (24 ounces) Basic Pâte à Choux for Eclairs

2 1/2 cups (20 ounces) Vanilla Pastry Cream

1 egg

1 cup (8 ounces) plus 1 teaspoon water

1/4 cup (1 ounce) cocoa powder

1/4 cup (1 1/2 ounces) sugar

1/2 cup (4 ounces) heavy cream

1 cup (6 ounces) semisweet chocolate morsels

1 Preheat oven to 350°.

2 Line the baking sheet with parchment paper. Squeeze out the prepared pâte à choux pastry into 2-inch diameter teardrop shapes and flatten the points (see Figure 4-7). Mix the egg and 1 teaspoon water in a bowl. Brush the puff pastry with the egg wash.

3 Bake for about 45 minutes or until golden-brown. (At this point, remove 1 from the oven to test it. Open the puff pastry when it has cooled slightly — the center should be moist but not wet.)

4 After the pastry has cooled (about 10 minutes), use a narrow object like a chopstick to make holes in the center of the bottom. Work the object around inside the pastry to open up the cavity. Set aside.

Chocolate Sauce

1 Bring 1 cup (8 ounces) water to a boil.

2 Sift together the cocoa and sugar into a bowl. Add this combination to the boiling water, while stirring. Return to a boil — be careful: Cocoa powder can make the liquid boil over quickly. Set aside.

3 In a separate pot, bring the heavy cream to a boil. Meanwhile, place the chocolate morsels in a bowl and pour the hot cocoa liquid and then the hot cream over them.

4 Stir to melt the chocolate. Strain and serve immediately or set aside and reheat over a double boiler before serving.

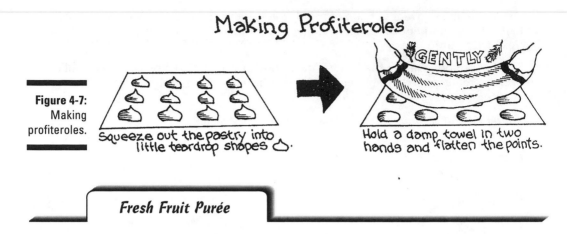

Figure 4-7:
Making
profiteroles.

Fresh Fruit Purée

If your guests are watching their calories, this twist on the traditional profiterole topping is a nice option. This combination isn't strictly lowfat because the pastry itself is quite rich — we'll call it sort of lowfat.

Tools: *Blender, sieve*

Preparation time: *5 minutes*

Yield: *1 ¹/₂ cups (12 ounces) sauce*

1 cup (8 ounces) fresh raspberries, strawberries (hulled), or blueberries

¹/₂ cup (4 ounces) water

2 tablespoons sugar

1 Place all ingredients in a blender. Liquefy.

2 Strain well, pushing the fruit through the mesh with the back of a wooden spoon or a spatula.

Absolutely fresh eclairs

Do you ever wonder why most commercial eclairs are slightly collapsed and have a dryish, leathery skin? Eclairs — which are sort of submarine-shaped as opposed to round profiteroles — have a very short shelf life. To be sure, the fresher these cream-filled pastries are served, the better they are. Don't stray too far from the kitchen.

Eclairs

After you try one of these fresh eclairs, you'll want to make them once a week (see photo). This recipe calls for medium eclairs — about 5 inches long. If you like, make small ones as finger snacks or giant ones for, well, whatever you want.

Tools: *Pastry bag with #6 to 8 tips, cooling rack, chopstick or pencil*

Preparation time: *45 minutes (not including Basic Pâte à Choux or Vanilla Pastry Cream)*

Baking time: *40 minutes*

3 cups (24 ounces) Basic Pâte à Choux   *2 cups (16 ounces) Vanilla Pastry Cream*

1 Preheat oven to 350°.

2 Using the pâte à choux and pastry bag with a #6 or 8 tip, squeeze the dough onto a baking sheet so that it makes a fat, thick shape. (You can make any size you like.) Leave spaces the width of one eclair between each eclair because they expand when baking.

3 Bake for about 40 minutes. Remove from oven, place on rack, and let cool.

4 Find a narrow object, like a chopstick, and poke a small hole in one end of the baked eclair pastry. Work the object around the inside of the pastry to open up the cavity.

5 Fill the pastry bag with pastry cream. Fully insert the tip into the eclair pastry and squeeze the bag. Fill fully, but not to the point where the eclair starts to come apart. (See Figure 4-8.)

Variation: *For coffee-flavored eclairs, put a tablespoon of instant coffee into the milk that you use to prepare the pastry cream. Or, for a more intense coffee flavor, crush about ¹/₂ cup (2 ounces) coffee beans in a towel (using a meat pounder or the back of a heavy saucepan). Boil the milk, remove from heat, and add the coffee beans. Cover and steep for 5 minutes. Strain well. Proceed with pastry cream recipe.*

Getting fancy: Making decorative pastry swans

You may think that making little swans out of pastry dough is a little bit out of your league — akin to making an ice sculpture of The White House with a Swiss Army knife. In fact, making pastry swans isn't much more challenging than making animal cookies or gingerbread men — and besides, we don't want you to get bored with all the really easy stuff in this book.

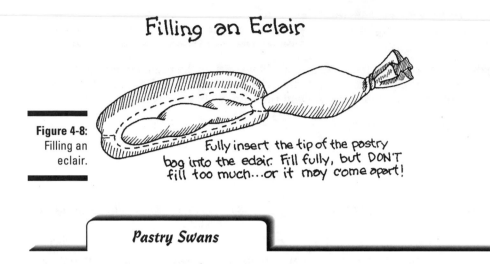

Figure 4-8:
Filling an
eclair.

Filling an Eclair

Fully insert the tip of the pastry bag into the eclair. Fill fully, but DON'T fill too much...or it may come apart!

Pastry Swans

You may not want to attempt this recipe during commercials for Monday night football (see photo). The recipe takes some uninterrupted attention. But the effort is worth it. If you have guests coming over on the weekend, these romantic, creamed-filled birds will blow their socks off! This recipe uses the same Basic Pâte à Choux dough and Vanilla Pastry Cream (see Napoleon with Strawberries recipe) described earlier in this chapter.

Tools: *Parchment paper, pastry brush, serrated knife, pastry bag with star-shaped #4 tip and #12 tip*

Preparation time: *20 minutes (not including Bâsic Pate à Choux or Cream)*

Baking time: *30 minutes*

Yield: *About 30 swans*

3 cups Basic Pâte à Choux

1 egg yolk, beaten

1 teaspoon water

1 cup (8 ounces) Vanilla Pastry Cream

1 Preheat oven to 350°.

2 Prepare a baking sheet with parchment paper cut out to fill the bottom of the sheet.

3 Fill a pastry bag half full with the pâte à choux. While holding the #4 tip to the parchment at a 45° angle, make the first swan as follows.

4 Make sort of a reverse S with the pastry bag to create a swan head by squeezing out a small amount of dough onto the sheet pan — barely touching the pan — into the reverse S pattern.

5 If the first few swan heads look more like miniature jumper cables, don't despair. Keep practicing. After you've mastered the S and want to get more anatomically correct, take a toothpick and create a little swan beak, as shown in Figure 4-9. The swan heads should be about 2 inches long; the beak just a fraction of an inch.

6 For the swan bodies, make a fat upside-down teardrop — wide on one end and tapering down to a point, as shown in Figure 4-9. The body should be about 2 to 3 inches long.

7 Mix the egg yolk and water. Brush the swan parts with the egg wash to give the pastry a nice shine. Don't brush on too much, however, because the egg wash can prevent the pastry from baking thoroughly.

8 Bake for about 30 minutes. The swans should be golden brown and puffed. Set aside and let cool slightly.

Assembly

1 Cut through the swan's body horizontally, using a serrated knife. Repeat with all baked pastry swans. Now, you want to make wings with one half of the swan body.

2 Take the top half of each swan body and place it cut-side down. Cut these in half lengthwise — each piece forms a wing.

3 Attach a #12 star-shaped tip to your pastry bag and fill it with pastry cream.

4 Take 1 of the large pastry halves and fill it with pastry cream. To do so, squeeze firmly at the wide end of the body and taper the filling back to the tail (see Figure 4-9).

5 Insert the swan head into the pastry cream. Attach the wings to either side of the body as shown — convex side out. Shake some confectioners' sugar through a sieve over the swans before serving.

Chocolate Glaze

This glaze for eclairs is one of the easiest to make because it has only 3 ingredients and is nearly foolproof.

Tools: *Double boiler*

Preparation time: *3 minutes*

Cooking time: *10 minutes*

¹/₂ cup (3 ounces) vegetable shortening (like Crisco)

3 ounces bittersweet chocolate, chopped

1 tablespoon corn syrup (optional)

(continued)

Pastry Swans

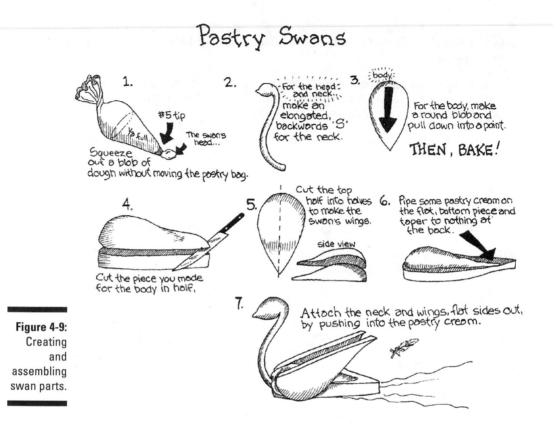

Figure 4-9: Creating and assembling swan parts.

1 In the top half of a double boiler, melt the shortening until it liquefies — about 5 minutes.

2 Add the chopped chocolate and corn syrup to the shortening and stir until the chocolate melts. Set aside the mixture to cool slightly and thicken.

> **Remember:** This mixture should not get so cool that it resembles fudge. If this happens, return the pot to low heat, whisking until the mixture reaches a thick liquid consistency.

3 When the chocolate reaches the proper consistency, dip the eclairs into the pot just enough to cover the top (see Figure 4-10, later in this chapter). Arrange the eclairs, chocolate side up, on a tray and let cool. If the chocolate starts to set while you're dipping, return it to low heat again to soften.

Caramel: Dentist's Best Friend or All-Around Dessert Sauce?

Caramel is one of the most basic sweet sauces — but it also requires considerable concentration to make it right. Caramel is the result of evaporating all the moisture from a mixture of sugar and water.

When cooked to 360°, caramel has a thick, liquid consistency and golden color. When it cools, caramel turns hard and brittle.

When cooking this simple sugar syrup, an even, consistent heat is vital. If the heat isn't uniform — and this can happen if you use a thin-bottomed pan that has hot spots and cool spots — the mixture will heat unevenly and burn. Professional chefs use unlined copper pans, which aren't generally available in kitchenware outlets. The next best pot is made of heavy-gauge stainless steel with a copper core.

When working with caramel, keep the following points in mind:

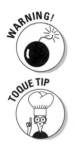

✔ **Be extra careful that absolutely no water hits the caramel when it's cooking or immediately after.** This causes dangerous steam that can scald your face or hands. Moreover, sugar turns to caramel at about 360°. Make sure that this scalding substance doesn't touch any of your skin.

✔ **Add a little lime juice or lemon juice to the caramel mixture before cooking to make the caramel smoother.** (See Figure 4-11.)

Dipping an Eclair

Turn the eclair over, flat side up!

Use a fork or tongs to grip the eclair.

Hot caramel can be dangerous! Be CAREFUL that no water hits the caramel! It can cause steam that can burn hands + face!

CHOCOLATE

CARAMEL 360°F

Figure 4-10: Dipping an eclair.

Dip the eclairs into the pot, just enough to cover the tops. Shake the eclair slightly, so it coats evenly.

✔ **Serve caramel glaze, whatever its use, within 3 to 4 hours.** After that, it starts to get gummy. Ideally, as you're dipping the pastries in caramel, have a teenager nearby who excels in short-distance dashes. Hand him two or three pastries at a time and aim him in the direction of the dinner table.

✔ **Stir the caramel periodically while it's cooking, but not constantly.** You don't want to whip air into it. When the sugar reaches the point where it is golden-brownish and liquid, instead of stirring, just swirl the pot to blend.

✔ **Pour leftover caramel over parchment paper to form various shaped candies: trees, houses, dogs, Ford Explorers, or whatever.**

✔ **After the pot has cooled, clean your pot by filling it with water and placing it on high heat.** Bring the water to a boil and watch most of the caramel separate from the surface.

Caramel Glaze

After you discover how to make caramel, you can use it on all kind of desserts: coated fruits and candies, eclairs and other pastry sweets, ice creams, custards, and much more.

Tools: *Heavy-bottomed stainless steel pot with a copper core, parchment paper or aluminum foil*

Preparation time: *2 minutes*

Cooking time: *5 minutes*

$^1/_4$ *cup ($1^1/_2$ ounces) sugar*

juice of $^1/_4$ lemon or lime (1 teaspoon)

bowl of very cold water, for dipping the pan

1 In a heavy-bottomed pot over high heat, combine the sugar and juice. Cook, stirring only occasionally, until it reaches a darkish golden color — about 5 minutes.

2 Remove from heat and immediately dip the bottom of the pan into a bowl of very cold water to stop the cooking process.

3 Very carefully, dip eclairs or profiteroles into the caramel to coat the surface of the eclair. (Refer Figure 4-10.)

4 Line a baking sheet with parchment paper or aluminum foil. Place the eclairs, caramel side up, on the baking sheet.

Dipping an Eclair

Turn the eclair over, flat side up!

Use a fork or tongs to grip the eclair.

CHOCOLATE

CARAMEL 360°F

Hot caramel can be dangerous! Be CAREFUL that no water hits the caramel! It can cause steam that can burn hands + face!

Figure 4-11: Dipping an eclair.

Dip the eclairs into the pot, just enough to cover the tops. Shake the eclair slightly, so it coats evenly.

Chapter 5
Crêpes and Blinis

In This Chapter

▶ Making the perfect golden crêpe

▶ Creative crêpe fillings

▶ What's a blini?

▶ Blini accompaniments

Crêpes are made with an eggy batter that's spread paper-thin. Crêpes are also for filling and rolling. Blinis, on the other hand, are more like pancakes. In this chapter, we show you how to make great crêpes and blinis.

Crêpes

"The first crêpe is for the dog," say French cooks, who know from experience that, no matter how many times you make crêpes, the first one off the pan will be a mess.

Making crêpes takes a bit of finesse; proper texture and color doesn't always come easily. The preceding French quote, purportedly attributed to Charlemagne (a notoriously inept crêpe maker) is all true. Think of the first crêpe off the pan as something like a baseball relief pitcher who is relaxing in the dugout reading comics before being called to the mound. What has he not done? Warm up! Exactly. The first inning will be disastrous, his pitches hitting the batter, landing up in the press booth, ricocheting off hot dog vendors. But before long he'll get warmed up, just like you. Then you're on a roll.

Crêpes have many regional variations in France. In Brittany, they're made with earthy buckwheat flour and filled with virtually everything, from country ham and melted cheese to seafood, vegetables, and, of course, sweets.

One element that distinguishes crêpes is their very liquid batter — the thinner the better.

Mastering the batter

Have you ever tried to put cocoa powder into a full glass of milk? What happens? The powder floats on the top in lumps, no matter how many hours you stand there stirring.

The bane of crêpes, like chocolate milk, is lumps. The lump factor in crêpes and many other batters is caused by the same sort of reaction. The crêpe recipe in this chapter eliminates lumps by first putting a flour and egg mixture together, without milk, in a mixing bowl. The egg smoothes and moistens the flour. (Please don't ask why. It just does.) So when the flour hits the milk, you don't have the "wet-dry chemical reaction."

If you follow these tips, your batter should be foolproof:

- ✒ **When making the batter, you want to add just enough milk to the egg and flour so that it still holds together, but no more.**

- ✒ **Make the batter as watery as you can.** If the batter is too thin, you can always thicken it a bit.

- ✒ **Crêpe batter is better if refrigerated overnight.** Resting the batter gives the flour time to absorb the milk evenly.

Achieving the proper texture and color

The major pitfall in making crêpes is a lumpy batter. Lumps are created when the flour is combined with the milk. To avoid lumps, combine the flour and egg first and then add the milk (gradually) while whisking vigorously. If you spot any lumps after all the milk is incorporated, break them down with a whisk.

Follow these tips when making crêpes:

- ✒ **A narrow spatula is much more efficient than a wide spatula for removing crêpes from the pan.** Because speed is so essential to avoid burning crêpes, a less efficient wide spatula can make the difference between a burned crêpe and a golden one.

- ✒ **Be careful not to let the pan get too hot.** If it sizzles too much, the batter will cook immediately upon hitting the pan instead of spreading out.

✔ **Use clarified butter.** Clarified butter is simply butter from which the solids have been removed. Clarifying butter prevents the butter from burning. To clarify, melt some butter in a pot. Pour the melted butter into a short, wide glass and let it sit. As the butter cools, tiny white particles rise to the surface and some sink to the bottom. When all particles have risen to the top, skim them. When you pour out the butter, don't pour the milk solids from the bottom of the glass onto the pan. The resulting golden liquid is clarified butter.

✔ **If you stack crêpes in the refrigerator or the freezer, sprinkle some sugar between them.** This way, they never stick together — and the sugar gives them a nice touch of sweetness.

✔ **Keep the ladle over the center of the pan as you pour in the batter.** You always want the batter to land in the center of the pan and spread outward for even distribution. (See Figure 5-1.)

Pouring Crêpe Batter into a Pan

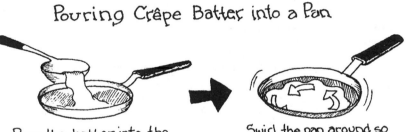

Figure 5-1:
Pouring
crêpe batter
into a pan.

Pour the batter into the crêpe pan with a ladle or measuring cup.

Swirl the pan around so the batter runs to the edges and covers the bottom of the pan.

✔ **Use a crêpe pan.** A proper crêpe pan (see Chapter 2) has a flat bottom with low sides rising at about 45° angle. Nonstick pans make the job of crêpe making easier, but the result is not as attractive — crêpes cooked in a nonstick pan tend to form a *skin*. Stainless steel or cast iron pans are best.

Basic Dessert Crêpes

Here is the basic, lumpless crêpes recipe that you can use in countless ways.

Tools: *Saucepan, electric mixer (optional), 8-inch crêpe pan, ladle, warm plate*

Preparation time: *5 minutes*

Cooking time: *15 minutes*

Yield: *6 to 8 servings*

(continued)

¹/₂ cup (4 ounces or 1 stick) butter	*1 teaspoon vegetable oil*
¹/₂ cup (3 ounces) sugar	*2 cups (16 ounces) milk*
1¹/₂ cups (6 ounces) cake flour	*1 tablespoon rum or Grand Marnier,*
pinch of salt	*or 1 vanilla bean, split lengthwise*
3 eggs	*zest of 1 lemon, finely grated*

1 Melt the butter in a saucepan over medium-high heat. Cook until the butter becomes brownish — this gives it a nutty flavor. Don't let any of the butter turn black. Have a small bowl nearby so that you can pour off the butter as soon as it turns brown. Let cool.

2 In a large mixing bowl, blend the sugar, cake flour, and salt. Add the eggs and whisk well. Whisk in the oil and the brown butter. Pour in about ¹/₂ cup (4 ounces) milk and whisk — the mixture should form a thick paste. Pour in the remaining milk a little at a time while mixing and then add the rum (or Grand Marnier or vanilla bean), and lemon zest.

3 Heat the crêpe pan over medium heat for about a minute. Cover the surface of the pan with clarified butter until it gets sizzling hot.

4 Ladle some batter onto the middle of the 8-inch crêpe pan (refer to Figure 5-1) and immediately start swirling the pan to distribute the batter over the surface. Pour the batter so that it's very thin on the pan — and remember, move the pan, not the ladle.

5 Cook the crêpe for about 30 to 60 seconds (heat may vary) or until it's brown around the edge and dry in the center. Using a thin spatula (it resembles a long tongue depressor), flip the crêpe quickly and cook for about 15 seconds.

6 Using the spatula, remove the crêpe to a warm plate. Sprinkle the crêpe with sugar. Repeat with the remaining batter. (After the first few crêpes, you shouldn't have to add more butter to the pan.)

Crêpes Suzette

This traditional dish is seen often in restaurants today. For sheer showmanship and a delicious citrus flavor, it can't be beat (see photo).

For this recipe, you need to make the Basic Dessert Crepes, earlier in this chapter.

Tools: Sauté pan, pot

Preparation time: 10 minutes (not including Basic Dessert Crêpes)

Cooking time: 15 minutes

Yield: 6 to 8 servings

juice of 5 navel oranges, or
1 cup (8 ounces) juice

1 tablespoon sugar

2 tablespoons Grand Marnier (optional)

6 navel oranges, skin removed and
sectioned

zest of 1 orange

$^1/_2$ cup (4 ounces) grenadine

15 crêpes

vanilla ice cream

1 In a sauté pan over high heat, bring the orange juice to a boil. Add the sugar, reduce to medium heat and simmer for 2 minutes.

2 Remove from heat and add the Grand Marnier and orange sections.

3 In a pot, combine the orange zest and grenadine. Bring to a boil, reduce heat, and simmer for 2 minutes. Set aside.

4 Gently place a crêpe into the pan holding the orange juice and orange sections. Leave for 1 minute to absorb some juice.

5 Using a narrow spatula, remove the crêpe to a warm serving plate. Roll the crêpe into a cylinder. Spoon on some orange sections. Using a fork, pick some orange zest from the grenadine syrup and distribute it over the crêpe. Top with vanilla ice cream and serve immediately.

If you make the Crêpes Suzette recipe, you can also try these variations:

✔ **Honey and Walnut Crêpes:** Heat $^1/_2$ cup (4 ounces) honey in a skillet and add $^1/_2$ cup (2 ounces) chopped walnuts. When the honey becomes warm and liquid, set the crêpe in the honey and fold it. Repeat with all crêpes. Serve with ice cream.

✔ **Bananas Foster Crêpes:** Melt $^1/_2$ cup ($3^1/_2$ ounces) brown sugar and 2 tablespoons butter in a skillet. Add 1 rum shot. Bring to a boil and then lower the heat. Add 2 sliced bananas. Cook 1 minute. Spoon this mixture over the crêpes.

✔ **Fresh Berries Crêpes:** Bring to a boil 1 cup (8 ounces) orange juice and $^1/_4$ cup ($1^1/_2$ ounces) sugar. Boil for 3 minutes. Distribute all the berries and spoon the combination over the crêpes.

ESSENTIAL SKILL

Getting the most zest possible

Orange and lemon zests are essential to so many desserts. Here's an easy technique for removing the flavor-packed zest without picking up the bitter white part while also separating the cleaned citrus sections.

1. **Using a potato peeler, remove strips of the orange rind (not the white pith).**

2. **Use a sharp chef's knife to slice the pieces of rind lengthwise as thinly as possible.**

3. **Cut off the white pith of the orange.**

4. **Slice off the ends of the orange widthwise (about ¼ inch deep).**

5. **Cut away the orange sections by running the blade along either side of the white membrane that separates them.**

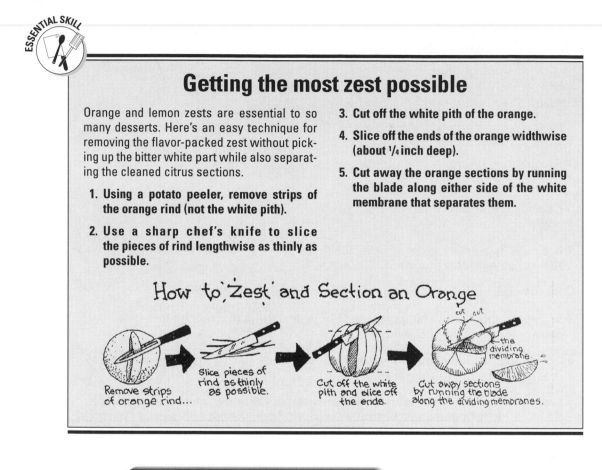

How to 'Zest' and Section an Orange

Remove strips of orange rind...

Slice pieces of rind as thinly as possible.

Cut off the white pith and slice off the ends.

cut cut
the dividing membrane

Cut away sections by running the blade along the dividing membranes.

Lemon Crêpes with Warm Raspberry Sauce

For this recipe, you need to make the Basic Dessert Crêpes, earlier in this chapter. When you make the crêpe batter, you need to add 3 tablespoons lemon zest and the juice of 1 lemon.

Serve this recipe with ice cream or sorbet.

Tools: *Medium pot*

Preparation time: *15 minutes (not including Basic Dessert Crêpes)*

Cooking time: *15 minutes*

Yield: *6 to 8 servings*

$^1/_2$ *cup (4 ounces) water*

$^1/_4$ *cup (1$^1/_2$ ounces) sugar*

juice and zest of 3 lemons, or $^1/_4$ cup (2 ounces) lemon juice

2 cups (16 ounces) raspberries

15 Basic Dessert Crêpes

In a medium pot, combine the water, sugar, lemon juice, and lemon zest. Bring to a boil. Remove from heat and add the raspberries. Place 2 crêpes per serving plate and pour warm raspberry sauce over the crêpes.

Blinis

Blini batter, as opposed to thin crêpe batter, is fluffy and airy. The original blini batter was made with yeast and left out to ferment before baking. We don't go through all that — egg whites provide the rocket booster in this recipe. Blinis can be made sweet or savory — the recipe is exactly the same except for the amount of sugar.

Blinis with Glazed Pineapple

This exotic tropical version of crêpes is great for entertaining.

To make a savory blini, remove the sugar from Step 1 and reduce the sugar in the meringue (Step 4) to 1 tablespoon. Savory blinis are traditionally served with caviar and sour cream.

Tools: *Electric mixer (optional), 8-inch crêpe pan, ladle*

Preparation time: *40 minutes*

Cooking time: *30 minutes*

Yield: *8 servings*

$1^1/_2$ *cups (6 ounces) plus 5 tablespoons cake flour*

$^1/_3$ *cup (2 ounces) plus 5 tablespoons sugar*

4 eggs, separated

$^3/_4$ *cup (6 ounces) milk*

1 tablespoon butter, melted

1 tablespoon clarified butter, for greasing the crêpe pan

$^1/_4$ *cup (2 ounces) sherry vinegar*

$^1/_2$ *cup (4 ounces) apple cider*

1 vanilla bean, split lengthwise, or 1 teaspoon vanilla extract

4 tablespoons cold butter, cut into small pieces

1 fresh pineapple, skinned, quartered, and cored

(continued)

Blinis

1 In a mixing bowl, combine the flour and $^1/_3$ cup (2 ounces) sugar. Add the egg yolks and whisk.

2 Add $^1/_2$ cup (4 ounces) milk to the mixture and whisk well. Gradually add the remaining milk while whisking. Then add the melted butter and whisk.

3 Whip the egg whites until they form stiff peaks.

4 Add 2 tablespoons sugar to the egg whites and continue whipping.

5 Fold the egg whites into the egg yolk mixture. The batter should be fluffy and airy. Don't overmix.

6 Heat an 8-inch crêpe pan over low heat. Coat with clarified butter. Ladle 3 blinis onto the pan (each 2 to 3 inches across). Cook the blinis for about 40 seconds per side over low heat. Set aside and keep warm.

Glazed Pineapple

1 In a pan, combine the sherry vinegar, apple cider, 3 tablespoons sugar, and vanilla. Bring to a boil and cook for 3 minutes.

2 Over medium heat, whisk in the cold butter, a few pieces at a time. The mixture should thicken as more butter is incorporated. When all the butter is blended, remove the vanilla bean and reduce to low heat.

3 Cut the pineapple quarters into $^1/_2$-inch slices and add to the pan. (See the following sidebar for tips on preparing the pineapple.) Cook for 1 minute over low heat. Serve with blinis and, if you want, vanilla ice cream.

Chocolate Blinis with Diced Bananas

This recipe is a variation on Blinis with Glazed Pineapple. You use the same blini recipe, but add 3 tablespoons sifted cocoa powder to the batter before you fold in the egg whites in Step 5.

For the chocolate sauce, you make the Hot Chocolate Fudge Sauce recipe in Chapter 4. If you want, you can serve this with your favorite ice cream.

Tools: *Paring knife*

Preparation time: *20 minutes (not including blinis or chocolate sauce)*

Cooking time: *None*

Yield: *8 to 10 servings*

2 ripe bananas	*8 to 10 blinis*
2 tablespoons confectioners' sugar	*Hot Chocolate Fudge Sauce*

1 Dice the bananas into $1/4$-inch cubes. Sprinkle with confectioners' sugar. Let the sugar seep in for 5 minutes.

2 Make the blinis and garnish each with about 1 tablespoon diced bananas and chocolate fudge sauce.

TOQUE TIP

Choosing, peeling, and coring pineapple

The task of choosing, peeling, and coring a pineapple doesn't have to be difficult. Simply follow these tips:

Pick a ripe pineapple that has golden tones on the surface and is not bright green (which means it's too young). When squeezed, the pineapple flesh should have slight resistance, but not be mushy.

Most importantly, smell the bottom of the pineapple; it should smell ripe and sweet.

After you have your pineapple picked out, you need to peel and core it.

1. **Slice the bottom off the pineapple so that it stands straight. Cut off the top, as shown in the figure. Cut it flat so that the pineapple can stand straight up.**

2. **Run a serrated knife lengthwise down the pineapple deep enough to eliminate the dark spots on the surface of the flesh, until all skin is removed.**

3. **Place the pineapple on its side and cut ¼-inch slices; spread the rings out on a cutting board.**

4. **With a sharp paring knife, remove the core from each slice.**

Peeling and Coring Pineapple

Slice the bottom off and cut off the top.

Run the knife down the pineapple to remove all skin.

Place on its side and cut into ¼" slices.

On a cutting board, remove cores from each slice with a sharp-paring knife.

Part III
Egging You On

The 5th Wave   By Rich Tennant

©RICHTENNANT

"OH, YOU'VE UPDATED YOUR BAKED ALASKA.
THAT WOULD EXPLAIN THE COOKIE OIL
TANKER LEAKING CHOCOLATE SAUCE
AROUND THE MERINGUE."

In this part . . .

The egg is the greatest invention since, well, the egg. Probably more than 75 percent of all desserts use this amazing switch hitter — the yolk and the white — and this part covers all its qualities and how to use them best.

We start with simple custards and puddings and move right on to meringues and classic desserts like floating islands and Baked Alaska.

Chapter 6
The Astonishing Egg

*W*hich came first, the egg or desserts? Who knows? But one thing is for sure: If it weren't for eggs, this book would be thinner than a pub guide to Teheran. Eggs — whites and yolks — do it all: moisten, emulsify, and make custards, batters, icings, soufflés, glazes, and more.

So, before you embark on a journey as a dessert cook, you need to know a little more about the makeup of eggs. In this chapter, you find out about the chemistry of eggs. For example, why do egg yolks bind and thicken foods so well? And why do egg whites froth up to four times their original volume? These properties come into play throughout this book.

What's in That Shell, Anyway?

You were probably told in school (unless you went to a strict vegetarian institution) that eggs are among the most perfect nutritional foods on earth. Mother Nature gave eggs all the nutrients necessary to support a chicken embryo until hatched — in the same way that milk, another complete food, supports calves.

Just as important for the dessert cook are the many properties of egg yolks and egg whites. You can use eggs to create dishes that leave guests moaning in ecstasy and offering to add you to their will if you divulge the recipe.

The major, but not only, property of the egg yolk is its ability to absorb flavors (liquid and solid) to create a rich-tasting base (as in chocolate mousse or custard).

The egg white has a remarkable *leavening* (foaming) quality, capable of foaming up to a volume many times its original size when whipped. You can sweeten this foam (as in meringue), fold it into flavored egg yolks (as in soufflés), or use it to lighten desserts (as in cakes and batters).

Buying Fresh Eggs

In most desserts, fresh eggs are critical because you want firm, absorbent yolks and whites that foam as much as possible. Both these capabilities diminish as an egg ages. When egg yolks age, the clear membrane encasing the yolk breaks down — when you cook it, the yolk falls apart. That might not be so bad in itself, but as egg yolks get older, they also can spoil.

Egg packages have expiration dates, sometimes two types. In any case, you don't want to buy eggs three or four weeks old. The normal expiration date is the government standard for freshness. When you see eggs that are close to or past that date, don't buy them. The other date is called the *Julian date* and indicates the date that the eggs were packed.

A short history of the egg

Eggs probably were around for a long time before anyone thought about eating one. The early Phoenicians somehow got the idea that the earth was formed when a giant egg cracked and opened and poured it out — lucky they didn't have such wacky ideas about navigation.

The chicken and egg were not widespread in Western Europe until the 18th century, according to Harold McGee's excellent book "On Food and Cooking: The Science and Lore of the Kitchen." The French picked up some new hatching techniques from the Egyptians. New breeds of hens, introduced from China, also

gave a boost to the egg industry, which was full blown in Europe and the United States by the late 1800s.

Technology has created modern egg factories that bear as much resemblance to the farm as a silicon chip factory. According to McGee, "Today's laying hen is born in an incubator, eats a diet that originates largely in the laboratory, lives and lays on a wire and under lights for about a year until she lays less regularly, and produces between 250 and 290 eggs."

With such an industrial egg industry in which eggs come from hundreds of miles away, assuring freshness is vital.

For example, 023 means that the eggs were packed on the 23rd day of the year, January 23. Add about four weeks to that to get the expiration dates. Look for these stamps on the tops or the sides of egg cartons.

Most American stores sell eggs that are AA and A. The quality difference is really negligible — both are good.

Egg sizes are calculated on a minimum weight per dozen:

- **Jumbo:** 30 ounces (840 g) per dozen
- **Extra large:** 27 ounces (756 g) per dozen
- **Large:** 24 ounces (672 g) per dozen
- **Medium:** 21 ounces (588 g) per dozen

Recipes in this book call for large eggs, but a grade either way won't make a difference.

Brown Eggs, Brown Chickens?

Shell color has nothing to do with egg quality. Different colors, and occasional speckling of the shell, come from the certain types of hens.

Little blood spots that are occasionally found in egg yolks are harmless as well. They're usually caused by a ruptured blood vessel on the surface of the yolk. Remove these spots with the tip of a knife.

You encounter the term *free-range chicken* more in restaurants than stores. Technically speaking, this term refers to chickens that aren't confined in large warehouses all their lives. The term *free range* can be misleading, however, because chickens often are confined to a fenced-in area and in such numbers to prevent any real extensive movement.

Don't confuse free range, which just means the chickens see some daylight in an open pen, with organic, which means that the chickens have been raised without growth hormones or other production-enhancing drugs. It's difficult to tell just by looking whether a chicken is organic (or even free range for that matter — although they usually have less excess fat). You have to check the source or ask for the source's license and check with the appropriate authority. (Different departments in various states oversee poultry production.)

Raw Eggs

Very few dessert recipes call for eggs that never get cooked, and none in this book do. A miniscule percentage of eggs, particularly those with cracked shells, can carry the salmonella bacteria. This bacteria is killed when eggs are cooked to 160° or beyond — such as when a cake is baked or a sauce is cooked — and held at that temperature for three minutes.

The best defense is to avoid eating raw eggs and to inspect eggs in the carton before buying them — don't buy cracked eggs.

The Cholesterol Issue

Cholesterol is largely a personal health issue. Those with elevated cholesterol levels or other problems may be advised to limit or eliminate egg consumption. A large egg contains 213 milligrams of cholesterol, although in recent years, speculation has risen that eggs may also carry within them a substance that limits the absorption of cholesterol.

The American Heart Association suggests that adults limit their daily cholesterol to no more than 300 milligrams.

To consider the cholesterol level of a dessert, calculate the number of egg yolks in it and divide that by the number of servings. For example, a pudding that has nine eggs and serves eight people works out to about 239 milligrams of cholesterol per person — a little less than the recommended daily maximum.

In recent years, modern feeding techniques have produced lowfat eggs that contain about half the cholesterol of regular eggs. These eggs have yet to reach beyond regional markets, however. (Currently, you can buy them only on the West coast, and they're being produced only on an experimental basis.)

Absorbent Yolks

A single egg yolk can *emulsify* (hold in suspension) many times its weight in vegetable oil. Adding a little water when whipping the yolk helps bind the emulsion. That's why we sometimes add water to egg yolks in this book — when making custards, soufflé bases, and even ice cream.

Hot, Hot, Hot

In recipes that call for adding hot milk or other liquids to egg yolks, we caution you to add a little bit at a time while whisking vigorously. Egg yolks have a tremendous capacity to absorb liquids, but when too much hot liquid hits them at once, they cook and turn hard. At that point, the dog has a nice chunky sauce for dinner.

 When working with egg yolks, make sure that they are chilled, mostly for hygiene reasons. Egg yolks, when warm, are more vulnerable to the salmonella bacteria. The bacteria also enters eggs through cracks in the shells, so inspect eggs in the store before buying. (For more information, see the section "Raw Eggs," earlier in this chapter.)

When working with egg whites, however, make sure that they're at room temperature to get the best foaming results — it's just the way the chemical reaction works. Because egg whites are mostly water, they are less prone to infection than egg yolks.

A Peak Experience

In many recipes, we talk about whipping egg whites and whipping chilled heavy cream to soft peaks or firm peaks. The distinction is important because it affects the texture of the dessert. In some cases, like meringues and cookies, you want a firm, thick texture from the egg whites. Other times, in batters and some cakes, you want a soft, looser texture.

- ✔ **Firm peaks:** Whip egg whites or heavy cream until they form sharp peaks that stand on their own — when you pull out a whisk, the peaks hold their position, like Green Berets.

- ✔ **Soft peaks:** Whip egg whites or cream until they form peaks that collapse under their own weight — when you pull out a whisk, the peaks fall back on themselves.

Separating Egg Whites and Yolks

Separating eggs, a common task in dessert-making, is sort of like parallel parking: Trying it for the first time can be frustrating, indeed embarrassing; with practice, however, you can do it so well you encourage spectators.

Folding egg whites

Folding egg whites is an instruction you'll find in many desserts recipes. To successfully accomplish this task (see the figure), follow these steps:

1. **Stir in about ¼ of the whipped egg whites into your yolk mixture (or whatever you're folding the egg whites into).**

2. **Place the remaining egg whites on top of the mixture.**

3. **Cut down through the egg whites as if you were cutting a cake.**

4. **Gently scoop the mixture from the bottom of the bowl and flip some of it onto the top of the whites.**

5. **Give the bowl a quarter turn and repeat Steps 3 and 4 (10 to 15 times) until the whites and mixture are combined.**

Make sure that you don't overblend, or the whites will deflate.

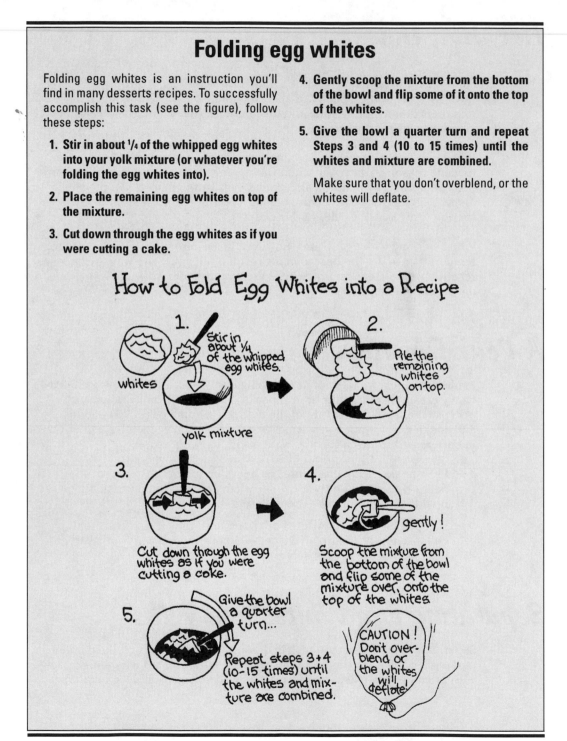

How to Fold Egg Whites into a Recipe

1. Stir in about ¼ of the whipped egg whites.
whites
yolk mixture

2. Pile the remaining whites on top.

3. Cut down through the egg whites as if you were cutting a coke.

4. gently! Scoop the mixture from the bottom of the bowl and flip some of the mixture over, onto the top of the whites

5. Give the bowl a quarter turn... Repeat steps 3+4 (10-15 times) until the whites and mixture are combined.

CAUTION! Don't over-blend or the whites will deflate!

To separate egg whites and yolks:

1. **Hold the egg in one hand and tap the center (widest) part of the egg against the rim of a bowl (glass, metal, ceramic) — tap it firmly without smashing it.**

   This step takes a little practice. You want to break the shell and the inner membrane, but not the yolk.

2. **With your two thumbs, pry open the egg shell at its crack to open the egg all the way, leaving the yolk in one half.**

   Let some of the egg white spill over into the bowl.

3. **Tilt the shell half that contains the yolk slightly, enough to make some of the egg white slide out; then, with the shell halves touching, carefully slide the egg yolk from one shell half to the other.**

   Do this two or three times, or until all the egg white falls into the bowl. (If the yolk breaks and a little falls into the bowl with the whites, remove the yolk with a paper towel or the edge of the empty egg shell.)

   If any little strips of white cling to the yolk, tilt the shell so that the white strips touch the edge of the shell and remove them carefully with your finger.

Chapter 7
Custards and Puddings

In This Chapter

▶ Two basic custards: Stirred versus baked

▶ Crème caramel and its many disguises

▶ Don't throw that out! Great bread puddings

▶ Rice pudding: The Rolls-Royce version

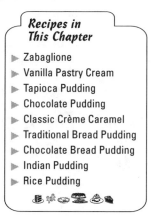

Recipes in This Chapter

▶ Zabaglione

▶ Vanilla Pastry Cream

▶ Tapioca Pudding

▶ Chocolate Pudding

▶ Classic Crème Caramel

▶ Traditional Bread Pudding

▶ Chocolate Bread Pudding

▶ Indian Pudding

▶ Rice Pudding

*1*f you're in a rush — and who isn't? — and yet you want to make special desserts for your family without relying on boxes, custards and puddings may be your first step toward liberation. Custards and puddings are a cinch to make and, if refrigerated, they hold well for several days — that is, if you can keep midnight marauders from snagging them prematurely.

Nearly every country in the Western Hemisphere has some sort of sweet custard dessert: crème caramel in France, flan in Spain, various custards in Italy, vanilla custards in Central and South America, rum-spiked puddings in Scandinavia, and more. In this chapter, we look at all kinds of custards and ways to jazz them up, as well as some terrific all-American puddings.

Custard's Best Stand

The great thing about custard is that it's a foundation food, sort of like rice, that can be combined with any number of ingredients, such as fruit, cookies, and cakes, to make different desserts. Fundamentally, custard is beaten eggs and milk, sweetened and then garnished in various ways.

But before you grab that whisk, you should know a few things about this most versatile dessert.

Is this a custard or a pudding?

The waters get a little murky when we try differentiating custards from puddings. In many cases, for example, a custard can also be defined as pudding. Suffice to say that puddings are flavored liquids, thickened with cooked eggs. Custards are beaten egg mixtures, sweetened with flavored liquids, that set and generally have a lighter, eggier consistency than pudding.

In both cases, the eggs coagulate during cooking — it's just the texture that is different. Think of the difference between an Indian pudding and a crème caramel.

The inside scoop

When you make custards or puddings, a few simple tips will assure success.

- As with any egg-based dessert, temperature is critical to get the right consistency. A *water bath (bain-marie)* is simply a way to make sure that custard mixes don't get too hot when cooking. To create a water bath, place a baking dish (or whatever you're baking in) in a high-sided baking pan or other container. Fill the container until water reaches halfway up the side of the dish holding the food. Because water can't get any hotter than boiling temperature (212°), the food can't get hotter than that, even if the oven is 300° or more.

  A *double boiler* serves a similar function to a water bath, only it's used on the stovetop. An egg-based sauce cooks in a pot that's set over another pot of boiling water. Hence, the steam (212°) provides steady, low heat. You can buy a double boiler or just improvise with your pots.

- When you're working with custard, be careful not to spill any water into it because it could cause a mini-steam explosion.

- A custard should be taken from the oven slightly before it's completely cooked because it continues to cook for another few minutes.

- Let custards and puddings sit for five minutes or so before serving so that they can cool and set.

Custard's Two Faces

Essentially, custard comes in two forms. One is the stirred type, which has the consistency of a thick sauce and is often served as such. Baked custard is the quivery one, like crème caramel.

Each custard has its own characteristics. For example, if you combine a stirred custard with Marsala wine, you get zabaglione (called *sabayon* by the French — see the section "Zabaglione," later in this chapter). When you thicken a stirred custard with cornstarch, it becomes pastry cream that you can use in tarts, eclairs, and cakes. (We talk more about those items in Chapter 4.)

You can combine baked custard, the more eggy and quivery kind, with chunks of old bread crumbs to make a bread pudding. When you add cornmeal and molasses to a baked custard, it becomes Indian pudding. Drenched in caramel, baked custard is called crème caramel. And, if you add chocolate to a baked custard as it cooks, it turns into a sinister pot de crème. (See recipes later in this chapter.)

We have divided the custards and puddings into two sections based upon whether they're cooked on the stovetop, as in most stirred custards, or in the oven (baked custards).

Stirred custards

For stirred custard, a beaten egg mixture is placed in a pan along with hot milk. The key is to bring the eggs to about 180°, just short of boiling, while stirring. (If the mixture boils, the eggs curdle and ruin the custard.) (See Figure 7-1.)

Use a cooking thermometer (see Chapter 2) to be exact. When done, the stirred custard mixture should coat the back of a wooden spoon without running off. Another way to test the custard is to hold the coated spoon over a pot and run your finger along the coated side to create a dry spot — sort of like Moses parting the Red Sea. The mixture should not run back over the dry spot.

Examples of stirred custards include crème anglaise or vanilla sauce, zabaglione (sabayon), all-around pastry cream, and even chocolate pudding. You might not think that a firm chocolate pudding would be a stirred custard, which we describe as saucelike. But chocolate pudding is one of the few exceptions. All recipes are included in this chapter.

Zabaglione

Zabaglione, a foamy, wine-sweetened sauce from Italy, is wonderful with any kind of fresh fruit or with cake. Zabaglione must be served immediately, if not sooner.

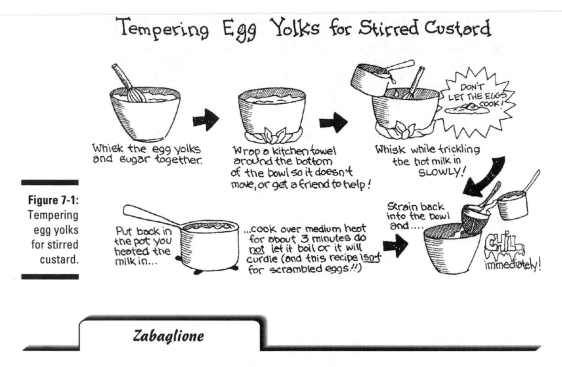

Tempering Egg Yolks for Stirred Custard

DON'T LET THE EGGS COOK!

Whisk the egg yolks and sugar together.

Wrap a kitchen towel around the bottom of the bowl so it doesn't move, or get a friend to help!

Whisk while trickling the hot milk in SLOWLY!

Put back in the pot you heated the milk in...

...cook over medium heat for about 3 minutes do not let it boil or it will curdle (and this recipe is not for scrambled eggs!!)

Strain back into the bowl and....

CHILL immediately!

Figure 7-1: Tempering egg yolks for stirred custard.

Zabaglione

The trick with this recipe is to keep whisking the mixture as it cooks in a double boiler (actually, in this case in a big mixing bowl over a pot of boiling water for ease of whisking) — if you stop even for a few seconds, the mixture may curdle, in which case the dog would have the most boozy snack of her life.

Marsala is a sweet wine, similar to sherry, that is served as an aperitif and also added to various dessert sauces.

Note: The mixture is cooked in a large mixing bowl over a pot of boiling water and not a double boiler. (See Figure 7-2.) That's because a big bowl is better for whisking.

Tools: *Pot*

Preparation time: *5 minutes*

Cooking time: *15 minutes*

Yield: *6 servings*

2 cups (16 ounces) dry white wine　　　*³/₄ cup (4¹/₂ ounces) sugar*

¹/₄ cup (2 ounces) Marsala　　　*5 egg yolks*

1 In a large bowl, combine the white wine, Marsala, sugar, and egg yolks.

2 Place the bowl over a pot of boiling water and begin to whisk in a clockwise motion, lifting the whisk out of the mixture each time and dipping it back into it.

This process ensures that you incorporate the maximum air possible. As the steam below the bowl cooks the mixture, it becomes opaque and starts to thicken — don't stop whisking!

3 Keep whisking, occasionally running the whisk around the sides of the bowl to prevent the eggs from sticking.

The mixture becomes very fluffy, and the bubbles get smaller as you whisk. This process takes about 15 minutes. The mixture is done when a dollop of it dropped on a plate holds its shape without breaking down.

4 Serve warm or cold with fresh ripe strawberries and a sprig of mint or with other fruits. Zabaglione also is good over any type of berry or high acid fruits, like peaches, apricots, or plums.

Variations: For a twist on traditional zabaglione, substitute 1/4 cup (2 ounces) Grand Marnier or other fruit-flavored liqueur for Marsala. If you don't want to add alcohol, substitute 2 cups (16 ounces) orange juice for the white wine and leave out the Marsala.

For a chocolate version, add 1/4 cup (1 ounce) cocoa powder in Step 1.

Double Boiler and Zabaglione Technique

Figure 7-2: Double boiler and zabaglione technique.

Combine the wine, Marsala, sugar, and yolks and place bowl over a pot of boiling water.

Begin to whisk in a clockwise motion, lifting whisk out each time and dipping back down...

KEEP WHISKING !!☆! Occasionally running the whisk around the sides of the bowl.

☆ The mixture is done when a dollop holds its shape.

Pastry cream

Pastry cream, made from stirred custard, is an all-important dessert component used in many kinds of pastries and other sweets. Pastry cream is nothing more than a stirred custard that is thickened with cornstarch or flour so that it holds its shape and doesn't make the pastry soggy. Pastry cream is the filling for eclairs, profiteroles, Napoleons, and other pastries. In addition, pastry cream is the base for hot dessert soufflés.

Vanilla Pastry Cream

We're getting a little ahead of ourselves here, because this pastry cream goes with desserts in the next chapter. But explaining it here makes sense because it belongs to the family of stirred custards.

You can flavor this particular pastry cream with chocolate, coffee, or various liqueurs to make all kinds of decadent desserts.

Tools: *Deep pot, plastic wrap*

Preparation time: *10 minutes*

Cooking time: *10 minutes*

Yield: *2 $1/2$ cups (10 ounces)*

2 cups (16 ounces) milk	*5 egg yolks*
$1/2$ cup (3 ounces) sugar	*$1/2$ cup (2 ounces) cornstarch*
1 vanilla bean, split lengthwise, or 1 teaspoon vanilla extract	

1 Combine the milk, sugar, and vanilla bean (not the vanilla extract yet) in a deep pot. Bring to a rolling boil. Reduce to simmer and let the vanilla bean steep for 5 minutes. Remove the vanilla pod.

2 In a large mixing bowl, combine the egg yolks and cornstarch and whisk well. While continuing to whisk, gradually add $1/2$ cup (4 ounces) of the hot milk mixture to the egg yolks. Be careful, because too much hot milk hitting the egg yolks at once may cook them.

3 Slowly add the remaining milk mixture while whisking. Return the mixture to the original pot and stir constantly over medium-high heat as you bring the mixture to a boil — stirring prevents the eggs from curdling.

The mixture reaches the consistency of a thick batter in about 10 minutes. When the mixture is smooth with no lumps and bubbles appear, remove from heat and keep whisking for another 3 minutes. If using vanilla extract, add it at this point.

4 Transfer mixture to a bowl. When it reaches room temperature, cover with plastic wrap and refrigerate for at least half an hour.

Tapioca

Tapioca pudding is a nostalgic American dessert that most people first taste when they're about six years old and then stop eating until sometime after college. Tapioca is a homey and relatively lowfat dessert that can surprise and delight your guests — and kids inhale the stuff. That's why we're bringing it back to you, in all of its granular glory.

Derived from the cassava root, which is widespread in South America, tapioca is a starch. In some countries, tapioca starch is used for thickening soups, stews, and sauces.

The type of tapioca used in desserts is called large pearl, or fish eye, tapioca. Raw tapioca must be soaked for hours to soften before using. That's why no one uses it. American supermarkets sell the quick-cooked version, which works fine.

Tapioca Pudding

This tapioca pudding is flavored with orange, vanilla, and cinnamon. You also can experiment with other seasonings, like nutmeg or almond extract.

Tools: *Pot*

Preparation time: *15 minutes (plus 2 hours chilling)*

Cooking time: *15 minutes*

Yield: *4 to 6 servings*

(continued)

2 cups (16 ounces) milk

1 cinnamon stick

zest of 1 orange

1 vanilla bean, split lengthwise

$^1/_3$ cup (1 $^1/_2$ ounces) quick-cooking tapioca

2 egg yolks

$^1/_3$ cup (1 $^1/_2$ ounces) sugar

1 Combine the milk, cinnamon stick, orange zest, and vanilla bean and seeds in a pot. Bring to a boil. Put the tapioca in a separate bowl. Slowly pour the hot milk mixture over the tapioca.

2 In a separate bowl, whisk together the egg yolks and sugar. Pour the hot tapioca mixture over this mixture. Stir together. Pour all this mixture back in the pot that was used to boil the milk and place over medium heat.

3 Bring to a boil, stir, reduce to simmer, and cook for 1 minute, continuing to stir.

4 Pour the pudding into a serving dish or individual dishes. Chill 2 hours.

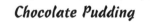

Chocolate Pudding

You may notice that this recipe for chocolate pudding is similar to that of vanilla pastry cream flavored with cocoa. Chocolate pudding is a great quick dessert that you can make ahead of time and garnish in all sorts of ways. Note that we allow 15 minutes of preparation time — that figure allows for phone calls, children falling off chairs, cats coughing up hairballs in the kitchen, and other normal household distractions.

Tools: Pot

Preparation time: 15 minutes

Cooking time: 15 minutes

Yield: 6 to 8 servings

9 egg yolks

1 $^1/_4$ cup (7$^1/_2$ ounces) sugar

$^1/_3$ cup (1$^1/_2$ ounces) cornstarch

1 vanilla bean, split lengthwise, or 1 teaspoon vanilla extract

2 cups (16 ounces) milk

4 ounces semisweet chocolate, chopped into dime-size pieces.

1 In a mixing bowl, combine the egg yolks, sugar, and cornstarch. Whisk well.

2 Place the vanilla bean and the seeds (not the vanilla extract yet) in a pot and add the milk. Stir to incorporate while bringing to a boil. When the milk boils, remove the vanilla bean.

3 Gradually pour the milk over the egg yolk mixture and whisk immediately. Continue whisking while pouring in all the milk and then return this mixture to the pot over medium heat. Stir constantly while bringing the mixture back to a boil.

4 Remove from heat and add the chocolate, stirring until it's melted and incorporated. If using vanilla extract, add at this point.

5 Spoon the pudding mixture into a serving bowl or individual bowls and refrigerate for several hours. Serve with whipped cream or Vanilla Pastry Cream (see recipe earlier in this chapter).

Baked custards

Baked custards are the second major variety of custard — and the base of many puddings. They usually have a more firm and eggy texture than loose stirred custards.

As in stirred custard, when you make baked custards you need to cook the egg mixture without letting it reach a boil. In this case, the mixture is baked in a water bath. (See the section "The inside scoop," earlier in this chapter, for more information on water baths.)

Examples of baked custards include crème caramels and flans, rice puddings, Indian puddings, and bread puddings. (See recipes in this chapter.)

Crème de la crème

Crème caramel is the most common of all baked custards. One difference between it and crème brûlée is that the former uses the whole egg while the latter uses only the egg yolks, so crème brûlée is richer.

Just about the only way to foul up the basic custard in crème caramel is by cooking it too fast and curdling the eggs. Don't get impatient and turn up the oven heat if you think it's taking too long to set. Once the eggs curdle, the party's over.

When making the caramel, don't overstir the mixture or else it can crystallize. Stir just enough to combine.

If caramel crystallizes while cooking, try adding a teaspoon of lemon juice and stir it in. The acid in the lemon breaks down the crystals and restores the texture of the caramel.

When a crème caramel is well made, it's pale yellow and dense enough to stand up by itself on the plate. The caramel shouldn't have a rubbery texture or tough skin. And the texture should be so light that a spoon can pass through the caramel by its own weight.

Classic Crème Caramel

Dozens of countries around the world have their own version of this classic egg dessert. Some, like Spain, like to add orange. Some South American countries add chocolate or tropical fruits. This is the basic recipe that you can vary later as you like.

Tools: *Heavy-bottomed pot, strainer, buttered 10-inch baking dish or individual ramekins of $^3/_4$ to 1-cup capacity, ladle*

Preparation time: *15 minutes (plus 2 hours chilling)*

Cooking/Baking time: *55 to 65 minutes*

Yield: *6 to 8 servings*

4 cups (32 ounces) milk

1 vanilla bean, split lengthwise, or 1 teaspoon vanilla extract

2$^1/_2$ cups (15 ounces) sugar

9 eggs

pinch of salt

1 teaspoon lemon juice

$^1/_2$ cup (4 ounces) warm water

Custard

1 In a heavy-bottomed pot, bring the milk to a boil and add the vanilla bean (not the vanilla extract yet). Remove from heat and cool slightly, about 10 minutes. Stir well; remove the vanilla bean.

2 In a bowl, whisk together 1$^1/_4$ cup (7$^1/_2$ ounces) sugar, eggs, salt, and vanilla extract until the mixture becomes frothy and lighter in color — about 5 minutes.

3 When the milk is cool enough for you to put your finger in without shouting, slowly pour it over the eggs while whisking. Strain. Transfer to a ceramic serving dish or to individual custard cups. Chill for 2 hours.

Caramel

1 Preheat oven to 300°.

2 Place ¼ cup (1½ ounces) sugar in a heavy-bottomed pot along with the lemon juice. Over medium heat, allow the sugar to melt and the caramel to form — it should be hazelnut or a toasty brown color.

3 Continue adding the rest of the sugar ¼ cup (1½ ounces) at a time as you stir occasionally. (Don't stir too much because the caramel can crystallize and form lumps.)

4 Reduce heat to low and gradually add drops of water to the pot while stirring. When the bubbling stops, add a little more water. Stir over the heat until the mixture is liquid and has no lumps.

5 Pour the caramel into the bottom of a buttered square baking dish — 10 inches square by 2 inches deep (or whatever you have close to that) — or pour into individual ramekins (individual baking dishes, like soufflé molds). (Remember, the cooking time is about a third less for ramekins.) Let the caramel cool until it reaches the consistency of molasses.

6 Ladle the custard mixture gradually over all the caramel. Fill to ¼ inch below the rim of the baking dish. Place baking dish in a larger pan. Pour enough water into the larger pan to reach halfway up the side of the crème caramel pan, or about an inch.

7 Bake for 45 minutes to an hour. To test the crème caramel, shake the dish — waves should appear in the custard. The custard should be relatively firm, like Jell-O. Remove, cool to room temperature, and then refrigerate for at least 1 hour.

8 To unmold, run a knife around the edge of the baking dish. Warm the baking dish slightly over a flame for about 30 seconds. Invert a serving dish and place it over the top of the crème caramel dish. Flip and unmold.

Old-fashioned puddings

These all-American puddings originally were cooked in iron pots hanging inside of hearths. Egg custard is the base for all these recipes. You can add many other ingredients, like bread, fruits, rice, and cornmeal.

Lots of things can go wrong when making puddings:

- ✔ **If your stirred pudding gets too thick when it's refrigerated, let it sit for 5 to 10 minutes at room temperature.** Then spoon the pudding into a bowl and whisk until it becomes smooth again. Refrigerate for only an hour or so before serving — much longer than that and the pudding could congeal again. (If your pudding is so dense that it can double as a tire block on steep hills, keep it in the trunk of your car for such eventualities.)

- ✔ **If your pudding comes out anemic and thin, fold in some whipped cream.**

Traditional Bread Pudding

This favorite dessert pudding no doubt came about generations ago. Frugal cooks never threw out any food that hadn't, through age, developed the ability to get up and walk on its own. Hence, bread pudding (see photo) is a way to use slightly stale bread. The foundation of the recipe is a basic baked custard.

You can serve bread pudding slightly warm (especially good with ice cream or whipped cream) or cool (maybe with Candied Orange Slices — see recipe in Chapter 16).

Tools: *Two 10-inch round baking dishes or 10-inch terrines, pan, heavy pot, slotted spoon, strainer*

Preparation time: *30 minutes*

Cooking/Baking time: *1 hour 50 minutes*

Yield: *8 to 10 servings*

$^1/_2$-inch pat of butter, for greasing the baking dishes

1 cup (8 ounces) chopped dried fruit (pears, apricots, apples, apricots, raisins, and so on)

2 cups (16 ounces) water for cooking fruit

$^1/_4$ cup (2 ounces) rum or alcohol of choice (optional)

$4^1/_2$ cups (36 ounces) milk

1 vanilla bean, split lengthwise, or 1 teaspoon vanilla extract

1 cinnamon stick

1 clove

$^1/_8$ teaspoon grated fresh nutmeg, or same amount dried

zest of 1 orange

$1^1/_4$ cup ($7^1/_2$ ounces) sugar

9 eggs

pinch of salt

10 slices of day-old white bread (preferably crusty country-style bread, crust removed), cut into 2-inch triangles

$^1/_8$ cup (2 ounces or $^1/_4$ stick) melted butter

1 Preheat oven to 300°. Butter two 10-inch round baking dishes or two 10-inch terrines.

2 Place the chopped fruits in a pan and cover with water. Bring to a boil. Let sit for 10 to 15 minutes. Strain. Douse with rum or other alcohol of choice (optional). Set aside.

3 In a heavy pot, combine 4 cups (32 ounces) milk, vanilla, cinnamon stick, clove, nutmeg, and orange zest.

4 Bring the milk and spices to a boil. Remove from heat and cool slightly, about 15 minutes. With a slotted spoon, remove the orange zest, clove, cinnamon stick, and vanilla bean. Strain the milk through a sieve into a bowl. Set aside as you prepare the egg mixture.

5 In a separate bowl, whisk together the sugar, eggs, and salt until the mixture becomes frothy and light in color.

6 Gradually pour the hot milk into the egg mixture while whisking. Strain into a bowl.

7 Soak the bread in the remaining $\frac{1}{2}$ cup (4 ounces) milk for 1 to 2 minutes. Don't let the bread get so soggy that it falls apart. It should just be moist all the way through.

8 Sprinkle $\frac{3}{4}$ of the fruit-rum mixture over the bottom of the baking dishes. Arrange the bread triangles over them, overlapping each other a little. Sprinkle remaining fruit on the top of the bread triangles. Quickly stir the custard mixture and then ladle it over the bread and fruit.

9 Drizzle the melted butter over the top.

10 Bake approximately 40 minutes or until the pudding feels slightly firm and a little resilient — it should also be browned slightly on the surface and resilient to the touch.

Chocolate Bread Pudding

This recipe is a variation on the preceding Traditional Bread Pudding. To get a sneak preview of how it will turn out, see the color photograph in this book.

Tools: *10 x 12-inch baking dish or individual 4-ounce baking dishes*

Preparation time: *30 minutes*

Baking time: *35 minutes*

Yield: *6 servings*

(continued)

¹/₂-inch pat of butter, for greasing the baking dish

5 eggs

2 egg yolks

¹/₂ cup (3 ounces) sugar

1 cup (8 ounces) milk

8 ounces chocolate, chopped into small pieces

1 cup (8 ounces) heavy cream

4 slices day-old white bread (preferably crusty country-style bread, crust removed), cut into 1-inch squares

1 Preheat oven to 300°. Butter the baking dish.

2 Whisk the eggs, yolks, and sugar together. Set aside.

3 Boil the milk. Remove from heat and pour the hot milk over the chocolate pieces.

4 Add the heavy cream. Pour the chocolate mixture over the egg mixture and strain.

5 Add the bread squares, stirring until well coated. Pour into the buttered baking dish.

6 Bake for 35 minutes or until firm. (The pudding should not move in the baking dish when jiggled.)

7 Allow to cool at room temperature for 30 minutes. Serve with whipped cream and chocolate sauce (see Chapter 4).

Indian pudding

When you look at the big picture, Native Americans in the 16th and 17th centuries probably made a big mistake by teaching Europeans anything at all that helped them survive in the wilderness — especially anything about cooking. If the American Indians had just left the Europeans alone, they probably would have become so sick of potatoes and dry turkey that they would have hopped onto their ships and gone home.

But, of course, that's not what happened. English colonists became particularly enamored with a food they called *Indian corn*. They ate it prepared many ways, a favorite being a sweetened pudding that was dubbed, naturally, *Indian pudding*.

When making Indian pudding, we find that stone-ground yellow cornmeal, widely available in grocery stores, has a nice grainy texture and good flavor.

Indian Pudding

This hearty cold-weather dessert is associated with New England, where it's believed to have originated with local Indians. It's delicious warm or at room temperature, and vanilla ice cream is a fine accompaniment.

Tools: *10-inch baking dish, medium pot, nutmeg grater, paring knife*

Preparation time: *10 minutes*

Cooking/Baking time: *1 hour 10 minutes*

Yield: *6 to 8 servings*

$1/2$-inch pat of butter, for greasing the baking dishes

4 cups (32 ounces) milk

$1/2$ cup (3$1/2$ ounces) cornmeal

$1/3$ cup (2 ounces) sugar

$1/2$ teaspoon ground cinnamon

pinch of salt

$1/2$ teaspoon ground ginger

10 scrapes of fresh nutmeg

$1/2$ cup (4 ounces) golden raisins

$1/3$ cup (2 $1/2$ ounces) molasses

$1/2$ cup (4 ounces or 1 stick) butter

4 eggs

1 Preheat oven to 350°. Grease a 10-inch baking dish.

2 In a medium pot, bring 2 cups (16 ounces) milk to a boil. Meanwhile, in a bowl, mix the cornmeal, sugar, cinnamon, salt, ginger, and nutmeg. Stir in the raisins.

3 When the milk boils, remove from heat. Stir in the dry ingredients. Return to medium-high heat and stir. When the mixture thickens, stir in the molasses.

4 When well blended, add the butter and stir until incorporated. Remove from heat and quickly whisk in the eggs.

5 Pour the mixture into the buttered 10-inch baking dish. Take a large wooden spoon and hold it over the pudding. Pour the remaining milk over the spoon so that it hits the pudding gently. (You want to avoid pouring the milk directly onto the pudding, which can cause an indentation.)

6 Bake for 1 hour. The pudding should be resilient to the touch.

Rice Pudding

Rice pudding has more faces than a circus clown. Everybody seems to make it differently, and everybody claims to have the best recipe. The old-fashioned authentic recipe calls for a basic crème anglaise (vanilla pastry cream) blended with cooked rice and flavorings. This version is the Rolls-Royce of rice puddings — rich with egg yolks and fluffed up with whipped cream. A little goes a long way. This pudding is at its fluffiest, awesome best when consumed within one day.

If you want, you can garnish with Candied Orange Slices (see recipe in Chapter 16) or sliced fresh fruit.

Tools: *Heavy-bottomed pot, strainer, wooden spoon, 12-inch glass pie shell, aluminum foil, platter*

Preparation time: *25 minutes*

Cooking/Baking time: *50 minutes*

Yield: *6 to 8 servings*

4 cups (32 ounces) water

$^3/_4$ cup (4 ounces) Carolina rice

2 cups (16 ounces) milk

$^1/_4$ cup ($1^1/_2$ ounces) plus 1 tablespoon sugar

zest of 1 orange

4 egg yolks

1 cup (8 ounces) heavy cream

Rice

1 Preheat oven to 325°.

2 In a pot, boil the water and plunge the rice into the water for 4 minutes. Pour through a strainer and discard water. While rice is still in the strainer, rinse with cold water and allow to drain well, about 5 minutes. (This process removes some starch from the rice.)

3 In a pot, combine $1^1/_2$ cups (12 ounces) milk with the sugar and orange zest. Bring to a boil and remove from heat. Place the drained rice in the milk mixture. Blend with a wooden spoon.

4 Transfer everything into a 12-inch glass pie shell or any shallow ovenproof container. Cover tightly with aluminum foil. Poke 4 holes in the top of the foil with a sharp knife.

5 Bake for 30 minutes or until all milk is absorbed by the rice.

6 When done, transfer the rice to a platter and spread out thinly so that it can cool at room temperature for 20 to 30 minutes.

Custard

1 In a heavy-bottomed pot, boil the remaining milk. In a bowl, combine the egg yolks and 1 tablespoon sugar. Whisk vigorously for a minute.

2 Pour a little bit of the boiled milk over the egg yolks while whisking. (This process is called *tempering,* which means to raise the temperature of the eggs slowly so that they don't cook or curdle.) While continuing to whisk, drizzle the remaining hot milk over the eggs. Pour this mixture back into the milk saucepan.

3 Place over medium heat and whisk. Whisk over heat until the mixture thickens — usually no more than 45 seconds. Be careful not to overcook. Quickly strain into another bowl. Set aside.

Whipped Cream

Whip the heavy cream with a mixer or whisk until it reaches soft peaks — shaving cream consistency, no thicker.

Assembly

In a bowl, add the custard to the rice and stir until blended. Gently break up any large lumps with a whisk. When the rice mixture is cool, take a rubber spatula and fold in the whipped cream. Don't overmix, or it will break down. Chill at least 30 minutes before serving.

Chapter 8

Things That Go Crunch in the Night: Meringues

*I*n terms of sheer fun, meringues have to rate near the top in the dessert world. Whisking clear, flat egg whites into a wondrous mound of snowy fluff is always uplifting. Once you discover all the things this airy substance can do — lighten cakes, puff soufflés, garnish pies — you can make desserts that are as festive as they are delicious.

In this chapter, we describe the major types of meringues and their functions. Then we hit the stove to create some classic French and American desserts.

Meringue 101

Think of meringues as essentially egg whites whipped with sugar until they become fluffy but firm. In many recipes, meringue is added primarily to add a little textural contrast to mousses, whipped cream, and the like. You use them in all kinds of desserts, including lemon meringue pie, *dacquoise* (a layered meringue-and-almond cake), meringue cookies, meringue cakes, *charlottes* (a meringue ladyfinger cake), *vacherin* (a meringue and cream cake), and much more.

When you know how to make one of the three major types of meringue, you can improvise and make your own elegant dessert with fruit, whipped cream, or ice cream.

Don't discard unused meringue down the sink! This gelatin-thickened meringue floats on water, so if it does go down the drain, it won't disintegrate fully.

Whipping Up Perfect Egg Whites

Egg whites are an amazing substance, capable of doing so many things, such as lightening other food and making meringues. The secret is the way that egg whites foam up — whisked egg whites can foam up to about eight times their volume, which has to be some sort of record in the food world. (We suspect that probably several dozen egg whites doused with food coloring was the substance slithering after Steve McQueen in the 1950s horror flick *The Blob*. The leftover egg yolks must have made for one whopper of an omelet.)

The reason egg whites foam up is essentially the same reason behind the head on a glass of beer: Tiny pockets of air get trapped inside sheets of water. The substance in egg whites that makes this expansion possible is *albumen protein*. You don't really want to know what this is, do you? If anybody asks, just say that it's the protein that traps air and causes foam.

Before you start cracking eggs, here are a few helpful tips to get the most mileage out of egg whites:

✔ **Use a copper bowl, if possible.** A copper bowl — for reasons that aren't entirely clear — yields rich, creamy egg whites for your meringue (better than those made in ceramic or stainless steel bowls). If you don't have a copper bowl, a pinch of cream of tartar causes a similar reaction in egg whites.

Chefs have been using copper bowls to whip egg whites for over 200 years, without knowing precisely why. The scientific explanation — having to do with copper ions, binding of proteins, and the like — is still being hashed out. Suffice to say that copper works. If you buy a copper bowl, get a relatively large one (2 quarts or more) because whisking egg whites is easier if your bowl isn't too small. Make sure that you clean and dry the bowl thoroughly after each use; copper is attractive, so you may want to hang it on the wall.

Copper discolors after a few weeks. Nothing is wrong with that, but for cosmetic reasons, you may want to clean it with a commercial copper cleaner. Or you can use a solution of lemon juice or vinegar and salt — just rub it on with a damp sponge and then rinse the bowl. (Mix the juice of one lemon with 2 tablespoons table salt.)

- ✔ **Your work bowl, whether it's copper or stainless steel, must be obsessively clean.** Any grease, dirt, or fat inhibits air bubbles from forming in the meringue — the whites just slosh around in the bowl, and your arm gets as sore as an overworked relief pitcher.

- ✔ **Egg whites to be whisked are best at room temperature.** This way, they're softer and looser, and thus can form air bubbles more easily. (Air bubbles cause the frothing.) Egg whites set out (covered with plastic wrap) at room temperature for 15 minutes become sufficiently warm to whisk. Don't leave egg whites out too long because of the threat of bacterial infection. (The threat is less than with egg yolks, but you can never be too careful.)

- ✔ **Adding cream of tartar to egg whites helps air bubbles form.**

- ✔ **Use egg whites that are at least a week old but less than a month old.** The whites have a chance to soften a bit, which allows them to foam better when whisked.

- ✔ **Don't overwhisk egg whites, or they won't expand properly.** Whisk them just until they form peaks that can stand on their own when plopped on a table.

French Meringues

French meringue is the simplest and most fragile of all meringues. You make it by folding sugar into whipped egg whites. This semisoft substance is used in Baked Alaska (see the recipe later in this chapter), mixed with chopped nuts to make layer cakes, or used as a lightening agent in mousses or cakes. You can also poach French meringue in milk to make the famous French dessert Floating Islands (Îles Flottantes).

When you bake a French meringue, it takes on another identity. It becomes hard and crumbly, suitable for a dacquoise or meringue cakes. Before baking a French meringue, however, you make one modification: You fold some confectioners' sugar into the meringue. Then it's baked for a long time at a low temperature to harden.

If you're in a puckish mood, try molding hard, baked meringue into a baseball — then pitch it to an unsuspecting batter.

Never refrigerate leftover baked French meringues — they'll soak up humidity and get soft. Keep them in an airtight plastic container.

Arguably, the most famous meringue recipe in the U.S. is lemon meringue pie. At its best, it has a slightly puckery and citric base, crowned with a soft, foamy meringue topping. The soft French-style meringue is best suited to this king of pies. It may seem ironic that a classic American dessert uses a French meringue, but it's the texture, not the nationality, that counts, and this is the best meringue for this type of pie, mais oui?

Lemon Meringue Pie

This classic lemon meringue pie uses the basic American-style pie crust from Chapter 3. The tart lemon flavor comes from fresh lemon juice (use only fresh) and lemon zest. Achieving the proper balance between tart and sweet is the key to a good lemon meringue pie. You don't want a guest looking like a trumpet player on break, nor should the guest be assaulted with sugar.

Note that you prepare the meringue last because uncooked meringue starts to deteriorate within 10 minutes. Have the crust and filling ready as you're finishing the meringue.

Tools: *Rolling pin, 9 or 10-inch pie pan, aluminum foil, dried beans (for weighing down the crust), cooling rack, medium pot, sieve, electric mixer (optional)*

Preparation time: *40 minutes*

Baking time: *40 minutes (plus 1 hour and 20 minutes for cooling/refrigeration)*

Yield: *8 to 10 servings*

1 Basic American Pie Dough	*1 cup (6 ounces) sugar*
juice of 5 lemons (7 tablespoons)	*grated zest of 2 lemons*
4 eggs	*5 egg whites, room temperature*
$^1/_2$ cup (4 ounces or 1 stick) butter, cut into 1-inch cubes	*$^1/_2$ teaspoon cream of tartar (if not using a copper bowl)*

American Pie Crust

1 Preheat oven to 375°.

2 Roll out the pie dough with a rolling pin. Place the dough in the pie pan. Line the pie crust with aluminum foil. Fill with dried beans.

3 Bake for 20 minutes. Remove the foil and beans.

4 Continue baking for about 10 minutes, or until the crust is brown.

5 Transfer the crust to a cooling rack.

Lemon Filling

1 Place the lemon juice, eggs, butter, and $^1/_2$ cup (3 ounces) sugar in a medium pot. Heat over medium heat. Whisk constantly until the mixture thickens.

2 Pass the mixture through a sieve into a bowl. Stir in the lemon zest. Cover and refrigerate until used.

French Meringue

Place the egg whites and cream of tartar in a bowl and beat until they form soft peaks. Gradually drizzle in the remaining sugar while beating until the mixture reaches stiff peaks (when you remove the whisk, meringue clings to it).

Assembly

1 Preheat oven to 375°.

2 Spoon the lemon filling into the prepared pie crust. With the back of a spoon, smooth the filling over the crust.

3 Using a spatula, spread the meringue over the top of the pie, forming occasional peaks. The meringue should be slightly thicker in the center than at the edges.

4 Bake the pie for about 10 minutes, or until the meringue browns slightly.

5 Remove from the oven and let cool for 20 minutes or so. Refrigerate for an hour or more before serving.

Another classic French recipe is Floating Islands, which is always festive and never goes out of style. This recipe is made with the soft and fragile French meringue that we use on the Lemon Meringue Pie. The "islands" are the puffs of meringue that float on a sea of vanilla sauce, called crème anglaise in French. These airy meringues are a perfect foil to the rich crème anglaise. By the way, you can use the irresistible crème anglaise as a sauce for dozens of desserts, including cakes, puddings, soufflés, and many more.

To clean the pot in which you make the caramel, fill the pot with water and place it on high heat. Bring to a boil. Most of the caramel will separate and rise to the surface.

Îles Flottantes (Floating Islands)

As with so many elegant desserts, you prepare this one in steps. First, you prepare the crème anglaise because you can make it ahead of time and chill it. Next, you make the caramel garnish because that, too, can hold. Third, you prepare the simple poaching liquid for the meringues. The fragile meringue is prepared last, and the dessert is then assembled immediately because meringue deteriorates within an hour.

Homemade caramel is exceedingly simple, but you must constantly watch the pot so that the caramel doesn't burn. You can use caramel on all kinds of desserts, especially ice cream.

Tools: *Electric mixer (optional), medium pot, sieve, slotted spoon, a wide (14 inches or more) pan*

Preparation time: *1 hour 5 minutes*

Cooking time: *1 hour*

Yield: *8 servings*

6 cups (48 ounces) milk	*1 cinnamon stick*
2 vanilla beans, split lengthwise, or 2 teaspoons vanilla extract	*zest of 1 orange (1 long strip, if possible, for easy removal when cooking)*
4 egg yolks	*8 egg whites, room temperature*
3¼ cups (19½ ounces) sugar	*¼ teaspoon cream of tartar*
½ teaspoon fresh lemon juice	*1 cup (4 ounces) sifted confectioners' sugar*
4½ cups (36 ounces) water	

Crème Anglaise (Vanilla Sauce)

1 Place 2 cups (16 ounces) milk and 1 vanilla bean (or 1 teaspoon vanilla extract) in a pot and bring to a boil. Remove from heat. Remove the vanilla bean and set aside.

2 In a bowl, whisk the egg yolks and ½ cup (3 ounces) sugar together for 3 minutes, until the mixture is pale yellow and smooth. Then drizzle some hot milk into the eggs while whisking. Continue whisking until all the hot milk is blended.

3 Return the mixture to the pot. Place the pot over medium heat while whisking vigorously. Whisk for about 2 minutes, or until thickened. Strain and chill, covered.

Liquid Caramel Sauce

1 In a pot over medium heat, heat 1 cup (6 ounces) sugar and the lemon juice until it caramelizes (turns darkish golden-brown) — about 3 minutes. Shake the pan back and forth gently to move the caramel around while cooking — but don't stir too much, or the caramel will get too thick.

2 Very carefully drizzle in $1/2$ cup (4 ounces) water and stir slowly. Return to a boil to finish the caramel. Shake the pan a little, and when the caramel looks fully developed (no water spots), strain it into a bowl and set aside. As the caramel reaches room temperature, it develops a soft caramel consistency. If the caramel gets too hard, return it to the stove over low heat until it softens.

Poaching Liquid

1 Combine 1 cup (6 ounces) sugar, the remaining milk and water, the cinnamon stick, orange zest, and the other vanilla bean or 1 teaspoon vanilla extract in a large, wide pan over high heat. Bring to a boil.

2 Reduce heat to simmer and cook for 5 minutes, stirring occasionally. Then remove the cinnamon stick, orange zest, and vanilla bean. Keep warm until needed.

French Meringue

1 With an electric mixer or a whisk, beat the egg whites and cream of tartar until soft peaks form. Slowly pour in the remaining sugar.

2 After the sugar is incorporated, stop whisking. With a rubber spatula, fold in the confectioners' sugar — do not overmix. Whisk gently to combine. Set aside.

3 To poach the meringue: Using a large serving spoon or a wooden spoon, scoop out a generous mound of the prepared meringue. With another spoon, mold the meringue into a thick, roughly pyramid shape — about 4 x 3 inches. Gently place the meringue onto the simmering poaching liquid, pointed side up. Repeat with the rest of the meringue — you should have about 8 meringues.

4 After the meringues have poached for 5 minutes, use a slotted spoon or wide spoon to tip the meringues on their sides. Poach for another 5 minutes.

5 Carefully remove the meringues to a damp (but not too wet!) kitchen towel and let them sit for about 3 minutes.

To Serve

1 Spoon some crème anglaise on the center of a plate.

2 With a spatula, carefully transfer a poached meringue onto the center of the crème anglaise.

3 Drizzle the liquid caramel sauce over the meringue. Serve within 1 hour.

Quick Strawberry Sauce

For a lighter version of floating islands (see preceding recipe), substitute strawberry sauce for the crème anglaise. You also can prepare a sauce with the same amount of pureéd fresh raspberries or blackberries. Just sweeten to taste with confectioners' sugar and strain.

If you want to vary the taste, add 10 fresh mint leaves or 2 tablespoons rum or liqueur to the blender before puréeing.

Tools: *Blender, sieve*

Preparation time: *10 minutes*

Cooking time: *None*

Yield: *4 to 6 servings*

2 cups (16 ounces) fresh strawberries, washed and hulled

2 tablespoons sugar

In a blender, purée the strawberries and sugar. Strain through a fine sieve.

Chocolate Meringue Cake

Giving meringue a chocolate twist is merely a matter of adding a little cocoa powder.

Tools: *Sifter, strainer, electric mixer (optional), pastry bag, parchment paper, medium pot*

Preparation time: *1 hour 10 minutes*

Cooking time: *2 hours 10 minutes (plus 50 minutes for chilling)*

Yield: *8 to 10 servings*

$^1/_2$ cup (2 ounces) confectioners' sugar

$^1/_2$ cup (2 ounces) cocoa powder

8 egg whites, room temperature

$^1/_4$ teaspoon cream of tartar

$1^1/_2$ cups (9 ounces) sugar

3 egg yolks

$^1/_4$ cup (2 ounces) water

$1^1/_4$ cups (10 ounces) heavy cream, very cold

8 ounces bittersweet chocolate

2 tablespoons butter

Chocolate Meringue

1 Preheat oven to 200°.

2 Sift the confectioners' sugar and cocoa powder together and set aside.

3 With a whisk or an electric mixer, whisk the egg whites and cream of tartar to form firm peaks. Then slowly add 1 cup (6 ounces) sugar while continuing to whisk for about 1 minute.

4 With a spatula, fold the sifted cocoa-sugar mixture into the egg white mixture (the meringue).

5 Fill the pastry bag with the meringue. Twist the top to eliminate air. Place the parchment paper on a large cookie sheet. On the parchment paper, squeeze out the meringue into three 8-inch-wide circles. Use the rest of the meringue to make 14-inch-long strips. (You'll break up the strips and use them for decoration.)

6 Bake for 2 hours, or until the meringue has completely dried out. To test the meringue, remove a small piece from the oven for a few minutes and let cool (the meringue will always be soft while it's in the oven). If it becomes hard and dry, the meringue is done.

Chocolate Mousse Filling

1 In a bowl, whisk the egg yolks for 5 minutes.

2 Place $1/2$ cup (3 ounces) sugar and the water in a pot and boil for 1 minute. Pour the boiled sugar-water mixture over the egg yolks, mixing, until the egg yolk mixture is lukewarm. Set aside.

3 In a separate bowl, whip the heavy cream to soft peaks.

4 Bring a pot of water to boil. Place the chocolate and the butter in a bowl and put the bowl over the pot of boiling water.

5 After the chocolate and butter have melted, stir the lukewarm yolk mixture into the chocolate. Remove from heat and stir to cool. When it's just warm to the touch, fold in the whipped cream.

6 Refrigerate 1 hour. (The mixture is very liquid at this point and needs about an hour to set.)

Assembly

1 Place a circle of chocolate meringue on the serving platter and cover entirely with a $1/4$-inch layer of chocolate mousse filling.

2 Repeat Step 1 twice with the other 2 meringue circles and the mousse. (Keep some mousse for Step 3.)

(continued)

3 Cover the cake with the rest of the mousse. Break the strips of meringue into 3-inch pieces and place all over the cake at odd angles.

Baked Alaska, an indulgent, all-American dessert, is always a crowd-pleaser. Baked Alaska is essentially ice cream set over a layer of cake, all covered with soft French meringue that is browned in the oven before serving. French meringue is perfect for this dish because it molds easily to the shape of the cake and ice cream.

Baked Alaska with Orange Grand Marnier Flambé Sauce

If you go through all the steps to make Baked Alaska, you may as well go for it and serve it in flames. The Orange Grand Marnier Flambé Sauce lets you do just that. (You also can use this quick sauce, flambéed or not, with all kinds of ice cream desserts as well as fruit desserts — especially those with whipped cream.)

We build Baked Alaska on top of a 4 x 8-inch cardboard rectangle. The cardboard base lets you pick up the cake easily and transfer it to a serving platter. For this recipe, you need a sponge cake (see the Whipped Cream Layer Cake in Chapter 9).

Tools: *Electric mixer (optional), 4 x 8-inch cardboard, aluminum foil, pastry bag with a #5 star tip, medium pot, matches*

Preparation time: *15 minutes (not including sponge cake)*

Cooking time: *15 minutes*

Yield: *10 to 12 servings*

5 egg whites, room temperature

pinch of cream of tartar (if not using a copper bowl)

1 cup (6 ounces) sugar

1 sponge cake

1 pint (2 cups) vanilla ice cream, very hard

¹/₂ cup (2 ounces) slivered almonds

2 tablespoons sifted confectioners' sugar

1 teaspoon vanilla extract

¹/₂ cup (4 ounces) orange juice (if fresh, strained of pulp)

¹/₂ cup (4 ounces) Grand Marnier (or Triple Sec, Cointreau, flavored vodka, Amaretto, or any liqueur that is at least 80 proof)

1 Whisk together 5 egg whites and the cream of tartar in a bowl until the whites triple in volume. At that point, slowly drizzle in the sugar while mixing. Continue mixing until the whites reach stiff peaks.

2 Wrap the cardboard in aluminum foil.

3 Cut a piece of sponge cake to the exact size of the cardboard by placing the cardboard on top of the cake and cutting around the cardboard. Repeat to cut out a second layer of sponge cake.

4 Remove the ice cream from the freezer. Run hot water around the container and remove the ice cream. With a long serrated knife, slice the ice cream into 2-inch-thick slices. Place the slices on top of the cake to form a rectangle that covers all but a 1-inch border at the edges of the cake.

5 Fill the pastry bag with the egg whites (the meringue). Twist the top to eliminate air. (See Chapter 4 for instructions on how to use a pastry bag.) Pipe a thin layer over the ice cream, starting on the sides, using a circular motion. Then cover the top in a similar manner.

6 Lay the second sponge cake on top. Squeeze meringue around the sides and on the top. Sprinkle some slivered almonds and confectioners' sugar on the top.

7 Place the cake under a broiler, about 6 inches from the heat source. Watch constantly as you broil for 45 seconds to a minute.

8 Carefully transfer the Baked Alaska to a serving plate.

Orange Grand Marnier Flambé Sauce

1 In a small pan, bring the vanilla and orange juice to a boil and continue boiling for 1 minute. Remove from heat and add the Grand Marnier.

2 At the table, in front of all the guests, tilt the pan to bring the liquid to one edge and ignite with a match. Pour carefully over the Baked Alaska. When the flames go out, serve.

Italian Meringues

Firmer and denser than French meringue, Italian meringue is the result of combining hot sugar syrup with stiffly beaten egg whites (see Figure 8-1). The hot syrup cooks the egg whites and makes them firm. They're often *piped* (squeezed through a pastry bag — see Figure 8-2) into decorative shapes or used to decorate cakes.

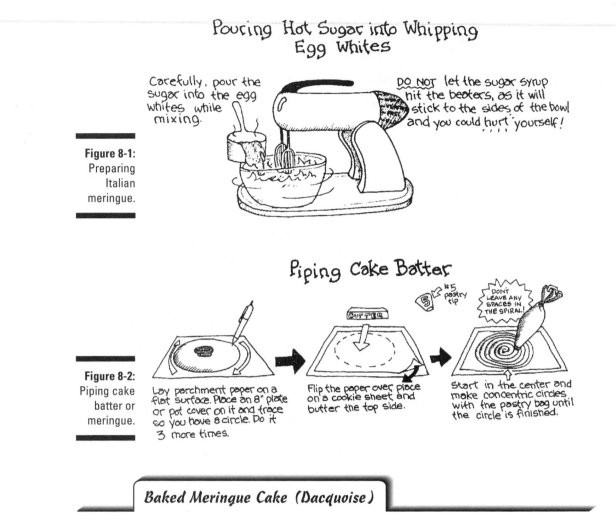

Figure 8-1:
Preparing
Italian
meringue.

Figure 8-2:
Piping cake
batter or
meringue.

Baked Meringue Cake (Dacquoise)

This famous dish is made with the Italian meringue that is sweetened with extra confectioners' sugar and then baked at a low temperature to make it hard and dry. For the dacquoise (dack-WHAZ), the meringue is flavored with almond. Think of a dacquoise as a baked meringue cake.

This recipe is broken down into 2 logical steps: First you make the Baked Meringue. (In this case, it holds because it's baked, unlike fragile French meringue.) Then you make the Buttercream Filling, which is a mixture of stirred custard, whipped butter, and Italian meringue. (You also can use this filling to garnish layer cakes as well.) This progression is not absolutely essential — all the ingredients hold, so you can modify the steps.

If you're not using a kitchen mixer (rather than a handheld mixer), you'll need a second pair of hands when you make the Italian Meringue.

Tools: *Food processor, electric mixer (optional), four 10-inch sheets of parchment paper, large pot, sieve, candy thermometer*

Preparation time: *1 hour 30 minutes*

Cooking/Baking time: *3 hours 30 minutes*

Yield: *8 to 10 servings*

¹/₂ cup (2 ounces) confectioners' sugar

1 cup (4 ounces) whole blanched almonds

13 egg whites

pinch of cream of tartar

1 cup (6 ounces) plus 1 tablespoon sugar

¹/₂ cup (4 ounces) milk

3 egg yolks

1³/₄ cups (14 ounces or 3¹/₂ sticks) soft butter, room temperature

3 tablespoons corn syrup

¹/₄ cup (2 ounces) water

Baked Meringue

1 Preheat oven to 250°.

2 In a food processor, combine the confectioners' sugar and almonds. Grind until it turns into a fine flour — about 2 minutes. Place in a bowl.

3 In a very clean bowl, whip 10 egg whites and the cream of tartar until frothy.

4 Add 1 tablespoon sugar to the egg whites. Whisk until the egg whites form stiff peaks. Whisk in ¹/₂ (3 ounces) cup sugar. With a rubber spatula, fold in the almond mixture a little at a time.

5 Scoop a fourth of the meringue out of the bowl onto the parchment paper and spread it out with the back of the spoon to form circles approximately 8 inches in diameter. (You want the rings of meringue to be about ¹/₂ inch thick.)

6 Repeat Step 5 for the rest of the meringue to form 4 circles.

7 Bake for 2 hours or until brittle.

Buttercream Filling

1 In a large pot, combine ¹/₂ cup (4 ounces) milk and ¹/₄ cup (1¹/₂ ounces) sugar. Bring to a boil over medium-high heat. Turn off heat and let it sit.

2 In a bowl, whisk the egg yolks. Drizzle the hot milk over the egg yolks while continuing to whisk. (This process is known as *tempering*.)

(continued)

3 Pour the milk-egg yolk mixture back into the milk saucepan. Whisk over medium heat until the mixture thickens — usually no more than 45 seconds. Be careful not to overcook and curdle the eggs. Quickly strain this custard into another bowl and whisk immediately to cool the mixture to room temperature quickly. Set aside.

4 Whisk the soft butter in a bowl until smooth. Set aside.

Italian Meringue

1 In a clean bowl, whisk 3 egg whites until they reach soft peaks and are frothy and white. Add $^1/_4$ ($1^1/_2$ ounces) cup sugar. Continue to whisk while you complete the next 2 steps. (If you don't have a kitchen mixer that operates on its own, you'll need a second person to help.)

2 In a clean, thick-bottomed, small saucepan, combine the corn syrup, water, and remaining sugar. Place a candy thermometer in the mixture. On high heat, cook the mixture until it reaches 254° or until it has boiled 5 minutes.

3 When the syrup reaches 254°, immediately pour it into the egg white mixture. Don't let the syrup touch the moving whisk (especially if you're using a fast-moving electric mixer) because the hot sugar syrup may stick to the cold whisk like glue. Continue mixing to cool down the egg whites (about 2 minutes).

Buttercream Filling Assembly

In a large bowl, blend well the custard (the milk-egg yolk mixture) and butter. Whisk in the Italian Meringue until fully blended. If the buttercream breaks up at the end of this procedure, just keep whisking. The buttercream may look broken because the butter may be cold and not ready to accept the liquids. The heat generated by whisking smooths out the buttercream again.

(If you're not going to use the buttercream right away, refrigerate it. To reconstitute, remove from the refrigerator and let the buttercream reach room temperature. Mix until the buttercream becomes smooth and shiny again. Don't worry at the early stage of mixing if the buttercream looks like something out of a cheap horror movie — keep mixing, and it'll come together.)

Dacquoise Assembly

1 Place a meringue circle on a flat serving platter. Using a spatula, spread a layer of buttercream (about 1 inch thick) over the circle. Place the second layer of meringue on top of the buttercream. Repeat for the other meringue circles. If the meringues break (they're brittle), glue them back together with the buttercream.

2 With a spatula, coat the sides and top of the cake with buttercream. Sift confectioners' sugar or cocoa over the top. Refrigerate.

3 Remove from the refrigerator 20 minutes before serving.

Flavoring buttercream

Buttercream is a delicious filler as it is, but for variety or for different recipes, you may want to give it a different flavor. Here are a few suggestions:

- **Hazelnut:** Fold in ¹/₂ cup (4 ounces) Nutella (a commercial hazelnut-chocolate spread that is found in most supermarkets) at the end of the buttercream recipe.

- **Peanut butter:** Fold in ¹/₂ cup (4 ounces) creamy style peanut butter at the end of the buttercream recipe. To make it blend more easily, stir a little buttercream in with the peanut butter to break it down before adding the peanut butter to the rest of the buttercream.

- **Chocolate buttercream:** Melt ¹/₂ cup (4 ounces) semisweet chocolate over a double boiler and stir quickly into the buttercream when it is still slightly warm.

- **Lemon buttercream:** Add the zest and juice of two lemons.

- **Raspberry buttercream:** Add ¹/₂ cup (4 ounces) seedless raspberry jam.

- **Coffee-flavored buttercream:** Dissolve 1 tablespoon instant coffee in the hot milk that you use to make the custard.

Baked Almond Meringue

This simple and quick version of the preceding recipe is a great summer treat (see photo). And if you serve this with sorbet, it's a great lowfat indulgence.

Tools: *Electric mixer (optional), parchment paper*

Preparation time: *30 minutes*

Baking time: *2 hours*

Yield: *6 servings*

6 egg whites, room temperature

³/₄ cup (4¹/₂ ounces) sugar

¹/₄ cup (1³/₄ ounces) brown sugar

¹/₄ cup (2 ounces) almonds, chopped fine

1 Preheat oven to 250°.

2 Place the egg whites into a bowl and beat until foamy. Add 2 tablespoons sugar.

3 Beat for 10 minutes. When the mixture is very white and foamy, add the remaining sugar and brown sugar. Continue to whisk for 15 minutes. Fold in the chopped almonds.

(continued)

4 Line the baking sheet with parchment paper. Using a large spoon, scoop 3 x 4-inch-high mounds of meringue onto the parchment paper. Bake for 2 hours.

5 Remove from oven and set aside to cool for 10 minutes. When cool, cut into 2 pieces vertically and fill with your favorite ice cream. Serve immediately.

Swiss Meringue

The heaviest of all, Swiss meringue is quite stable. You make it by whisking sugar and egg whites over a double boiler. Because of its chewy texture, Swiss meringue is most commonly used in coconut macaroons and other cookies.

For a recipe that uses Swiss meringue, see Coconut Macaroons in Chapter 16.

Part IV
A Real Cake Walk

The 5th Wave By Rich Tennant

"WHY DO I SENSE YOU'RE UPSET? BECAUSE YOU'RE PIPING THAT CAKE WITH HAND GRENADES INSTEAD OF ROSETTES."

In this part . . .

Throw that cake mix down the basement stairs. After you find out how to appreciate the resilient, moist delights of homemade cakes, you'll be hooked. In this part, we cover cakes of all kinds, from sponge cakes to layer cakes to shortcakes.

And because fillings and icings are essential to a festive and flavorful cake, we also load you up with terrific combinations.

Chapter 9

The World's Easiest Homemade Cakes

Making the perfect cake is like creating the perfect painting. Sometimes it's best to remain simple and do the things you know how to do best. The recipes in this chapter are time-tested classics — crowd-pleasers all — that home bakers have been making for generations.

Think of it this way: A cake is composed of eggs, flour, sugar, salt, and often some kind of shortening. To that, cooks add all kinds of flavoring and garnishes. Cakes also come in variety of shapes and sizes. The techniques of combining these ingredients also vary, and we show you that. But for starters, just think of these basic building blocks and how they interact.

We recommend using the freshest ingredients — eggs, butter, ripe fruits, and such. The recipes in this chapter are not complex. The goal is to introduce you to basic cake-making methods so that you understand how different flavors and textures are achieved. Then you can take off on your own. The natural harmony of a few good ingredients is what you strive for — not a clash of all kinds of competing flavors.

Creating a Basic Layer Cake

The layer cake is one of the best-known cakes around the world. It's simply alternate layers of cake (usually sponge cake of some sort) and a cream-based filling. The number of layers varies, but two or three is most common for the home cook.

You can layer many types of cake — angel food cake, chiffon cake, gingerbread, biscuits, and flourless chocolate cakes — but we start with the most common, the sponge cake. Discovering how to make a most, flavorful sponge cake gives you a base for dozens of desserts.

The term *sponge* comes from this cake's airy, pliant texture. This texture comes from the combination of whipped eggs and sifted flour, which are the base of most layer cakes. Sponge cakes freeze well, but they're best eaten the day they're baked. If you make sponge cakes often, an electric mixer is a great kitchen companion (see Chapter 2) — either the inexpensive hand-held version or the standup machine with its own bowl. With a mixer, you can whip a sponge cake batter together in five minutes. By hand with a whisk, the process takes about 15 minutes.

By embellishing a basic layer cake batter, you can end up with several different desserts (see Figure 9-1). Here are just a few:

Figure 9-1:
The sponge cake family tree.

✔ Classic Chocolate Mousse Layer Cake (see recipe in this chapter)

✔ Layer Cake filled with Buttercream (see the Wedding Cake recipe in Chapter 15)

✔ Whipped Cream Layer Cake (see recipe in this chapter)

✔ Layer cake filled with Vanilla Pastry Cream (see Chapter 7) and fruits

✔ Ganache

✔ Single layer cake dusted with sugar (sift the sugar over the top of the cake)

✔ Single layer cake garnished with sabayon (see Chapter 19) or Zabaglione (see Chapter 7)

✔ Ladyfingers (see Chapter 10)

✔ Charlottes (see Chapter 10)

When you try these recipes, keep the following tips in mind:

✔ **Before you whisk or mix by hand in a bowl, twist a dishcloth loosely and wrap it around the bottom of the mixing bowl, tying a knot to secure it.** The dishcloth keeps the bowl from flying all over the place. (See Figure 9-2.)

Figure 9-2:
A dishcloth keeps your bowl from moving around.

When there's nobody to help you whisk... twist a dishcloth loosely and wrap it around the bottom of the mixing bowl, tying a knot to secure it.

✔ **Use a bottomless cake ring mold (see Chapter 2) to make layer cakes.** A cake ring mold is just a stainless steel circle that measures 3 or 4 inches high and 10 inches or more in diameter. It helps eggy batters set better and cook more evenly. Place the mold on a flat cookie sheet, with the sheet serving as the bottom. Pour the batter nearly to the top.

✔ **Refrigerate chocolate mousse mixture to be used in a layer cake for an hour before serving.** Chilling allows the texture to firm up.

✔ **You've finished baking your cake when its surface is golden-brown and a toothpick inserted into the center comes out clean.**

✔ **If you burn the cake, all may not be lost.** Take a serrated knife and carefully slice off the burnt part. (Save the burnt section for practical jokes — serve with ice cream and garnish with matches.) If the interior is moist and doesn't smell burned, it's fine.

Whipped Cream Layer Cake

This is the easiest layer cake you'll ever do — it's simply filled with whipped cream. This fluffy and festive cake is ideal for kids' birthday parties (or for tossing in someone's face during fun-filled food fights). What's more, you can make the sponge cake part ahead of time, cover it tightly in plastic wrap, and freeze it for up to a month.

Apply the whipped cream filling as close to serving time as possible. Within 4 hours, the whipped cream starts breaking down and becomes less fluffy. (Very cold cream is easier to whip than moderately cool cream. You also might want to chill the bowl used for whipping.)

We use canned mandarin oranges for this recipe — mandarin oranges hold up well when canned, and you can use the sweet packing liquid to moisten the cake. If you use fresh fruit to garnish the cake, moisten the sponge cake by brushing the top of each layer with a simple syrup of 50 percent sugar and 50 percent water boiled together until thick and smooth and then cooled. You also can use fruit liqueurs.

Tools: *Electric mixer (optional), sifter, 9-inch cake mold, pastry brush*

Preparation time: *30 minutes*

Baking time: *25 minutes*

Yield: *10 to 12 servings*

6 eggs

1/2 cup (3 ounces) sugar

1 cup (4 ounces) cake flour

1 tablespoon butter, melted

1/2-inch pat of butter, for greasing cake mold

2 cups (16 ounces) heavy cream, very cold

1 teaspoon vanilla extract

2 tablespoons confectioners' sugar

1 15-ounce can mandarin oranges (or cherries or apricots), drained (reserve juice)

Sponge Cake

1 Preheat oven to 400°.

2 Whip the eggs and sugar for about 5 minutes or until fluffy. (By hand, it takes about 15 minutes.) Sift the flour into the egg mixture while folding with a spatula (it helps to have an extra person to hold the bowl) — don't overmix. Drizzle in the melted butter as you finish folding in the flour.

3 Butter the cake mold. Pour the batter out over the cake mold. Using a spatula, spread the batter evenly and smoothly inside the cake mold.

4 Bake for 25 minutes.

5 Let cool completely (about 30 minutes) before cutting.

6 Slice the sponge cake horizontally into three layers. With a long, serrated knife, start cutting horizontally — gradually penetrate a few inches while rotating the cake. Continue rotating the cake while gradually cutting deeper and deeper. Eventually, you'll cut all the way through.

Whipped Cream Filling

In a bowl, combine the heavy cream and vanilla extract with the confectioners' sugar and whip until the mixture reaches stiff peaks. (Make sure that the cake is sliced and ready for assembling before making the whipped cream.)

Assembly

1 Using a pastry brush, paint the bottom layer of the cake with some juice from the mandarin oranges or with some fresh orange juice — moisten the cake well, but don't drench it.

2 Spread a $1/4$-inch thick layer of the whipped cream mixture over the bottom layer of the cake. Arrange 6 mandarin slices around the perimeter of the cake so that they're visible from the side of the cake.

3 Place the second layer of cake over the the bottom layer. Brush liberally with the fruit juice. Spread a layer of whipped cream over the top. Arrange more mandarin slices around the perimeter and add the top cake layer. ***Remember:*** Always place this top layer cut side up. This step presents a more uniform look, and the cut side absorbs the fruit syrup more readily.

4 Decorate the top of the cake with the remaining whipped cream and add more mandarin slices. Chill immediately. The cake can sit in the refrigerator for 4 to 6 hours. Make sure that you refrigerate any leftover cake.

Variations: *Sprinkle chopped nuts (green pistachios are good) or shredded coconut on top of the cake. Substitute strawberries or other berries for the mandarin orange slices.*

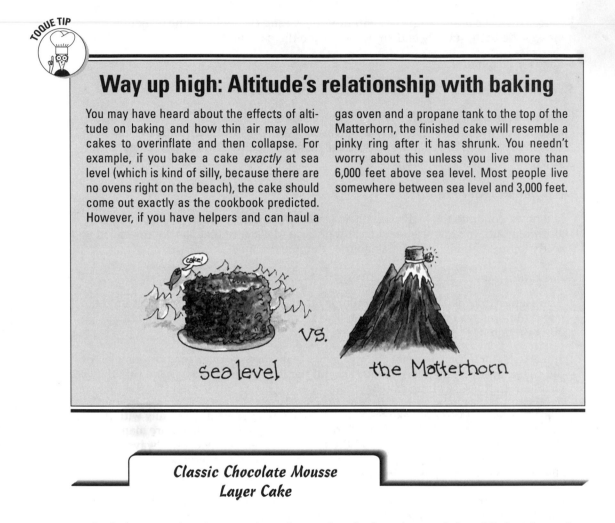

TOQUE TIP

Way up high: Altitude's relationship with baking

You may have heard about the effects of altitude on baking and how thin air may allow cakes to overinflate and then collapse. For example, if you bake a cake *exactly* at sea level (which is kind of silly, because there are no ovens right on the beach), the cake should come out exactly as the cookbook predicted. However, if you have helpers and can haul a gas oven and a propane tank to the top of the Matterhorn, the finished cake will resemble a pinky ring after it has shrunk. You needn't worry about this unless you live more than 6,000 feet above sea level. Most people live somewhere between sea level and 3,000 feet.

cake!

sea level   VS.   the Matterhorn

Classic Chocolate Mousse Layer Cake

In this recipe, the sponge cake is flavored with chocolate and then filled with a rich chocolate mousse filling (see photo). We use the basic simple syrup — just sugar and water flavored with cocoa powder — to moisten the chocolate sponge cake. If you want, you can omit the chocolate syrup and still follow the same recipe. You also can chill any extra chocolate mousse and serve it on its own. If you want a shiny surface, prepare the Chocolate Glaze later in this chapter.

Tools: 10-inch cake mold, electric mixer (optional), sifter, cooling rack (optional), medium saucepan, double boiler, pastry brush

Preparation time: 2 hours

Baking time: 35 to 50 minutes (plus 2 hours refrigeration)

Yield: 10 servings

$^1/_2$ -inch pat of butter, for greasing the cake mold

10 eggs

2 cups (12 ounces) plus 2 tablespoons sugar

2 cups (8 ounces) cake flour

$^1/_2$ cup (2 ounces) plus 1 tablespoon cocoa powder

1 tablespoon melted butter, cooled to room temperature

$^1/_2$ cup (4 ounces) water

2 tablespoons butter

$^1/_2$ cup (4 ounces) milk

10 ounces semisweet or bittersweet chocolate, in $^1/_2$-inch cubes

4 eggs, separated

1 cup (8 ounces) heavy cream, very cold

Chocolate Sponge Cake

1 Preheat oven to 400°. Grease a 10-inch cake mold.

2 In a bowl, whip the eggs and 1 cup (6 ounces) sugar until fluffy (about 5 minutes with a mixer, 15 minutes by hand).

3 Slowly sift the flour and $^1/_2$ cup (2 ounces) cocoa into the egg mixture while folding with a rubber spatula (it helps to have an extra person to hold the bowl) — don't overmix. At the end, fold in the melted butter.

4 Pour the mixture into the greased cake mold and bake for 35 minutes or until a toothpick comes out clean.

5 Cool the cake on a rack and then unmold it (turn it upside down onto a plate).

Simple Syrup Flavored with Chocolate

Combine the water, $^1/_2$ cup (3 ounces) sugar, and 1 tablespoon cocoa in a saucepan and bring to a boil, stirring occasionally. Remove from heat.

Chocolate Mousse Filling

1 Place the butter and milk into the top pan of a double boiler (or 1 saucepan placed above a slightly larger 1 that is holding boiling water). When the milk gets very hot, add the chocolate cubes and stir until melted. Turn off the heat, but leave the bowl over the hot water.

2 Meanwhile, in a bowl, whisk the egg yolks with 2 tablespoons of sugar until pale yellow and frothy. Place over a double boiler or a pot holding boiling water and continue whisking for another 5 minutes to heat the yolks. Keep the mixture moving so as not to scramble the eggs.

(continued)

3 Place the heavy cream in a chilled bowl and place in the freezer for just 5 minutes. Whip the cream until it forms soft peaks (shaving cream consistency). Refrigerate until needed.

4 Place the egg whites in a bowl and whisk. When whites start to rise, add a few tablespoons of sugar. Continue whipping and add the remaining sugar. Meanwhile, remove the whipped cream from the refrigerator.

5 When the chocolate is melted and stirred (it should be lukewarm), whisk the egg yolks into the chocolate mixture. Then, as quickly as possible, fold in the egg whites and whipped cream. The mixture should be smooth with no lumps of cream left unblended. You fold in the whipped cream immediately because the chocolate could begin to solidify if you wait.

Assembly

1 Cut the cake into 3 horizontal layers. Using a pastry brush, dab some chocolate syrup onto the bottom layer. Spread a ¼-inch layer of chocolate mousse. Repeat with the next 2 layers.

2 With a spatula, smooth the remaining chocolate mousse over the top and sides of the cake. Refrigerate for 2 hours.

Chocolate Mousse Cones

You can use the chocolate mousse from the preceding recipe to make a nontraditional presentation (see photo). You'll need to make paper cones (see Chapter 18).

Tools: *Parchment paper cones, strainer*

Preparation time: *15 minutes (not including chocolate mousse)*

Freezing time: *2 hours*

Yield: *5 servings*

3½ cups (28 ounces) chocolate mousse   *10 strawberries, sliced*

3 tablespoons cocoa powder

1 Make parchment paper cones 8 inches long according to instructions in Chapter 18, but leave the tops open. Fill the cones 2 inches from the top with chocolate mousse and place in the freezer for 2 hours.

2 When the mousse is cold, peel the paper from the outside and cut the bottom to a flat plane so that the cone can stand up straight. Place the cone on a flat cookie sheet.

3 Using a fine strainer, sift cocoa over the top liberally until the mousse is well covered.

4 Transfer the chocolate cones to the serving plates and serve with fresh strawberries cut into narrow slices. Place strawberry slices around the chocolate cones.

Gina's Puckering Glazed Lemon Cake

This terrific lemon cake recipe, another twist on the basic sponge cake layer cake, came from our friend Gina Fox in Rhinebeck, New York, who is a first-rate baker and winner of many blue ribbons at the Dutchess Country Fair and other competitions. We were lucky to have her drop in on our kitchen while we were putting together this book.

This cake is wonderfully citric — with its lemon zest *and* fresh lemon juice — and tart, thanks to the buttermilk. The lemon glaze is quick and simple (all you have to do is combine the ingredients and bring them to a boil), and you can use it for many types of cakes.

Tools: *Bundt pan or 10-inch cake pan, electric mixer (optional), sifter*

Preparation time: *40 minutes*

Baking time: *45 to 55 minutes*

Yield: *10 to 12 servings*

¹/₂-inch pat of butter, for greasing the pan

1 cup (8 ounces or 2 sticks) butter, soft

2 cups (12 ounces) sugar

3 eggs

3 cups (12 ounces) unbleached flour

¹/₂ teaspoon baking soda

¹/₂ teaspoon salt

1 cup (8 ounces) buttermilk

3¹/₂ tablespoons grated lemon zest

juice of 5 lemons (1¹/₂ cups or 12 ounces)

4 tablespoons melted butter

2 cups (8 ounces) confectioners' sugar

The Lemon Cake

1 Preheat oven to 325°.

2 Grease and flour a Bundt pan or a 10-inch cake pan.

(continued)

3 With an electric mixer or a wooden spoon, combine the soft butter and sugar and beat until creamy and light-textured.

4 Add the eggs, one at a time, while beating.

5 In a separate bowl, sift the flour, baking soda, and salt. Stir to combine.

6 Shake a little of the flour mixture into the egg batter while stirring (it's much easier with an electric mixer). Then add a little of the buttermilk. Continue alternating between adding the flour mixture and adding the buttermilk, making sure that the last thing you add is the flour mixture (that way, the cake pulls away from the bowl so that it's easier to pour out).

7 Add 2 tablespoons lemon zest and $1^1/_4$ cups (10 ounces) lemon juice and stir. Pour into the Bundt pan or cake pan.

8 Bake for 45 to 55 minutes or until the cake pulls away slightly from the edge of the pan (or a toothpick inserted comes out clean). Cool for 10 minutes and then remove from the pan onto a cooling rack.

Lemon Glaze

Combine the 4 tablespoons butter, confectioners' sugar, $1^1/_2$ tablespoons lemon zest, and $^1/_4$ cup lemon juice in a bowl and whisk until smooth. Pour over the warm cake — haphazardly, if you want, as long as you cover the cake evenly.

Blueberry Poppy Seed Cake

This holiday cake (see photo) is relatively light, ideal for the finale of long, caloric celebrations. It also makes a great breakfast snack.

Tools: *8 to 10-inch springform pan, electric mixer (optional)*

Preparation time: *25 minutes*

Baking time: *45 to 55 minutes*

Yield: *10 to 12 servings*

^{1}/$_2$-inch pat of butter, for greasing the pan

1^1/$_2$ cups (9 ounces) sugar

^{1}/$_2$ cup (4 ounces or 1 stick) softened butter

2 teaspoons grated lemon zest

1 egg

1^1/$_2$ cups (6 ounces) plus 2 teaspoons flour, sifted

2 tablespoons poppy seeds

^{1}/$_4$ teaspoon salt

^{1}/$_2$ cup (4 ounces) sour cream

2 cups (16 ounces) blueberries, washed and drained, stems removed

^{1}/$_4$ teaspoon nutmeg

3 tablespoons fresh lemon juice

zest of 1 lemon

Batter

1 Grease and flour the springform pan.

2 With an electric mixer or wooden spoon, beat ^{2}/$_3$ cup (5 ounces) sugar and the butter until fluffy. Add the grated lemon zest and egg. Beat for 2 minutes more at medium speed (or 4 minutes by hand).

3 In a bowl, combine 1^1/$_2$ cups (6 ounces) flour, the poppy seeds, and salt. Stir to blend well.

4 Add a little of the flour mixture to the sugar-butter mixture (the batter). Stir. Then add a little sour cream. Keep alternating between the two until well blended.

Topping

Combine the blueberries, ^{1}/$_3$ cup (2 ounces) sugar, 2 teaspoons flour, and the nutmeg in a bowl and stir.

Assembly

1 Preheat oven to 350°.

2 Spread the batter over the bottom of the pan (about ^{1}/$_4$ inch thick in the center, higher around the edges).

3 Spoon the topping evenly over the batter.

4 Bake for 45 to 55 minutes, or until golden-brown. Remove from oven and cool slightly before removing from the pan.

Quick Lemon Glaze

Boil the lemon juice, zest of 1 lemon, and remaining sugar together until the sugar melts. Drizzle the warm glaze over the cake before serving.

Jelly rolls: Another variation on the sponge cake

Jelly rolls are a cinch to make, and you can fill them in many different ways. Jelly rolls are basically sponge cake sheets (made in sheet pans) that are swathed with jelly or jam and then rolled. However, the sponge cake you use for a jelly roll is slightly different from the one you use for layer cakes. This cake must be more eggy and pliant or else it won't roll easily.

Jelly Roll

It's best to use this jelly roll right away. If you want to save it for the next day, wrap it well in plastic wrap and refrigerate.

Tools: *Cookie sheet, parchment paper, electric mixer (optional), sifter*

Preparation time: *45 minutes*

Baking time: *25 minutes*

Yield: *1 jelly roll*

¹/₂-inch pat of butter, for greasing the parchment paper

5 eggs

1 cup (6 ounces) sugar

1 teaspoon baking powder

¹/₄ teaspoon salt

1 cup (4 ounces) cake flour

3 tablespoons milk

1 teaspoon vanilla extract

preserves, jam, or homemade compote

small amounts of sugar and confectioners' sugar

1 Preheat oven to 350°. Line the cookie sheet with parchment paper and grease well.

2 In a bowl, whisk together the eggs and sugar.

3 Sift the baking powder, salt, and flour into a bowl.

4 Sprinkle the flour mixture into the egg mixture a little at a time, mixing by hand (a second pair of hands to hold the bowl comes in handy here).

5 Add the milk and vanilla and fold until smooth. Spread the mixture out on the cookie sheet.

6 Bake for 25 minutes or until golden-brown. Let cool slightly, but not all the way.

Assembly

1 Take a smooth cotton towel (not terrycloth) that's larger than the cookie sheet and lay it on a flat surface. (See Figure 9-3.) Sprinkle lightly with granulated sugar all over.

2 Unmold the cake by grabbing the edges of the parchment paper and gently transferring the cake to the sugared towel, parchment side up. Gently peel away all the parchment paper.

3 Layer the cake with preserves, jam, or homemade compote, about $1/4$ inch thick.

4 Lift the towel from the end closest to you to and begin rolling the jelly roll away from you. While pressing down lightly on the cake, continue to lift the towel so that the cake rolls over onto itself evenly. The first full turn must be very tight so that the jelly roll comes out round and without gaps in the middle. After you've nearly made a complete turn, pick up the cotton cloth and use that to help continue rolling.

5 When you reach the end of the jelly roll, transfer to a serving platter or baking sheet. Bring the 4 corners of the towel together and lift the jelly roll onto the platter or sheet. Slide the jelly roll off the towel, cover with plastic wrap, and refrigerate. Dust with confectioners' sugar when ready to serve. It will last 2 days in the refrigerator.

Rolling Up a Cake or Strudel

1. Lay a smooth, cotton towel on a flat surface. Sprinkle all over with sugar.

2. Remove the cake by grabbing the edges of the parchment, transfer to towel, parchment side up and peel the parchment away.

Figure 9-3: How to assemble a jelly roll.

3. Layer the cake with filling.

4. Start at one end and roll the cake or strudel towards you. After nearly a complete turn, pick up the cloth and use to continue rolling.

Chiffon cakes

Chiffon is another type of cake in the sponge family (genoise is the better known cousin). All you have to remember is that chiffon cake is more dense than sponge cake. The heavier density makes chiffon cake more suitable for hearty layer cakes or wedding cakes. This cake starts with vegetable oil, sugar, and egg yolks getting whipped up and then combined with flour and egg whites. Sponge cake, on the other hand, starts with the eggs and sugar first, and then you fold in the flour.

Yellow Chiffon Cake with Chocolate Frosting

This easy chiffon cake makes the basic yellow cake that boxed mixes try to approximate. Believe us, this cake is much better. If you doubt that, make them side by side and do a blind taste test. If the boxed cake wins, send it to us, and we'll eat it.

This recipe makes one very high cake or two thin ones. The chiffon cake itself freezes well for a month or so if covered in plastic wrap.

You also can spread whipped cream over each level of chocolate frosting or arrange fresh berries on top of the cake.

Tools: *10-inch cake pan, food processor (optional), medium pot*

Preparation time: *35 minutes*

Baking time: *50 minutes*

Yield: *8 to 10 servings*

$^1/_2$inch pat of butter, room temperature, for greasing cake mold

$2^1/_2$ cups (10 ounces) cake flour

1 tablespoon baking powder

$1^1/_2$ cups (9 ounces) plus 1 tablespoon sugar

1 teaspoon salt

$^1/_2$ cup (4 ounces) vegetable oil (safflower, peanut, or corn)

3 egg yolks

$^3/_4$ cup (6 ounces) milk, cold

1 vanilla bean, split lengthwise, or 1 teaspoon vanilla extract

8 egg whites

8 ounces bittersweet chocolate

1 cup (8 ounces) heavy cream

3 tablespoons corn syrup

Chiffon Cake

1 Preheat oven to 350°. Grease a 10-inch cake pan with butter.

2 Sift together the flour, baking powder, $3/4$ cup ($4^1/2$ ounces) sugar, and salt. Mix well in a bowl and then add the vegetable oil, egg yolks, milk, and vanilla. Mix well.

3 Place the egg whites in a mixing bowl and whisk until frothy with 1 tablespoon sugar. When stiff peaks appear, add $3/4$ cup ($4^1/2$ ounces) sugar slowly.

4 Whisk the whites for another minute and then fold into the egg yolk mixture.

5 Pour the batter into the greased cake pan and bake for 50 minutes or until a toothpick comes out clean.

6 Set aside to cool (the cake will pull away from pan as it cools).

7 Run a knife along the edge of the cake pan to loosen further. Shake the pan back and forth, tapping the side gently, to be sure that it loosens enough. (If the pan is greased thoroughly, the cake should come out easily.)

Chocolate Frosting

1 Chop up the chocolate (in a food processor or with a knife) into dime-size pieces.

2 In a medium pot, bring the heavy cream and corn syrup to a boil.

3 While the processor is running, pour in the cream mixture gradually. Stop to scrape down the sides of the work bowl from time to time. Process until smooth. If mixing by hand, whisk the chocolate while pouring the hot cream over it and continue whisking for 3 minutes. Place mixture in a bowl and chill if not using immediately.

4 When ready to apply frosting, place the bowl (stainless steel is best) atop a warm stove to soften. Whisk well to bring back the smooth texture.

Assembly

1 Slice the cake in thirds horizontally. (See Chapter 15.) Place one layer on a flat surface and, using a spatula, spread frosting generously and evenly all over the surface. Place the next layer of cake over it and repeat.

2 Cover the top surface and the sides with frosting.

Glazing and Frosting Techniques

Glazes and frostings are very different. A *glaze* is a thick liquid that's poured over a cake while the glaze is warm. It then sets in the refrigerator and develops a nice shine. A *frosting* is a thick, whipped substance that is usually applied with a spatula. The texture is much richer than that of a glaze. They both serve to add flavor and smooth texture and to keep baked cake from drying out.

To glaze a cake:

1. **Place the cake and its cardboard base on a wide tin can and then place the tin can on a baking sheet with sides.**

2. **When the glaze is lukewarm (if colder, it won't run; if too warm, it'll be runny), gradually pour some glaze over the center of the cake and immediately grab the cake off the tin can and tilt it in all directions so that the glaze runs off the edges.**

   The whole top should be covered. (It's critical that you start rotating the cake as soon as the glaze hits so that it does not congeal in one spot.) Continue pouring the glaze until the cake is completely covered.

Pouring too much glaze on the cake is better than pouring too little. You have only one shot to make the glaze smooth. Adding more glaze later results in an uneven coating.

Making a cardboard base

When you glaze cakes, use a cardboard base to hold the cake. For the base to work effectively, you need to elevate the cake while glazing it. That way, you can glaze all around the cake. To elevate the cake, place the cake on a cardboard base and then place the base on top of a wide tin can (or a new paint can).

To make a cardboard base, cut a piece of thick cardboard to the circumference of the cake ring — to be precise, place the ring over the cardboard and draw a line around it.

Chocolate Glaze

Here's a recipe for a chocolate glaze. You also can make chocolate curls for garnish. Take a block of semisweet or bittersweet chocolate. Using a vegetable peeler, scrape off curls (see the sidebar "Making chocolate curls"). Sprinkle these curls decoratively over the top of the cake.

Tools: *Saucepan, fine sieve*

Preparation time: *5 minutes*

Cooking time: *10 minutes*

Yield: *About 2 cups*

1 cup (8 ounces) heavy cream

2 tablespoons vegetable shortening

$^1/_4$ cup (2 ounces) corn syrup

4 ounces bittersweet chocolate, chopped

1 In a saucepan, combine the heavy cream, shortening, and corn syrup. Bring to a boil. Stir once.

2 Place the chocolate pieces into the hot cream mixture. Stir with a whisk until the chocolate is melted.

3 Strain through a fine sieve into another bowl.

4 Let cool to lukewarm.

Cutting a Cake

No matter how great your cake looks, the way you cut it can make or break it.

An 8-inch cake should yield 12 generous pieces or 16 regular-size pieces. A 10-inch cake should yield 16 generous pieces or 20 regular-size pieces.

Follow these tips when you cut your cake:

- ✔ **When serving a cake to guests, count the number of guests and then determine the number of pieces (and sizes) needed.** Symmetry is the key.

- ✔ **The best knife for cutting cakes and tarts is a 12- to 14-inch long serrated knife.**

> ✔ **Have a deep container of hot water (or a warm, wet towel or sponge) nearby to plunge your knife into between slices.** You want to remove crumbs clinging to the blade between slices — they mar the surface of the next cut. Also, a wet knife cuts through cake easier and cleaner.
>
> ✔ **When you cut, use a gentle sawing motion.**

Making chocolate curls

Shaved chocolate curls can be the finishing touch on all types of desserts. To make them:

1. **Take a block of bittersweet chocolate and run a large, sharp knife across the surface, scraping off curls of chocolate.**

This step is easier to do if you place the chocolate block against a wall or counter. Make sure that you scrape the chocolate away from you and toward the wall.

2. **Place the curls on a chilled plate and keep in a cool place — not refrigerated.**

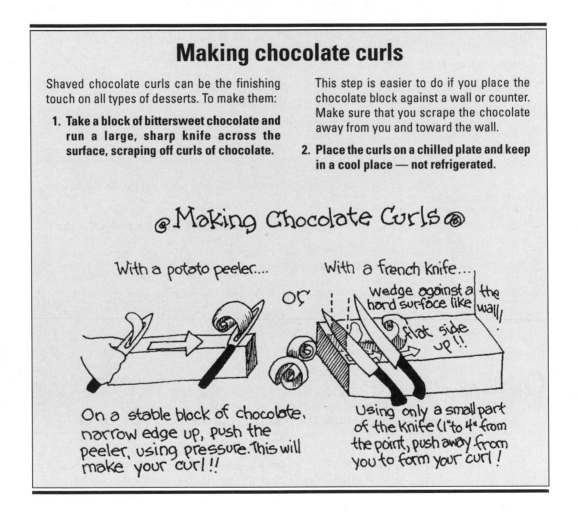

Making Chocolate Curls

With a potato peeler....   or   With a french knife...

wedge against a hard surface like the wall!

flat side up!!

On a stable block of chocolate, narrow edge up, push the peeler, using pressure. This will make your curl!!

Using only a small part of the knife (1" to 4" from the point, push away from you to form your curl!

What if you have more guests than cake?

Occasionally, you may find yourself with more guests than you have cake — relatives you hardly know have a tendency to show up at holiday time. In this case, exercise your knife skills to cut even thinner portions of cake and jazz them up with ice cream, whipped cream (maybe sprinkled with powdered chocolate), berries, or candied fruit.

If you really find yourself in a bind, try whispering to one or more of your guests that they had a call from the fire department but that the call got cut off before you could get details.

To cut your cake (see Figure 9-4):

1. **Cut the cake in half.**

   Think of a cake as a clock, with 12 o'clock at the far end. Plunge the tip of the knife at 12 o'clock and cut straight down, sliding the knife out beneath 6 o'clock (without raising the knife).

   The cake is now halved and easier to work with.

2. **Cut across the cake from 9 o'clock to 3 o'clock.**

   The cake is now cut into quarters and is easier to divide evenly.

3. **To get 16 even slices from a 10-inch cake, take one quarter of the cake and, using the knife, cut it in half; cut each half again in half and repeat with the remaining cake quarters.**

How to Cut a Cake or Tart

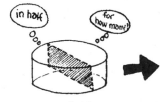

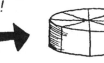

Go for an even number. It's MUCH easier !!

Mentally, divide your cake in half and decide how many pieces you need.

Then, imagine it in 4 quarters and...

Make multiple cuts till you have the right amount !

Remember to keep a glass of water or wet towel near by so you can clean your knife. OTHERWISE, you will drag loose pieces of cake across the top of the beautiful cake you just worked so hard on !

Figure 9-4: Cutting your cake so there's enough to go around.

Punching the cake

Because sponge cake tends to be drier than other cakes, bakers punch the cake. The term *punching* refers to moistening the cake with a simple sugar syrup when assembling it. See figure.

Soaking or 'Punching' the Cake

SYRUP

or

POW

BAM!

Brush the bottom layer of the cake with some of the fruit juice...do not DRENCH!

Chapter 10
Ladyfingers and the Real Tiramisu

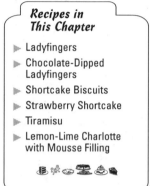

*I*n this chapter, we walk you down the lady-finger highway all the way, including tiramisu, strawberry shortcake, and the famous French dessert called charlotte, which in this rendition is filled with lemon-lime mousse.

What Are Ladyfingers, Anyway?

You probably wanted to skip this chapter just because of the name. Ladyfingers don't exactly sound like the kind of good-time dessert that you dig into after a mosquito-infested backyard barbecue or even a Saturday night pot-luck dinner with the neighbors. They sound so effete, like something they passed around at the court of Louis IV.

Okay, so maybe we have a PR problem here, but believe us, when you find out how to make these little tongue-shaped cakes, you can make all sorts of double-barreled desserts. Think of ladyfingers as a twist on basic sponge cake. The main difference is that ladyfingers are lighter and more elastic because of the sweetened egg whites in them. Hence, ladyfingers are good for molding around ice cream and other wonderful things. The added lightness comes from using half cornstarch and half flour rather than all flour.

You've probably seen ladyfingers in the supermarket, stored in those cardboard boxes with a see-through cellophane window. What you can't see is how dry they are. Ladyfingers should be used right away or frozen shortly after baking. Otherwise, they dry out in a couple of days. At that point, they become cookies — and not bad ones at that — but they're no longer useable in some of the desserts we prepare in this chapter.

Ladyfingers are baked in strips of about 16 connected cakes that are a little larger than a man's thumb. After you get the texture and flavor right, you can use these cakes for all kinds of desserts, from the most basic to the most outrageous. For example, the second recipe in this chapter calls for just dipping individual ladyfingers into melted chocolate, chilling, and serving.

To get your ladyfingers just right, follow these tips:

- ✔ **If you don't use ladyfingers right away, store them in an airtight plastic container.** Ladyfingers slowly lose their moisture and become more like cookies than cake. Or you can cover tightly in plastic wrap and freeze. Ladyfingers remain moist for several months this way.

- ✔ **If your ladyfingers dry out before you have a chance to use them, consider them cookies.** Dip in melted chocolate, dust with confectioners' sugar or a combination of confectioners' sugar and cocoa, or serve plain with ice cream.

- ✔ **You can also soak dry ladyfingers in a little homemade syrup.** Combine 1 cup (8 ounces) water and $1/2$ cup (3 ounces) sugar in a pot, bring to a boil, and then cool. Float the ladyfingers on the syrup for about 15 seconds and remove to a plate with a fork. The ladyfingers absorb the syrup and become pliant again.

- ✔ **Make sure that your mixing bowl is antiseptically clean before you use it to whip the egg whites.** Otherwise, the whites won't rise fully.

- ✔ **Before whipping egg whites, make sure that you have all your ingredients on hand, weighed out (if necessary), and ready to go.** You can't let whipped egg whites sit on the counter as you fumble about because they immediately start to break down.

Ladyfingers

This light and airy batter yields a cake that's durable and elastic, making it extremely versatile. This recipe makes about 50 ladyfingers. If you prefer, make one single cake with the batter and slice it up as you want.

Tools: *12 x 15-inch baking sheet, parchment paper, electric mixer (optional), pastry bag with #5 tip, sieve, mister*

Preparation time: *30 minutes*

Baking time: *10 to 12 minutes*

Yield: *Three 15-inch strips of ladyfingers or about 50 ladyfingers*

6 eggs, separated	¹/₂ cup (2 ounces) cake flour
1 cup (6 ounces) sugar	¹/₂ cup (2 ounces) cornstarch
drop of lemon juice	¹/₄ cup (1 ounce) confectioners' sugar

1 Preheat oven to 400°.

2 Line a 12 x 15-inch baking sheet with parchment paper. Using a straight object (like a ruler) and a marking pen, make two sets of parallel lines, 3 inches apart. This process makes three template strips for your ladyfingers so that they all come out the same size.

3 In a bowl, whisk the egg yolks with ¹/₂ cup (3 ounces) sugar until the mixture is fluffy and lemon colored. If you're using an electric mixer, whisk for about 10 minutes.

4 Scrape all the egg yolks into a large mixing bowl and set aside. Clean the work bowl and whisk or beaters very well and pour in the egg whites.

5 Whisk the egg whites with a drop of lemon juice and 1 tablespoon sugar. Whisk until the whites are fluffy and form peaks — about 10 minutes. While continuing to whisk, slowly pour in the remaining granulated sugar. Mix for another 2 minutes.

6 Sift together the cake flour and cornstarch into a bowl. Set aside.

7 Working quickly, pour one-third of the egg white mixture onto the egg yolks and then immediately sprinkle in one-third of the flour mixture.

8 Immediately, use a rubber spatula to fold the eggs and flour mixture (give it two turns, just enough to mix a little). Repeat with the remaining egg white and flour mixtures. Thoroughly and quickly fold the batter just to incorporate — don't overmix. (You want the batter to be as fluffy as possible.)

(continued)

9 Insert a #5 tip into a pastry bag. Fill a pastry bag half full with batter. Pipe out roughly 1 inch wide ladyfingers between the lines that you've drawn on the parchment paper. You should have strips of 16 ladyfingers each. (Make sure that each hump-shaped ladyfinger touches the next one so that, when you have finished each strip, you have one long, connected strip.)

10 Through a fine sieve, sprinkle confectioners' sugar over the ladyfingers. Mist with water (very, very lightly) and place in the oven immediately. (The misting forms a nice crust on the top of the ladyfingers.)

11 Bake for 10 to 12 minutes. Make sure that the ladyfingers don't start to turn brown — at that point, they start to overcook and lose their flexibility.

12 Remove the ladyfingers and cool slightly (not totally). Place the ladyfinger strips on a work surface, paper side up, and peel off the paper. (It should come off easily.) Cut off 1 or 2 ladyfingers on each end of the strip — these tend to brown and get brittle.

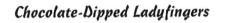

Chocolate-Dipped Ladyfingers

Whether your ladyfingers are fresh and elastic or more firm like cookies, a nice quick way to serve them is dipped in melted chocolate, maybe with some ice cream or whipped cream on the side.

If you want to get fancy, dip them in melted chocolate and then in chopped nuts (walnuts, hazelnuts, pistachios). You aren't limited to bittersweet or semisweet chocolate, though; you also can use white chocolate or milk chocolate. Don't add flavorings to the chocolate, however, because it can change the chemistry and make the melted chocolate too runny to properly coat the ladyfingers.

Tools: *Parchment paper*

Preparation time: *30 minutes (not including ladyfingers)*

Baking time: *None*

Yield: *25 ladyfingers*

1¹/₂ cups (6 ounces) chopped walnuts, pistachios, hazelnuts, or almonds (or any combination you like), minced fine

4 ounces bittersweet or semisweet chocolate, roughly chopped

25 ladyfingers

1 Place the chopped nuts on a plate.

2 Place a stainless steel bowl over a smaller bowl filled with hot (not boiling) water. Place the chopped chocolate in the big bowl on top and let it melt, stirring occasionally.

3 Dip a ladyfinger halfway into the chocolate, turning to cover all around. Let excess chocolate drain off. Gently scrape the coated end of the ladyfinger over the lip of the bowl to remove any excess.

4 Roll the chocolate-coated half of the ladyfinger over the minced nuts to cover evenly and then set on clean parchment paper. (If you put the ladyfinger on a serving plate immediately, it can stick. Repeat this process with all ladyfingers, melting a little more chocolate, if needed.) You can refrigerate these, especially if the temperature in the kitchen is 72° or higher.

Shortcake Biscuits

This recipe is an elegant version of strawberry shortcake. You can make this recipe in a baking dish and refrigerate until serving. But you aren't limited to strawberries; you can make this recipe with all kinds of fresh summer fruits.

Tools: *Sifter, rolling pin, plastic wrap, drinking glass*

Preparation time: *10 minutes (plus 45 minutes refrigeration)*

Baking time: *30 minutes*

Yield: *8 servings*

2 cups (8 ounces) cake flour

1 teaspoon salt

1 tablespoon baking powder

3 tablespoons sugar

$^1/_2$ cup (4 ounces) vegetable shortening

$^1/_2$ cup (4 ounces) sour cream or heavy cream

$^1/_2$-inch pat of butter, for greasing the baking sheet

1 Preheat oven to 350°.

2 In a bowl, sift together the flour, salt, baking powder, and sugar.

3 Break up the vegetable shortening into nickel-size pieces and add to the flour mixture (try to coat each piece of shortening with flour so that the pieces remain separate). Add the sour cream or heavy cream.

(continued)

4 Mix the ingredients with a wooden spoon. As soon as the dough is dry enough to work with, mold it into a ball and transfer to a lightly floured work surface.

5 Flatten out the dough with your hands. Fold the dough over onto itself, dust lightly with flour, roll out with a rolling pin, and repeat. Do this 10 times.

6 Wrap the dough with plastic wrap and refrigerate for 45 minutes.

7 When ready to use, roll out to ³/₄ inch thickness. Using a drinking glass about 2¹/₂ inches in diameter, cut out 8 rounds. (The excess can by rewrapped and refrigerated — you have to roll it out again before using.)

8 Place the eight dough circles on a lightly buttered baking sheet. (You can brush the rounds with melted butter or a beaten whole egg to achieve a golden crust.)

9 Bake for 30 minutes or until a toothpick inserted in the center comes out clean. Let cool.

Note: If using the shortcake biscuits, slice them in half horizontally and proceed from Step 2 in the following recipe.

Strawberry Shortcake

This recipe is a variation on an all-American dessert that dates back to the early 1800s. The original *short cake*, or *short dough*, generally refers to a biscuit-type pastry made with shortening rather than butter. We break tradition here and give you a ladyfinger version, just for fun. For this recipe, you need to make the Ladyfingers earlier in this chapter or the preceding Shortcake Biscuits.

Tools: Rolling pin, wide-bottomed bowl, paring knife, cookie cutter or drinking glass

Preparation time: 30 minutes (not including ladyfingers or biscuits)

Cooking time: None

Yield: 6 servings

about 50 fresh ladyfingers in strips or 6 shortcake biscuits (see preceding recipe)

4 cups (32 ounces) fresh strawberries, cleaned and hulled

¹/₂ cup (3 ounces) sugar

1 tablespoon confectioners' sugar

2 cups (16 ounces) heavy cream, very cold, or 1 pint vanilla ice cream

1 teaspoon vanilla extract

2 tablespoons confectioners' sugar

1 bunch fresh mint (optional)

Building a Charlotte

Charlotte, a French dessert, is a wonderful centerpiece for a festive occasion. Sometimes called Charlotte Russe, it was invented by the legendary pastry chef Carême.

Lemon-Lime Charlotte with Mousse Filling

This recipe is essentially ladyfinger cake filled with a flavored mousse — in this case, a refreshing lemon-lime mousse. You need to make the Ladyfingers earlier in this chapter.

You need to have all the elements ready to go when you get to the assembly stage. If you take too much time assembling the cake, the gelatin may seize up and become too hard to work with. If the gelatin does get too thick before you pour it into the charlotte mold, place it in a stainless steel bowl over a pot of boiling water and whisk until it reaches the proper consistency.

Tools: *12 x 16-inch baking pan, parchment paper, 8-inch cake mold, pastry bag with #5 tip, sieve, mister, cake rack, pastry brush, grater, electric mixer (optional), pot*

Preparation time: *1 hour (not including ladyfingers)*

Cooking time: *50 minutes*

Yield: *25 ladyfingers (9 servings)*

¹/₂-inch pat of butter, for greasing the cake mold

³/₄ cup (3 ounces) cake flour

³/₄ cup (3 ounces) cornstarch

12 eggs, separated

1¹/₂ cups (9 ounces) confectioners' sugar

25 ladyfingers

¹/₄ cup (2 ounces) orange juice, for moistening the cooked ladyfingers before placing in mold

3 large lemons

3 limes

¹/₄ cup (2 ounces) water

1 envelope gelatin

³/₄ cup (4¹/₂ ounces) sugar

2 cups (16 ounces) heavy cream, very cold

1 Preheat oven to 350°.

2 Line a 12 x 16-inch baking pan with parchment paper. Butter an 8-inch round cake mold.

3 In a mixing bowl, sift together the cake flour and cornstarch. Set aside.

(continued)

4 Whip 9 egg yolks with ¹/₂ cup (3 ounces) confectioners' sugar until fluffy and lemon-colored — about 7 minutes. Transfer to a large bowl. Set aside.

5 Clean the mixing bowl very well and dry. Add the 9 egg whites. Whisk until the egg whites are fluffy and reach soft peaks — about 7 minutes. Slowly add the remaining confectioners' sugar while whisking. Mix for another 3 minutes.

6 Place the bowls holding the egg whites, the egg yolk mixture, and the sifted flour mixture side by side. Using the egg yolks as the base, sprinkle one-third of the flour mixture over the egg yolks. Then spoon one-third of the egg whites over the egg yolks and flour. Fold the ingredients. Repeat this process until all ingredients are combined. (Make sure to scrape all the batter from the bottom of the bowl because flour tends to sink to the bottom.)

7 Insert a #5 tip in a pastry bag. Fill the pastry bag halfway with batter. Pipe out 1-inch thick ladyfingers on the baking pan until you have 3 strips about 15 inches long. Pour remaining batter into the greased round 8-inch cake mold.

8 Through a fine sieve, dust the ladyfingers with some of the confectioners' sugar. Mist with water (very, very lightly). Immediately place the ladyfingers and the 8-inch cake mold into the oven.

9 Bake the ladyfingers for 10 to 12 minutes — the 2 ladyfingers at each end of the strip can get slightly browned (they're trimmed off), but the rest should be pale yellow and spring back to the touch. Make sure that they don't start to turn brown or else they'll lose their flexibility. Bake the cake about 20 minutes.

10 Remove the ladyfingers and cool slightly (not totally). Place a ladyfinger strip on a work surface, paper-side up, and peel off the paper. (It should come off easily.) Cut off one or two ladyfingers on each end of the strip — these tend to brown and get brittle, and they shouldn't be part of the charlotte. Using a pastry brush, moisten the ladyfingers with the orange juice.

11 Remove the cake mold when done, let cool for 5 minutes, and then demold it upside down onto a cake rack. Set aside the cake mold and make the lime mousse. (We suggest you make the mousse at the last minute so that it can be poured into the mold while it is still semiliquid.)

Lemon-Lime Mousse

1 Using a grater, remove the zest of 1 lemon and 1 lime.

2 Remove the juice from the 3 lemons and 3 limes and strain it. You should have about ¹/₂ cup (4 ounces).

3 In a large bowl, combine ¹/₄ cup (2 ounces) water with the gelatin. Let the gelatin soften.

4 In a pot, combine ¹/₄ cup (1¹/₂ ounces) sugar with the lemon and lime juice and bring to a boil.

5 Place the 3 egg yolks in a mixing bowl. Pour the hot citrus juice over the yolks, whisking rapidly. When thoroughly blended, pour into the bowl holding the gelatin. Whisk to combine.

6 In a bowl, whip the cold heavy cream to soft peaks. Refrigerate.

7 In a bowl, whisk the 3 egg whites until they form soft peaks. (If whisking by hand, add a drop of lemon juice to boost foaming.) Add ½ cup (3 ounces) sugar and continue whisking for another 5 minutes.

8 Whisk the gelatin mixture several times to make sure that it's not getting too firm — it can be thick, but it should break into pieces when you run a whisk through it.

9 Use a whisk to fold the egg whites into the gelatin mixture. You use a whisk to make sure that the egg whites are thoroughly incorporated. Fold in the heavy cream.

10 Build your charlotte (see the following instructions).

A charlotte is built from the outside toward the center. First you build the outer walls with the ladyfingers (see recipe earlier in this chapter) and then lay the sponge cake foundation inside before adding the mousse. Because ladyfingers can stick to the side of a cake mold, we line the mold with parchment paper.

To build any charlotte:

1. **Cut a strip of parchment paper about 32 inches long (a little longer than the circumference of the cake mold) and about 4 inches high.**

2. **Place a 9-inch cake mold (or the ring from a springform cake) on the serving platter for the charlotte or atop a corrugated cardboard cake circle, available at cake decorating stores and some bakeries (see Chapter 8).**

3. **Press the parchment strip against the inside of the mold.**

4. **With a pastry brush and fruit juice, moisten the flat side of the ladyfingers to make them more moist and flexible.**

   If the recipe you're making already has you moistening the ladyfingers with juice, you can skip this step.

5. **Lay a moistened strip of ladyfingers against the parchment paper, flat side facing inward. Repeat with a second strip.**

   If the second strip overlaps, trim off some ladyfingers. If you have gaps or areas that need to be covered, use the leftover ladyfingers. Store the unused ladyfingers in an airtight plastic container.

6. **Using a serrated knife, slice the sponge cake in half horizontally.**

   To make sure that this cake round will fit inside the ladyfinger circle (it all depends on the thickness of the ladyfingers), hold one layer of the cake directly over the ladyfinger round. If your cake fits into the circle of ladyfingers, lower it, cut side up, and press lightly to secure it at the bottom. If it's too big, trim the circumference with large scissors until it fits.

   Pour half of the lemon-lime mousse into the center of the ladyfinger mold.

7. **At this point, you can add any favorite fruits to the charlotte. Take the remaining half of the cake and place it, cut side up, on top of this mixture. Pour the remaining lime mousse over that. If the lime mousse is a little too thick at this point, tap the charlotte plate against the table to settle it. Refrigerate.**

8. **Garnish with fresh berries and, if you want, serve with a dollop of sweetened whipped cream.**

Chapter 11

Attack of the Killer Cakes

In This Chapter

▶ Making chocolate cake for lumberjacks

▶ How to make a soufflé collapse

▶ A wild British party dessert

▶ Charlemagne's favorite victory tart

▶ Why eat a cake upside-down?

▶ The secret to awesome cheesecake

*T*here are desserts, and there are *desserts*. The former, we prepare with great precision and an eye to presentation. Then when they're done, we carry them to the table on appropriate little plates (prompting the requisite oohs and aahs). Your guests nibble politely, all the while offering mock expressions of guilt: "Oh, this is sooooo goooood! Tomorrow, I'll have to run 47 miles along the interstate with a station wagon roped to my back." This ritual is all part of the peculiar guilt etiquette surrounding desserts.

Granted, those desserts taste good, but then you have desserts that are beyond good. When you eat these *real* desserts, no such public expression of contrition is necessary. Sweets falling into this category are usually as heavy as a Cadillac tire. Many of these monster desserts are found at diners or maybe at church suppers, wedding receptions, or anyplace where two people meet.

This chapter is devoted to no-holds-barred-as-rich-as-Bill-Gates-blowout desserts. (We could have named this chapter "Too Much Ain't Enough: Why It's Good and Patriotic to Splurge Once in a While.") We begin with classic German-style Black Forest Cake, which is suitable for birthdays and other caloric occasions. Then come fallen soufflés, which in some ways can be better — at least richer — than the perfectly puffed version. Try the British trifle; after that is a staggering Normandy tart (Princess Cake), which is sort of like a cake that had a head-on collision with a crème brûlée. Finally, we show you how to prepare a big gooey pineapple upside-down cake (another good option for parties), as well as a terrific cheesecake.

The Cake of German Olympians

So, you thought that the most famous German exports were muscle-bound young gymnasts, Mercedes-Benz automobiles, and Leica cameras? Think again — in a given week, we bet that more Black Forest cakes (or variations of this rich chocolate cake) are consumed worldwide than all the gold medals, luxury cars, and high-end cameras produced in Germany in a single year.

The following recipe for Black Forest Cake is a favorite among Germans and nonGermans, alike.

Black Forest Cake

This traditional German chocolate cake is a favorite on both sides of the Atlantic and is surprisingly simple to make. We have broken down the steps into making the cake; making the chocolate *ganache* (pronounced "Gone – aash"), which is pure chocolate and cream; and putting it together with the whipped cream and cherry garnish.

You also can decorate the cake with shaved chocolate curls (see Chapters 9 and 18).

Tools: *8-inch cake mold, electric mixer (optional), cooling rack, pot*

Preparation time: *25 minutes*

Baking time: *35 minutes*

Yield: *8 to 10 servings*

$^1/_2$-inch pat of butter, for greasing the cake mold	1 tablespoon clarified butter
	8 ounces semisweet chocolate
6 eggs	4 cups (32 ounces) heavy cream, very cold
$^3/_4$ cup (4$^1/_2$ ounces) plus 3 tablespoons sugar	3 tablespoons confectioners' sugar
1 teaspoon almond extract	$^1/_2$ cup (4 ounces) water
1$^1/_2$ cups (6 ounces) cake flour	12-ounce can cherries, pitted and drained
$^1/_4$ cup (1 ounce) cocoa powder	

Cake

1 Preheat oven to 400°. Grease an 8-inch cake mold.

2 Blend the eggs, $^3/_4$ cup (4$^1/_2$ ounces) sugar, and almond extract until fluffy and pale yellow. (Mix on high speed for 5 minutes to achieve maximum volume.)

3 In another bowl, sift together the cake flour and cocoa. Sprinkle this into the egg mixture while folding with a spatula. Drizzle in the melted clarified butter and fold that in — just until incorporated, no more. (See the sidebar "Clarifying butter," later in this chapter.)

4 Pour the batter into a greased 8-inch cake mold and place on a baking sheet. Fill the baking sheet with enough water to go $^1/_3$ up the side of the cake mold. Bake for 35 minutes or until an inserted toothpick comes out clean. Let cool slightly. Unmold and remove to a cooling rack.

Ganache

1 Chop the chocolate into quarter-size chunks and place in a bowl.

2 In a pot, bring 2 cups (16 ounces) heavy cream to a boil. Pour the hot cream over the chocolate and whisk, working from the center outwards. Keep whisking until the mixture becomes very smooth — 3 to 5 minutes (see Figure 11-1). Set aside to cool (ganache is spreadable at room temperature).

Whipped Cream

1 Whisk 2 cups (16 ounces) heavy cream and the confectioners' sugar until it reaches soft peaks.

2 In a pot, bring to a boil $^1/_2$ cup (4 ounces) water and 3 tablespoons sugar. Add the cherries. Bring to a boil again and cook cherries 3 minutes. Drain, reserving the cooking liquid.

Assembly

1 Cut the chocolate sponge cake horizontally in 3 equal layers (see Chapter 15). Place the bottom layer, cut side up, on a serving platter or a cardboard circle.

2 Spread about $^3/_4$ of the ganache over the surface of the bottom layer and reserve the rest for the sides. Place $^1/_3$ of the cherries on the ganache and cover with the second layer of sponge cake.

3 Moisten the second layer with cherry juice and cover with whipped cream. Distribute $^1/_3$ of the cherries over the whipped cream. Repeat with the third layer of cake and the remaining cherries and whipped cream. Use the remaining ganache to frost the sides of the cake.

Figure 11-1:
Pour hot
cream
over the
chocolate
to create
ganache.

Fallen Soufflés: Not Always a Blunder?

In the past, when your dessert soufflé collapsed, you cowered in the kitchen, ashamed to face your dinner guests. You may have considered sneaking down to the garage and careening out the driveway to the ocean or the mountains. Alone, as the sun rose, you would contemplate your failure, your silly bravado in even attempting something so ambitious. How could you ever face your children again?

In today's tolerant society, when grade inflation is rampant and fatuous scribbling is hailed as fine art, even the fallen soufflé has been rehabilitated — but unlike bad art, fallen soufflés offer pleasure. The ingredients in, say, a chocolate soufflé — flour, bittersweet chocolate, cream, butter, sugar — are appealing in almost any configuration. When puffed up and airy, the result is delightful. But when the soufflé collapses (it does so naturally when you let it sit and get cool), you alter only the texture, not the flavor. Instead of an ethereal creation, you have a very moist, rich, eggy cake. Of course, the cake may look as if a horse stepped in it, but no matter — a little ice cream or even some confectioners' sugar on top can make it appear absolutely artistic.

Clarifying butter

Butter contains little white solids, and if it gets too hot in a pan, these solids can burn. If a recipe calls for very hot butter, you need to eliminate these white solids. To do so, melt the butter in a saucepan. Some solids will float to the top; other solids will sink to the bottom. With a spoon, skim off all the floating solids.

Then carefully pour the butter into a bowl, stopping before the white sunken solids fall out. The clear butter you have left is called clarified butter.

Another way to prevent butter from burning at high heat is to cut it with $1/3$ part of vegetable or olive oil.

Fallen Chocolate Soufflé

Today, chic restaurants from coast to coast feature fallen soufflés on their menus. Sometimes they're called *soufflé cakes*. The version you have here is exceptionally light because it contains very little flour.

Tools: *8-inch cake pan, electric mixer (optional), medium pot, strainer*

Preparation time: *30 minutes*

Baking time: *20 minutes*

Yield: *10 to 12 servings*

$1/2$-inch pat of butter, for greasing the cake pan

11 ounces bittersweet chocolate, chopped coarsely

$1/3$ cup (3 ounces or $3/4$ stick) butter

$3/4$ cup (6 ounces) heavy cream

5 eggs, separated

$1/2$ cup (3 ounces) sugar

3 tablespoons flour, sifted

1 teaspoon baking powder

$1/2$ cup (2 ounces) chopped walnuts or hazelnuts (optional)

$1/2$ cup (4 ounces) milk

$1/4$ cup (1 ounce) confectioners' sugar

Soufflé

1 Preheat oven to 400°. Grease an 8-inch cake pan.

2 Place a large bowl over a pot of boiling water (you're simulating a double boiler). Combine 7 ounces chocolate, the butter, and $1/3$ cup (2 ounces) heavy cream, stirring occasionally. When the mixture has melted, stir to combine. Set aside in a warm place (such as the stovetop).

3 Add the egg yolks to the chocolate mixture. Stir well.

4 In another bowl, whisk the egg whites until they reach firm peaks. Add the sugar and whisk for another minute (If you're using an electric mixer, turn it to high speed as soon as you add the sugar to get the maximum volume from the whites). Immediately fold the egg whites into the chocolate mixture.

5 In a bowl, combine the flour, baking powder, and chopped nuts. Fold into the chocolate mixture.

6 Pour the mixture into an 8-inch round buttered cake pan.

7 Bake for 20 minutes. Allow to cool in the cake pan.

Bittersweet Chocolate Sauce

1 In a medium pot, combine the remaining heavy cream and the milk and bring to a boil.

2 Place 4 ounces chocolate in a mixing bowl and pour the hot milk mixture over it. Stir until all the chocolate melts.

3 Strain into another bowl. Cover and set aside in a cool place (not refrigerated) until ready to use. If the sauce starts to get solid before you use it, return to a pot over low heat, stirring constantly until it is liquid again.

Assembly

When the soufflé is cool, invert on a serving platter and sprinkle with confectioners' sugar. Serve warm or cool with the Bittersweet Chocolate Sauce.

You can make a quick decoration for your fallen soufflé cake by cutting a simple stencil and shaking confectioners' sugar over it:

1. **Find a photograph or a design that you want to put on your cake — or make your own.**

   Make your design simple — the cathedral of Notre Dame or the Woodstock Festival would take too long, plus you'll wear out many razor blades. Start with a flower, a star pattern, or a tree, for example.

2. **Place a sheet of blank white paper over the design or trace the design onto thin cardboard.**

3. **With a razor or sharp knife, cut out the pattern so that it's smaller than the diameter of the cake.**

4. **Sift an even layer of cocoa powder over the cake and then place the stencil over the cake (see Figure 11-2).**

   You may want to ask someone to help you hold down the stencil so that it's flush with the top of the cake.

5. **Sift an even layer of confectioners' sugar over the stencil.**

   Voilà!

Using Stencils to Decorate a Cake

Figure 11-2:
Creating
unique
patterns
with a
stencil.

The cutout should be smaller than the cake.

Make a template out of thin cardboard. Make sure it's CLEAN!

For a dark cake, sprinkle powdered sugar over the top.

For a light cake, sift cocoa powder on top as a base, then use the stencil and sprinkle with powdered sugar so you will see the design.

Not Trifling Around Anymore: English Trifles

The classic English trifle is sometimes referred to as *tipsy cake,* because some cooks like to spike it with rum or sherry. If you like, douse some of the finished sponge cake in the following recipe with some flavored alcohol.

English Trifle

This wonderfully excessive British dessert is made by layering sponge cake and cooked fruits with a vanilla custard sauce (see photo). It's ideal for a party because you can quickly and easily scoop out portions. Also, it's easier to transport than cakes. You can easily double this recipe and serve it in one giant bowl or in two smaller ones.

Tools: *12 x 16-inch baking sheet, electric mixer (optional), cake rack or parchment paper, 4 medium pots, trifle or serving bowl (about 10 to 12 inches in diameter at the top and about 8 inches deep)*

Preparation time: *1 hour 50 minutes*

Cooking/Baking time: *1 hour*

Yield: *15 servings*

$^{1}/_{2}$ *inch pat of butter, for greasing the baking sheet*

10 eggs

1$^{3}/_{4}$ cups (10$^{1}/_{2}$ ounces) sugar

2 cups (8 ounces) flour, sifted

$^{1}/_{4}$ cup (2 ounces or $^{1}/_{2}$ stick) butter, melted

1 tablespoon confectioners' sugar (optional)

2 cups (16 ounces) water

1 cup (6 ounces) plus 5 tablespoons sugar

5 ripe plums, pitted and quartered

5 apricots, pitted and quartered

2 cups (16 ounces) blueberries, stems removed, washed and drained

2 mangoes, pitted and diced

1 cup (8 ounces) milk

1 vanilla bean, split lengthwise or 1 teaspoon vanilla extract

2 egg yolks

mint leaves (optional)

Sponge Cake

1 Preheat oven to 375°. Grease a 12 x 16-inch baking sheet with low sides.

2 Whisk the eggs and 1 cup (6 ounces) sugar until lemony-yellow and frothy — they should froth up to four times their original volume or more.

3 Sprinkle the flour over the egg mixture while folding with a rubber spatula.

4 Drizzle in the butter while continuing to mix. As soon as the butter is blended in, stop mixing. Pour into a buttered 12 x 16-inch baking sheet.

5 Bake for 25 minutes or until golden-brown. Cool for 5 minutes. Transfer to a cake rack (it will come out easily) or to a sheet of parchment paper dusted with confectioners' sugar. Set aside.

Fruit Filling

1 Take 4 medium pots and place in each $^1/_2$ cup (4 ounces) water and 3 tablespoons sugar. (This way, the fruit colors remain separated.)

2 Bring to a boil. Place 1 batch of each fruit in each pot.

3 Reduce to simmer and cook for 4 to 5 minutes, or until fruits are soft to the touch.

4 Remove from heat and let cool until ready to use.

Vanilla Custard

1 Place the milk, vanilla, and 2 tablespoons sugar in a medium pot and bring to a boil.

2 Remove from heat. Remove the vanilla bean.

3 In a bowl, whisk the egg yolks while drizzling in the hot milk. When all the milk is added, return the mixture to the pot in which the milk was boiled. Over medium heat (do not boil the milk mixture), whisk constantly for 2 minutes — the mixture should become frothy and a little thicker. Set aside to cool. Refrigerate for at least 10 minutes.

Assembly

1 With a serrated knife, cut out 3-inch squares of the sponge cake — you should have 15 portions for the trifle and some extra portions for the cook.

2 Place 5 sponge cake squares on the bottom of the trifle bowl. Cover with the plum compote mixture. Cover the plum compote with 5 more squares of sponge cake. Cover this layer of sponge cake with the apricots. Place another 5 squares of sponge cake over this.

3 Pour the chilled custard over this layer. Decorate the top with pieces of mangoes and blueberries. Arrange the blueberries in the center and the mangoes around the edges. If you desire, also add some decorative mint leaves.

Normandy Tart (Tart Normande)

The Princess Cake, a Normandy tart and an ultra-rich dessert, is from the French seaside province of Normandy, where rich food takes on near-religious dimensions. Normandy is particularly known for its dairy products. The Tart Normande is essentially an apple tart to which custard has been added. It has two layers: one of baked fruit and custard, and the other, called a *chiboust,* which is nothing more than pastry cream (made with lemon juice rather than milk). The pastry cream is lightened with meringue and held together with gelatin.

Princess Cake

Princess Cake is a Normandy tart (see photo). We divided this recipe into four sections, which is the easiest way to approach it: the tart shell, the tart filling, the chiboust, and the glazing. For the first section (the tart shell), you need to make the French Tart Shell (pâte sablé) recipe in Chapter 3.

Tools: *Medium pot, large pan, electric mixer (optional), sifter*

Preparation time: *10 minutes (not including tart shell)*

Baking time: *30 minutes*

Yield: *8 to 10 servings*

2 eggs

1 cup (6 ounces) plus 2 tablespoons sugar

2^1/$_2$ cups (20 ounces) heavy cream

2 tablespoons butter

5 Granny Smith or golden apples, peeled, cored, and cut into eighths

1 vanilla bean, split lengthwise and inside seeds scraped out, or 1 teaspoon vanilla extract

2 cinnamon sticks

^{1}/$_8$ teaspoon grated nutmeg

zest of 1 lemon

1 tart shell

4 eggs, separated

^{1}/$_2$ cup fresh lemon juice (3 large lemons)

2 tablespoons cornstarch

1 package gelatin, softened

^{1}/$_4$ cup (1^1/$_2$ ounces) brown sugar

Tart Filling

1 Preheat oven to 400°.

2 In a large bowl, whisk together eggs and ^{1}/$_4$ cup (1^1/$_2$ ounces) sugar.

(continued)

3 In a medium pot, bring 2 cups (16 ounces) heavy cream to a boil. Remove from heat and slowly pour the cream into the egg mixture while whisking. Set aside.

4 In a large pan, heat the butter and ¼ cup (1½ ounces) sugar over medium-high heat until it caramelizes. (The mixture should turn dark golden.)

5 Add the apples, vanilla, cinnamon sticks, nutmeg, and lemon zest to the pan and cook, shaking the pan occasionally so that the apples don't stick to the pan, until soft — about 10 minutes, also stirring occasionally. Remove the cinnamon sticks.

6 Pour the caramelized apples into the cream mixture. Pour everything into the tart shell. Bake for about 30 minutes.

7 Meanwhile, prepare the chiboust.

Chiboust

1 In a bowl, combine the egg yolks and lemon juice. Whisk until smooth.

2 In a separate bowl, sift together 2 tablespoons sugar and the cornstarch. Whisk into the egg yolks.

3 In a pot, bring ½ cup (4 ounces) heavy cream to a boil. Pour the cream gradually into the egg mixture while whisking. Place the bowl over a pot holding boiling water and stir until thickened — about 10 minutes. Add the gelatin and stir thoroughly over the steam. Remove from heat and set aside in a warm place, like the stovetop.

4 Whisk the egg whites in a bowl along with a pinch of sugar. When the whites have formed stiff peaks, add the remaining ½ cup (3 ounces) sugar. Mix for 30 seconds. Quickly fold this meringue into the egg mixture.

5 When the tart is at room temperature, pour this mixture over the filling and use a spatula to make a level surface on the top. Place in the freezer for 20 minutes.

To Glaze

1 Sift the brown sugar over the top of the cake. Make sure that none of the creamy top shows through and that the sugar is applied evenly.

2 Place the pie under a broiler. Move the pie as necessary as it glazes. The sugar should melt and start to smoke. As soon as it starts to blacken, move the pie around to glaze evenly — a little blackening is okay. Serve warm.

Upside-Down Cakes

Extensive research has failed to uncover the inventor of the upside-down cake. Our inquiries took us as far away as New Zealand and Patagonia in distant southern Argentina, which, as everyone knows, are upside-down on the globe. We were very tempted to make up an outlandish tale about how upside-down cake came about just for a few cheap laughs, but we decided against it.

Pineapple Upside-Down Cake

The upside-down cake (see photo) in this recipe develops a nice caramelized bottom (or is it top?) because of the caramel. And here's a good question for a game show: "If you flip an upside-down cake before you eat it, are you eating plain pineapple cake or what?"

Tools: *Heavy skillet or 10-inch cake mold, electric mixer (optional), sieve*

Preparation time: *30 minutes*

Baking time: *40 minutes*

Yield: *8 to 10 servings*

6 tablespoons butter

1 cup (7 ounces) brown sugar

1 pineapple, peeled, sliced, and cored into 10 equal pieces about $^1/_4$ inch thick

$^1/_2$ cup (2 ounces) chopped walnuts

3 eggs, separated

$1^1/_2$ cups (9 ounces) sugar

1 vanilla bean, split lengthwise, or 1 teaspoon vanilla extract

$^1/_2$ cup (4 ounces) orange juice or pineapple juice

$1^1/_2$ cups (6 ounces) cake flour

$1^1/_2$ teaspoons baking powder

1 Preheat oven to 350°.

2 Melt the butter and brown sugar in a large, heavy skillet or cake mold.

3 Cut the pineapples slices in half crosswise. Arrange them tightly in the cake mold.

4 Sprinkle the chopped walnuts over the pineapple slices.

5 Mix the egg yolks with 1 cup (6 ounces) sugar, the vanilla, and orange juice. Blend for about 5 minutes or until frothy and pale yellow.

6 Meanwhile, sift together the cake flour and baking powder. Pour the egg mixture over the sifted flour mixture. Stir well.

(continued)

7 Whisk the egg whites with 1 teaspoon sugar until they rise and fluff. Add the remaining ¹/₂ cup (3 ounces) sugar gradually while mixing.

8 When the egg whites reach stiff peaks, fold them, a little at a time, into the egg-flour mixture.

9 Spread the mixture evenly over the pineapple slices. Bake for 40 minutes or until a toothpick comes out clean. To unmold: Let the cake cool. Run a knife around the perimeter and place a serving platter on top. Flip over.

I'll Just Have a Sliver: The Awesome Cheesecake

Any discussion of killer cakes has to include cheesecake, even though a strong argument can be made that it's not a cake at all but a pie. Cakes generally have a bit of air in them and a somewhat crumbly texture.

Whatever its true identity, cheesecakes are more popular in America than anywhere else. The two major categories are

- **Eastern European:** Most associated with Jewish cooking, these cheesecakes are dense, smooth, and made with cream cheese. The term *New York cheesecake* generally refers to this style, and these have been a staple in New York steakhouses for decades.

- **Italian-style:** These cheesecakes use ricotta cheese and have a lighter texture.

Aside from cream cheese and ricotta, you can use curd cheese, fresh farmer cheese, mascarpone, or even yogurt. If you can find fresh farmer-style cream cheese in your local market, it makes an excellent cheesecake. Commercial cream cheese usually contains binders like gum or agar (a seaweed derivative) that makes it heavy.

- **Put topping on your cheesecake, if you want.** See the section "Topping Off Your Cheesecake," later in this chapter, for two ideas.

- **Use some extra graham cracker crumbs to coat the strip of sour cream around the side of the cheesecake (or coat with toasted slivered almonds).**

- **Garnish the cheesecake artistically with fresh raspberries, strawberries (if they are large, slice them in half lengthwise), or blueberries.** If fresh fruits are not in season, canned mandarin sections or canned whole cherries (both well-drained) are good substitutes.

Mamie Eisenhower Cheesecake with Graham Cracker Crust

This recipe calls for a graham cracker crust, which is an American twist on the European pastry crust (see photo).

Tools: *10-inch cake mold or 10-inch springform pan, electric mixer (optional)*

Preparation time: *20 minutes*

Baking time: *1 hour*

Yield: *10 servings*

$1/2$-inch pat of butter, for greasing the cake pan

2 tablespoons butter

$1/2$ cup ($3 1/2$ ounces) graham cracker crumbs

$1 1/4$ cup (8 ounces) plus 1 tablespoon sugar

3 cups (three 8-ounce packages) cream cheese, room temperature

zest of 1 lemon

5 eggs, room temperature

1 cup (8 ounces) heavy cream

$1/4$ cup (2 ounces) milk

1 vanilla bean, split lengthwise and seeds removed, or 1 tablespoon vanilla extract

1 Preheat the oven to 325°. Grease a 10-inch springform pan or regular 10-inch cake mold.

3 In a pan, melt the butter. Stir the melted butter into the graham cracker crumbs. Add 1 tablespoon sugar and blend well. Coat the cake mold evenly with the graham cracker crumbs, including the sides of the mold. Pat the crumbs with the back of a fork so that they adhere to the cake mold.

4 In the bowl, blend the cream cheese and lemon zest. Mix until the cheese is very smooth. (If you leave lumps at this point, they'll show up in your cheesecake.)

5 When the cream cheese is smooth, add the remaining sugar gradually. Add the eggs, one at a time, to the cream cheese mixture — if you're using an electric mixer, it should be on medium-slow speed and running the entire time. Stop occasionally to scrape down cream cheese that clings to the side of the bowl. Add the heavy cream while mixing and then add the milk. If anything sticks to the side of the bowl, scrape it down into the mixture. Add the vanilla. Stir.

6 Pour the batter into the prepared pan or mold. Bake for 1 hour. To check for doneness, tap the edge of the mold — if the whole cheesecake moves as a unit (not in waves), it's done. Cool at room temperature.

7 Chill completely — overnight is best.

8 Unmold the cheesecake. (See the following sidebar, "Unmolding a cheesecake.")

Unmolding a cheesecake

Cheesecake is easier to unmold in a springform pan than in a conventional cake pan. To unmold a springform pan, rinse a knife under hot water, run it around the perimeter of the mold, and then open the pan.

To unmold a cheesecake in a conventional cake pan:

1. **Refrigerate the cheesecake for at least 2 hours.**

2. **Rinse a knife under hot water and run it around the perimeter of the mold (see figure).**

3. **Cover the cheesecake with plastic wrap; place a flat dish (it should not slope on the sides) over the cheesecake mold.**

   The plastic wrap prevents the cheesecake from sticking to the plate.

4. **Turn an oven burner on low; place the cheesecake mold on the burner and move it constantly.**

   Do not leave any plastic wrap extending over the edge of the cake mold.

Be careful not to burn the plastic wrap. This melts the butter that coats the pan and the cheesecake becomes loose.

5. **Hold the flat dish against the mold tightly and, in one swift movement, reverse the cheesecake so that it transfers to the flat dish bottom side up; take your serving plate and, in one swift movement, flip again.**

6. **Remove plastic wrap.**

What if, when you're unmolding the cheesecake, it falls and breaks apart, disintegrating into odd-sized chunks? Gently scrape the cheesecake all together again and pat into the same mold. Rechill and unmold. It should bind again. After you unmold it, use a spatula to smooth over rough spots.

What if, when unmolding over a gas flame or electric coil, you let the cheesecake pan get too hot over the burner? Just place the cheesecake pan back in refrigerator and then repeat.

How to Unmold a Cheesecake Baked in a Cake Mold

Turn an oven burner on LOW. Place the mold on the burner and keep it moving! The cheesecake will move in the pan.

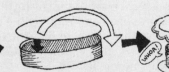

Place a flat plate on top and hold tightly against the mold. In one swift movement reverse to cookie side up↑. Then lift off cake mold.

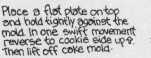

Place your serving plate on top of your upside down cheesecake and flip =SWIFTLY! Now, it's right side up!

Topping Off Your Cheesecake

We offer two easy and tasty toppings for your cheesecakes: One is made with sweetened sour cream, which has a nice tart edge; the other is a traditional cherry topping.

Sour Cream Frosting

This frosting is the traditional covering for cheesecake. It makes a tart contrast to the sweet and creamy center.

Tools: *No special tools*

Preparation time: *5 minutes*

Cooking time: *None*

Yield: *Enough for 1 cheesecake*

1 cup (8 ounces) sour cream

2 tablespoons sugar

2 tablespoons confectioners' sugar

1 Combine the sour cream and sugars in a bowl. Stir well with a wooden spoon.

2 Spread most of the frosting onto the center of the cheesecake. Using the back of a wooden spoon, spread out the sour cream in concentric circles, making sure not to press down onto the top of the cheesecake — pressing down could mar the surface and result in uneven frosting.

3 Take more frosting and coat the side of the cake about halfway up from the bottom.

Cherry Topping for Cheesecake

Instead of sweetened sour cream as a topping for your cheesecake, you can make a simple cherry garnish. This one is made with canned cherries, which are quite acceptable in the off-season.

(continued)

Tools: *Small pot, sieve, slotted spoon*

Preparation time: *10 minutes*

Cooking time: *10 minutes*

Yield: *Enough for 1 cheesecake*

16-ounce can red pitted cherries

1 tablespoon sugar

1 tablespoon cornstarch

1 Drain the cherries well, reserving juice. Remove any crushed or smashed cherries.

2 In a pot, bring the cherry juice to a boil.

3 In a bowl, sift together the sugar and cornstarch. (Be sure to sift; otherwise, it will be lumpy.)

4 Gradually whisk the hot juice into the cornstarch and sugar mixture. Return to heat and bring to a boil, stirring until the mixture thickens slightly. Remove from heat and return the cherries to the pot. Gently — and we mean gently! — stir the cherries to coat thoroughly. Allow to cool slightly. With a slotted spoon, spread the cherries onto the top of the cheesecake.

Part V
Good Cold Things

The 5th Wave   By Rich Tennant

In this part . . .

The fundamentals of making great ice cream are disarmingly simple — discover how to make a base and then flavor it and freeze it. You can make well-textured ice cream in simple, hand-cranked devices that cost less than $40 or sit back and watch a refrigerated unit do it — but it will cost $250 or more for a good one. Either way, the fundamental technique is the same, and that's the heart of Part V.

Sorbets, too, are easy to make after you know the techniques. And we also talk about the easiest frozen dessert of all, granités. All you need is fruit-flavored frozen water and a fork to stir one up — and a spoon to savor it.

Chapter 12

Granités, Sorbets, and Ice Creams

. . . .

In This Chapter

▶ Stirring things up: Fresh fruit granités

▶ Getting dessert from a tea bag: Frozen infusions

▶ Making homemade sorbets

▶ A dubious history of ice cream

▶ Eat your heart out, Ben and Jerry

. . . .

This chapter describes three kinds of frozen desserts, starting with the granité, which is little more than fruit-flavored water that is scraped periodically during the freezing process to create little shards of flavored ice. Granités are unbeatable hot weather coolers.

The second category is sorbets. These fruit-flavored ices have a higher sugar content than granites, which makes them softer and sweeter. Sorbets also are churned in an ice cream machine, making them more uniform in texture. Lastly, we cover ice cream.

A word about equipment: Contrary to widespread belief, you don't always need an expensive machine to make great frozen desserts. For many fresh fruit granités and infusion granités, all you need are a blender and a fork. (Some, like apple granités, require a juicer.) And even for sorbets and ice creams, inexpensive hand-cranking machines ($40 or under) do the job quite well. If you make larger quantities of frozen desserts, however, a refrigerated machine is a worthwhile investment (see Chapter 2).

Groovin' with Granités

Granités are a cinch. Technically speaking, a granité is fruit juice or flavored water that's sweetened with sugar and churned up with a fork several times during freezing to create an ice crystal effect. Granités are among the purest fruit desserts because they call for less sugar than ice cream or sorbets — thus, you get more natural fruit flavor.

You can make granités with many kinds of fruits — apples, cherries, oranges, lemons, limes, grapes — as long as the juice is well strained to eliminate pulp. You want a clean, melt-on-the-tongue sensation, so fibrous fruits don't work as well. In the fibrous fruit category are mangos, apricots, plums, figs, papayas, and bananas. However, these fruits do work well in sorbets and ice creams, where the churning process breaks up much of the fiber and makes the texture thicker and creamier.

You also can experiment with frozen or canned fruit juices, which eliminate the juicing and straining.

If you try to make granité with plain water, you end up with a chunky mess because plain water freezes into a block at 32°. Adding sugar makes it melt more softly.

By adding sugar to the water and fruit juice (25 percent sugar to liquid by weight, or about 5 tablespoons sugar per cup of liquid), the freezing point goes down. Most of the following recipes call for 2 cups (16 ounces) juice and 10 table-spoons of sugar, which brings the exact freezing temperature closer to 20°.

The 25-percent-sugar-to-water ratio (or 5 tablespoons for every cup (8 ounces) of liquid) yields a mix that freezes slowly and softly, allowing you to churn it with a fork two or three times, every 30 minutes apart, to create thin shards (flakes) of ice. When these flakes of flavored ice hit your tongue, they melt instantly, cooling your mouth like nothing else. If the ice shards are too thick, they linger in your mouth, and the sensation is not the same.

Picking out the perfect fruit for a granité or sorbet

Sorbets and granités require fruit that's very ripe and soft. For example, when you buy mangoes for sorbet or ice cream, look for ones that have a yellowish, unblemished skin tinted with red. They should feel soft to the touch all over. To ripen an underripe mango, put it in a paper bag at room temperature overnight.

Apples should be unblemished and firm, not mushy. Citrus should also be firm — if it feels soft to the touch, it's old and probably drying up inside. Mint leaves should also be unblemished. Although berries can be very ripe — that is, getting a little soft, which is when they have peak flavor — they should not have mold on them.

TOQUE TIP

Some granité tips:

✔ Adding lemon juice to granité mixtures brings out the flavor of the fruit and also provides a nice flavor counterpoint to the sugar.

✔ Adding a crushed vitamin C tablet or powdered vitamin C to fresh fruit juice (especially apples and some berries) after they're puréed prevents the fruit from discoloring. This isn't necessary for frozen or canned juices.

✔ If the granité freezes like a rock before you have a chance to scrape it with a fork, put the ice in a metal bowl (the sturdiest type) at room temperature and, after the ice starts to melt a little, mash it with the back of a fork. It'll break into big chunks at first; just mash the chunks down further until it's reduced to shards of ice.

An alternative is to let the whole mixture melt and start all over again, pouring the mixture into a shallow metal pan or ice cube trays and freezing them, scraping every 30 minutes with the tines of a fork. But if you do, refreeze immediately to avoid bacterial contamination.

Apple Granité

Commercial apple juice works well in this recipe. To make a good apple granité from fresh apples, use firm, fresh green apples, like Granny Smiths, because they yield the cleanest and most fiber-free juice. For information about fruit juicers, see Chapter 2.

Tools: *Shallow metal pan or 3 metal ice cube trays without dividers*

Preparation time: *10 minutes*

Freezing time: *90 minutes*

Yield: *6 servings*

2 cups (16 ounces) apple juice (if making it fresh, use Granny Smith apples)

10 tablespoons sugar

1 tablespoon lemon juice

¹/₂ cup (4 ounces) water

1 tablet vitamin C (500 mg), crushed fine, or ¹/₄ teaspoon powdered vitamin C (for fresh juice only)

2 tablespoons apple-flavored liqueur, like Apple Jack or Calvados (optional)

1 In a large mixing bowl, stir together all the ingredients until the sugar dissolves.

2 Pour into a shallow metal pan (or ice cube trays without dividers) and place in the freezer.

(continued)

3 Every 30 minutes, scrape the surface of the ice with a fork and continue working back and forth until you reach all the way to the bottom. Break up any big ice chunks with the fork. After the third time (that is, after 90 minutes), the ice should be broken up into many little shards without big chunks.

Blueberry Granité

Blueberry granité is one of the most luscious types you can make. Lemon juice is critical in this recipe, to maintain the blueberry color.

As a twist, add 10 fresh mint leaves to the pot before you boil the blueberry mixture.

Tools: *Blender, medium pot, strainer, shallow metal pan or metal ice cube trays without dividers*

Preparation time: *10 minutes*

Freezing time: *90 minutes*

Yield: *6 servings*

2 cups (16 ounces) fresh blueberries washed, with stems removed

10 tablespoons sugar

juice of 1 lemon

¹/₂ cup (4 ounces) water

1 In a blender, purée the blueberries. Transfer them to a medium pot.

2 Add the sugar, lemon juice, and water to the pot. Bring to a boil and remove from the heat.

3 Strain and pour into a shallow metal pan (or ice cube trays without dividers). Place in the freezer.

4 Every 30 minutes, scrape the surface of the ice with a fork and continue working back and forth until you reach all the way to the bottom. Break up any big ice chunks with the fork. After the third time (that is, after 90 minutes), the ice should be broken up into many little shards without big chunks.

Concord Grape Granité

Grapes have a high sugar content and make a terrific granité. Don't worry about the seeds — you strain them out.

Tools: *Blender, medium pot, strainer, shallow metal pan or metal ice cube trays without dividers*

Preparation time: *10 minutes*

Freezing time: *90 minutes*

Yield: *6 servings*

8 cups (64 ounces) Concord grapes, washed, with stems removed

5 tablespoons sugar

juice of 1 lemon

$^1/_2$ cup (4 ounces) water

1 Place the grapes in a blender (in batches, if necessary) and purée briefly. Transfer to a pot.

2 Add the sugar, lemon juice, and water to the pot. Bring to a boil and remove from heat.

3 Strain and pour into a shallow metal pan (or ice cube trays without dividers). Place in the freezer.

4 Every 30 minutes, scrape the surface of the ice with a fork and continue working back and forth until you reach all the way to the bottom. Break up any big ice chunks with the fork. After the third time (that is, after 90 minutes), the ice should be broken up into many little shards without big chunks.

Lemon Granité

This tart, palate-cleansing dessert is essentially fresh lemonade turned to ice crystals. You can also make a lemon-lime granité by combining $^1/_4$ cup lemon juice and $^1/_4$ cup lime juice.

Tools: *Medium pot, shallow metal pan or metal ice cube trays without dividers*

Preparation time: *10 minutes*

Freezing time: *90 minutes*

Yield: *6 servings*

(continued)

¹/₂ cup (4 ounces) fresh lemon juice (about 4 or 5 lemons), strained

8 tablespoons sugar

1 cup (8 ounces) water

1 In a pot, combine the lemon juice, water, and sugar. Bring to a boil and remove from heat.

2 Pour into a shallow metal pan or ice cube trays without dividers. Place in the freezer.

3 Every 30 minutes, scrape the surface of the ice with a fork and continue working back and forth until you reach all the way to the bottom. Break up any big ice chunks with the fork. After the third time (that is, after 90 minutes), the ice should be broken up into many little shards without big chunks.

Raspberry Tea Granité

An *infused granité* is simply a granité made with tea. You can use any of your favorite teas, including fruit teas and herb teas.

You also can make your own combination of flavors with cinnamon sticks, vanilla beans, star anise, mint leaves, fresh herbs, and other flavorings. Just like when you're making tea to drink, the longer the ingredients steep in the hot water, the stronger the flavor of the granité. Ten minutes should be enough for a very strong flavor. Most fruit teas work well in this recipe.

Tools: *Medium pot, shallow metal pan or metal ice cube trays without dividers*

Preparation time: *10 minutes*

Freezing time: *90 minutes*

Yield: *6 servings*

2 cups (16 ounces) water

2 raspberry flavored tea bags

¹/₂ cup (3 ounces) sugar

1 In a pot, combine the water and sugar and bring to a boil. Add the tea bags and let them steep for 5 minutes. Remove the tea bags.

2 Transfer to a shallow metal pan or ice cube trays without dividers and place in the freezer.

3 Every 30 minutes, scrape the surface of the ice with a fork and continue working back and forth until you reach all the way to the bottom. Break up any big ice chunks with the fork. After the third time (that is, after 90 minutes), the ice should be broken up into little shards with no big chunks left.

Tropical Granité

Tropical Granité is the kind of dessert you expect at Club Med in Guadeloupe. We use the skin of a pineapple rather than the flesh because the skin exudes so much flavor when boiled — the flesh is half water. So what do you do with the remaining skinless pineapple? Serve the granité over thick slices or cubes of the pineapple, garnished with fresh mint.

Tools: *Medium pot, strainer, shallow metal pan or metal ice cube trays without dividers*

Preparation time: *10 minutes*

Freezing time: *90 minutes*

Yield: *6 servings*

2 vanilla beans, split lengthwise, or 1 teaspoon vanilla extract

skin of a whole fresh pineapple

zest of 1 orange

zest of 1 lemon

2 cups (16 ounces) water

8 tablespoons sugar

1 Combine all ingredients in a medium pot and bring to a boil. Simmer for 5 minutes.

2 Strain into a bowl and pour into a shallow metal pan (or ice cube trays without dividers). Place in the freezer.

3 Every 30 minutes, scrape the surface of the ice with a fork and continue working back and forth until you reach all the way to the bottom. Break up any big ice chunks with the fork. After the third time (that is, after 90 minutes), the ice should be broken up into many little shards without big chunks.

Cinnamon Granité

The cinnamon sticks give this granité a nice, sharp bite, which makes this dessert especially cleansing and cooling on sweltering summer days. We leave the cinnamon sticks in the frozen granité for extra zip. Just scoop around them.

Tools: *Medium pot, shallow metal pan or metal ice cube trays without dividers*

Preparation time: *10 minutes*

Freezing time: *90 minutes*

Yield: *6 servings*

2 cups (16 ounces) water

3 cinnamon sticks

¹/₂ cup (3 ounces) sugar

1 In a medium pot, combine the water and sugar and bring to a boil. Add the cinnamon sticks and continue to boil for another minute. Remove from heat.

2 Transfer to a shallow metal pan or ice cube trays (leave the cinnamon sticks in for extra flavor) and place in the freezer.

3 Every 30 minutes, scrape the surface of the ice with a fork and continue working back and forth until you reach all the way to the bottom. Break up any big ice chunks with the fork (work around the cinnamon sticks). After the third time (that is, after 90 minutes), the ice should be broken up into many little shards without big chunks.

A cool-looking fruit: Star anise

Star anise is a fruit of shrub that is native to the Far East — it should not be confused with star fruit, a yellow star-shaped tropical fruit with a lemony flavor. In Europe, star anise was used in various drinks, and in other countries, it's used in desserts for its licorice flavor. The star-shaped fruit is usually steeped in boiling liquids and then the liquid is added to other ingredients.

Blueberry Poppy Seed Cake, Chapter 9

All photographs by Lou Manna

Cheese and Cherry Strudel, Chapter 16

Linzertorte, Chapter 3

Angel Food Cake with Orange Glaze and
Plum Compote, Chapter 17

Wedding Cake, Chapter 15

Classic Puff Pastry, Chapter 4

French Tart Shell, Chapter 3

Nectarine Pie, Chapter 3

Lowfat Cheese-Filled Phyllo Napoleon, Chapter 17

Tea Cake, Chapter 16

Profiteroles, Chapter 4

Apricot Tart, Chapter 3

Plum Tart, Chapter 3

Chocolate Mousse Cone, Chapter 9

Soft Almond Cookies and Chocolate Truffles, both in Chapter 16

Classic Chocolate Mousse
Layer Cake, Chapter 9

Chocolate Bread Pudding, Chapter 7

Mamie Eisenhower Cheesecake with Graham Cracker Crust, Chapter 11

Raspberry Tart, Chapter 3

Princess Cake, Chapter 11

Crêpes Suzette, Chapter 5

Chocolate Chip Cookies, Chapter 16

Basic Pound Cake, Chapter 16

Pastry Swans and Eclairs, both in Chapter 4

Classic Chocolate Mousse Layer Cake
with Chocolate Shavings, Chapters 9 (cake)
and 18 (chocolate shavings)

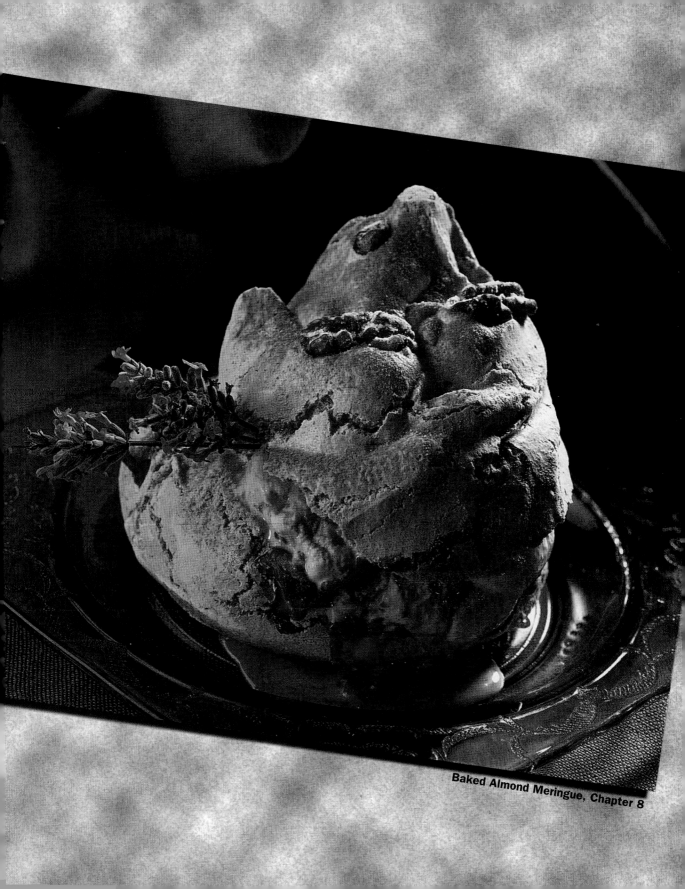

Baked Almond Meringue, Chapter 8

Traditional Bread Pudding, Chapter 7

Pineapple Upside-Down Cake, Chapter 11

Cherry and Pistachio Parfait
(Nougat Glacé), Chapter 13

Forty Mint Leaves Granité

If you happen to be in a part of the country where fresh mint grows like grass, this recipe is a great way to use it — almost as good as mint juleps.

Tools: *Medium pot, strainer, shallow metal pan or metal ice cube trays without dividers*

Preparation time: *10 minutes*

Freezing time: *90 minutes*

Yield: *10 servings*

40 leaves of fresh mint (no stems)	*1 cup (6 ounces) sugar*
3 twigs of fresh thyme	*1 vanilla bean, split lengthwise, or 1 teaspoon vanilla extract*
3 star anise, left whole (see the sidebar "A cool-looking fruit: Star anise" for more about star anise)	*zest of 1 lemon*
	zest of 1 orange
4 cups (32 ounces) water	

1 In a medium pot, combine all the ingredients. Bring to a boil and remove from heat.

2 Strain and pour into a shallow metal pan (or ice cube trays without dividers). Place in the freezer.

3 Every 30 minutes, scrape the surface of the ice with a fork and continue working back and forth until you reach all the way to the bottom. Break up any big ice chunks with the fork. After the third time (that is, after 90 minutes), the ice should be broken up into many little shards without big chunks.

Making simple desserts look great

Fresh granité served in a simple bowl is great in itself. But with a little effort, you can make it look as if it came from a $125-a-plate caterer. Scoop the granité on one of the following:

✔ Fresh fruits (sliced, if desired).

✔ A frozen lemon or orange shell, garnished with fresh mint leaves. (To make the shell, just halve the lemon or orange widthwise; use a sharp paring knife to remove all the pulp and fiber. Slice or grate the bottom so that the shell stands upright without tipping over and freeze the shell for at least an hour before filling with granité and serving.)

✔ A wide martini glass lined with fresh mint.

Try any of these presentations with the granité recipes in this chapter.

Sumptuous Sorbets

Sorbets differ from granités in two ways. First, sorbets have a higher sugar content, which obviously makes them sweeter but also gives them a softer texture (the higher the sugar ratio, the lower the freezing temperature).

The second difference is that sorbets are churned in some sort of ice cream machine, giving them a smooth, even texture.

Granités have 25 percent sugar content by weight — that's what gives them a flaky texture when scraped with a fork. Sorbets should be even softer so that they can be scooped. For that reason, the sugar content is jacked up to as much as 35 percent. Never exceed 35 percent, however, because after that point, the fruit and the syrup can't meld; instead, the sugar syrup rises to the top during freezing, and the fruit becomes mealy textured.

Some sorbet tips:

- ✔ Sorbet can get rock hard if left in the freezer for several days. To reconstitute it, you can just leave it out at room temperature for a while and then stir it with a fork. Putting sorbet in a microwave at a very low heat setting works well, too, because that causes the ice to soften from the inside. Be extremely careful not to melt the sorbet.

    Don't try to refreeze leftover sorbet that has melted and set for more than 10 minutes. For one thing, the texture will never be the same. But more important, bacteria may have contaminated the melted liquid. Refreezing won't kill the bacteria. Don't take any chances.

- ✔ Most sorbets call for brief boiling of the ingredients to meld the flavors and, most important, to preserve their colors. Grapes and blueberries, for example, turn gray when exposed to air during churning in the ice cream machine. Cooking briefly stabilizes the color.

- ✔ When sorbets come out of the ice cream machine, they're still quite soft. You could serve them that way, but they'd begin to melt very quickly. Instead, pack the sorbet tightly into an airtight container and freeze for 1 hour before scooping the sorbet onto serving plates.

- ✔ Flavored alcohol, such as fruit-flavored vodkas, kirsch, and Grand Marnier, can add a nice edge to sorbets. Keep in mind that alcohol lowers the freezing temperature of the sorbet (alcohol's freezing point is lower than water's). As a rule, add 2 tablespoons alcohol per quart of sorbet mix to keep the proper texture — this will make a sorbet slightly softer but not enough to adversely affect the texture. Of course, you can always douse the sorbets after they're on serving plates.

Apple Sorbet

Commercial apple juice works fine for sorbets. If you have a juicer and want to make the juice fresh, the best apples for making frozen desserts are the firm, tart variety, especially green ones like Granny Smiths.

Tools: *Ice cream machine*

Preparation time: *30 minutes*

Freezing time: *1 hour*

Yield: *6 servings*

2 cups (16 ounces) apple juice (if making it fresh, use Granny Smith apples)

³/₄ cup (4 ¹/₂ ounces) sugar

1 tablespoon lemon juice

¹/₂ cup (4 ounces) water

1 tablet vitamin C (500 mg), crushed fine, or ¹/₄ teaspoon powdered vitamin C (if using fresh apple juice)

2 tablespoons apple-flavored liqueur like Apple Jack or Calvados (optional)

1 In a large mixing bowl, stir together all the ingredients until the sugar dissolves.

2 Place in an ice cream machine and churn until the mixture sets — about 20 minutes (machines vary). The sorbet should be fully frozen but easily scoopable.

3 Pack the sorbet tightly into an airtight container and freeze for 1 hour. Scoop onto serving plates.

Blueberry Sorbet

Blueberry sorbet has an appealing deep blue color that looks terrific on all different color plates, maybe garnished with fresh blueberries and fresh mint. It also makes an indelible stain on clothing, so beware.

One variation on this recipe is to add 10 fresh mint leaves to the blueberry puree in Step 1, before boiling.

Tools: *Blender, medium pot, strainer, ice cream machine*

Preparation time: *30 minutes*

Freezing time: *1 hour*

Yield: *6 servings*

(continued)

8 cups (64 ounces) fresh blueberries, washed, with stems removed

³/₄ cup (4¹/₂ ounces) sugar

juice of 1 lemon

¹/₂ cup (4 ounces) water

1 In a blender, purée the blueberries. Transfer them to a medium pot.

2 Add the sugar, lemon juice, and water. Bring to a boil and remove from heat.

3 Strain into an ice cream machine and churn for about 20 minutes. The sorbet should be thoroughly frozen but easily scoopable. If you're using a hand-cranking machine (without a refrigeration unit), you should let the liquid cool to room temperature before placing in the ice cream machine.

4 Pack the sorbet tightly into an airtight container and freeze for 1 hour. Scoop onto serving plates.

Concord Grape Sorbet

Grape sorbet has a highly intense flavor, especially if you use Concord grapes.

Tools: *Blender, strainer, medium pot, ice cream machine*

Preparation time: *20 minutes*

Freezing time: *1 hour*

Yield: *6 servings*

8 cups (64 ounces) grapes (Concord grapes are best), washed, and stems removed

7 tablespoons sugar

juice of 1 lemon

¹/₂ cup (4 ounces) water

1 Place the grapes in a blender (in batches, if necessary) and purée well. Strain into a medium pot.

2 Add the sugar, lemon juice, and water to the pot. Bring to a boil, transfer to a bowl, and let cool to room temperature. (Placing the bowl over a bowl of ice hastens the cooling.)

3 Pour the cooled liquid into an ice cream machine and churn for about 20 minutes. The sorbet should be thoroughly frozen but easily scoopable. If you're using a hand-cranking machine (without a refrigeration unit), you should let the liquid cool to room temperature before placing into the ice cream machine.

4 Pack the sorbet tightly into an airtight container and freeze for 1 hour. Scoop onto serving plates.

Lemon Sorbet

Making sorbets doesn't get any easier than this: lemon juice, water, and sugar. You can have all kinds of fun adding fresh mint, fresh rosemary (just the leaves), fresh chervil, or the liqueur of your choice.

You can also make a lemon-lime sorbet by using ½ cup (4 ounces) lemon juice and ½ cup (4 ounces) lime juice.

Tools: *Strainer, ice cream machine*

Preparation time: *20 minutes*

Freezing time: *1 hour*

Yield: *6 servings*

1 cup (8 ounces) fresh lemon juice (about 10 lemons)

3 cups (24 ounces) water

1 cup (6 ounces) sugar

1 Place all ingredients in a bowl and whisk to dissolve the sugar.

2 Strain into an ice cream machine and churn for about 20 minutes. The sorbet should be thoroughly frozen but easily scoopable.

3 Pack the sorbet tightly into an airtight container and freeze for 1 hour. Scoop onto serving plates.

Raspberry Sorbet

Make this luxurious sorbet only when you can find very ripe raspberries or else it could be bitter.

Tools: *Blender, strainer, ice cream machine*

Preparation time: *20 minutes*

Freezing time: *1 hour*

Yield: *6 servings*

6 cups (48 ounces) raspberries, washed

6 tablespoons sugar

½ cup (4 ounces) water

juice of 1 lemon

1 Place all ingredients in a blender and purée well.

2 Strain into an ice cream machine and churn for about 20 minutes. The sorbet should be thoroughly frozen but easily scoopable.

3 Pack the sorbet tightly into an airtight container and freeze for 1 hour. Scoop onto serving plates.

Mango Sorbet

You can replace the mangoes in this recipe with papayas (2 papayas, peeled in the same manner as mangoes) or very ripe bananas (6 peeled).

Tools: Blender, strainer, ice cream machine

Preparation time: 20 minutes

Freezing time: 1 hour

Yield: 6 servings

2 ripe mangoes	*6 tablespoons sugar*
¹/₂ cup (4 ounces) water	*juice of 1 lemon*

1 With a sharp knife, peel the skin from the mango. Place the mango on a work surface and carefully cut the flesh away from the center pit (it will be slippery — grasp with a towel if necessary).

2 Place the mango flesh, water, sugar, and lemon juice in a blender and purée well. (Blend in batches if it doesn't all fit at once.)

3 Strain into an ice cream machine and churn for about 20 minutes. The sorbet should be thoroughly frozen but easily scoopable.

4 Pack the sorbet tightly into an airtight container and freeze for 1 hour. Scoop onto serving plates.

Ice Cream

To be sure, some good commercial ice creams are available. But once you make your own ice cream and develop special flavors that suit your taste, you'll have trouble going back to the supermarket freezer section.

Ice cream has many definitions around the world, ranging from the light and airy *gelato* in Italy to the creamy and rich blends of some Western European countries. In this section, we concentrate on American-style ice cream, which is also a rich blend of milk, sugar, egg yolks, and flavorings.

You can flavor ice creams in endless ways, but you always have to be mindful of texture. For example, if you add a strawberry purée, it should be thick and not too liquid because that could dilute the ice cream and make it too loose. In almost all cases, the addition of sugar thickens the purée and prevents it from forming ice crystals.

Also, if you want to add fresh berries to your ice cream, do so toward the end of the churning process in the ice cream machine. If you add them too soon, they'll be crushed.

Always use ripe fruit (peaches, apricots, figs, nectarines), cut up into very small pieces. Cook 2 cups (16 ounces) chopped fruit in $\frac{1}{4}$ cup (2 ounces) water, with $\frac{1}{4}$ cup ($1\frac{1}{2}$ ounces) sugar, for 5 minutes. If too much water evaporates during cooking, add some more.

Ice Cream Base

This mixture has everything you need to make a rich, smooth ice cream. Whatever type of machine you use (see Chapter 2 for more about ice cream machines), keep an eye on the mixture and don't let it get too hard while churning. Remove the mixture when it reaches the consistency of soft ice cream. It firms up in the freezer.

You can serve the ice cream base recipe in this chapter as is because it's essentially vanilla ice cream. It's also a base to which you can add all kinds of flavorings — coffee, hazelnut, strawberry — to create your favorite flavor.

Tools: *Thick pot ($1\frac{1}{2}$ quart or bigger), candy thermometer, ice cream machine*

Preparation time: *25 minutes*

Freezing time: *1 hour*

Yield: *6 servings*

(continued)

4 cups (32 ounces) milk

1 cup (6 ounces) sugar

1 vanilla bean, split lengthwise, or 1 teaspoon vanilla extract

9 egg yolks

1 In a thick pot, bring the milk, sugar, and vanilla to a boil. Remove from heat.

2 Place the egg yolks in a large mixing bowl. Slowly pour some hot milk over the egg yolks while whisking (not too quickly, or the hot milk may cook the eggs). Gradually pour in all the milk while whisking.

3 Carefully return the liquid to the cooking pot. Over medium heat, whisk until it reaches 180° (use a candy thermometer). Pasteurization occurs during the approximately 3 minutes in which the temperature rises from 160° to 180°.

4 Remove the vanilla bean with tongs or a slotted spoon and strain the mixture into a clean bowl. Set this bowl over a larger bowl that's full of ice. Stir periodically to chill (about 15 minutes).

5 When the base is cool, pour it into the ice cream machine and follow the machine's instructions. (If you're adding more flavorings, see following instructions.)

6 Remove the ice cream from the machine with a spatula and place in a covered container. Freeze for at least 1 hour.

Variations

Coffee: *Replace the vanilla bean with ¹/₂ cup (2 ounces) crushed whole coffee beans (you strain them out after cooking). Or add 1 tablespoon instant coffee to the boiled milk in Step 1.*

Cinnamon: *Replace the vanilla bean with 2 cinnamon sticks.*

Chocolate: *Add 3 tablespoons sifted cocoa powder to the milk when it just starts to boil in Step 1 (watch the milk carefully to keep it from foaming up and spilling over the edge of the pot). Or after straining the milk in Step 4, add 4 ounces chopped bittersweet chocolate to the mixture and stir to dissolve before placing the bowl over the ice to chill.*

Hazelnut: *After straining the milk in Step 4, add ¹/₂ cup (4 ounces) hazelnut paste (spread or paste) — (usually sold under the name Nutella; for mail-order information, see Appendix C) and stir to dissolve.*

Strawberry: *Hull and wash 2 cups (16 ounces) strawberries. Purée in a blender. Strain into a bowl. Add 4 tablespoons sugar and stir to dissolve (the sugar thickens the strawberry purée and prevents the formation of ice crystals in the ice cream). Add to the ice cream base, stir, and place in ice cream machine.*

If you want to add little chunks of strawberries to the ice cream, add them to the ice cream in the last few minutes of churning — that way, the chunks won't get crushed.

Chapter 13
Parfaits and Frozen Soufflés

· ·

In This Chapter

▶ Cooling off with frozen parfaits

▶ Easy frozen soufflés

▶ Eat your tea: Making frozen soufflés with tea

· ·

*F*rozen desserts are a busy cook's best ally. After you grasp the basic techniques, you can make frozen desserts days ahead of time and pull them out of the freezer just before serving. In this chapter, we explore three specific types of frozen desserts that are ideal for entertaining guests or for snacking on in the middle of the night: frozen parfaits, frozen soufflés, and a variation called tea-flavored frozen soufflés.

What Is a Frozen Parfait?

For most people, the term *parfait* conjures images of tall, tulip-shaped glasses holding Everests of ice cream under glaciers of whipped cream — with a cherry at the summit. That mental picture is more of a sundae, really. A *frozen parfait,* technically speaking, is a rich, ice cream-type dessert that doesn't have to be churned the way regular ice cream does. Frozen parfaits are made with a base of beaten eggs that are sweetened, flavored, and then folded with meringue (and sometimes whipped cream) to impart lightness and texture. Parfaits are usually poured into rectangular terrine molds (like loaf pans) and then frozen.

The wonderful thing about frozen parfaits is that variations on the basic technique are endless. After you know how to make one, you can improvise in dozens of ways by adding chocolate, coffee, fresh fruit, praline, and more. We show you several variations in this chapter.

Parfaits and bombes

You may come across the word *bombe* in magazines and books. Bombes are whipped egg yolks and sugar, which are the base of a parfait. That's really all you need to know.

Throughout this parfait section, you make bombes when you cook the egg yolks and sugar over a double boiler. The most important thing at this point is to know when the mixture is just thick enough, and to remove it from the heat at that point.

The bombe (or parfait base) should be thick and frothy (and no liquid should be visible on the bottom of the bowl when you whisk all the way to the bottom).

Strawberry Frozen Parfait

This is a simple fruit parfait. Always try to use seasonal fruits that are ripe to get the most flavor. If you substitute other fruits for strawberries, use the same quantities listed in this recipe.

Tools: *Blender, sieve, ladle, medium pot, electric mixer (optional), 9 x 5 x 3-inch loaf pan or a 10-inch cake pan, plastic wrap*

Preparation time: *20 minutes*

Cooking/Freezing time: *2 hours and 20 minutes (15 to 20 minutes cooking and 2 hours freezing)*

Yield: *10 to 12 servings*

15 large strawberries, hulled and washed

³/₄ cup (4¹/₂ ounces) plus 1 tablespoon sugar

¹/₄ cup (2 ounces) water

5 eggs, separated

¹/₄ teaspoon cream of tartar

2 cups (16 ounces) heavy cream, very cold

1 Place the strawberries in a blender with 1 tablespoon sugar and the water. Purée well. Pass through a sieve into a bowl, pushing the purée through the sieve with the back of a ladle.

2 Bring a medium pot of water to a boil. Place the egg yolks in a large stainless steel or ceramic bowl and add ¹/₂ cup (3 ounces) sugar. Place the bowl snugly over the pot of boiling water and whisk until the mixture becomes thick and frothy.

3 Add the strawberry purée to the egg yolk mixture. Stir well. Remove from heat and set aside.

4 In a bowl, combine the egg whites and cream of tartar and whisk. After the egg whites triple in volume, add $^1/_4$ cup ($1^1/_2$ ounces) sugar in a slow drizzle while mixing. Continue mixing until the whites reach stiff peaks to form a meringue.

5 Fold the egg whites into the strawberry-egg yolk mixture, all at once.

6 In a chilled bowl, whip the heavy cream to soft peaks. Fold the whipped cream gently into the strawberry-meringue mixture.

7 Line a 9 x 5 x 3-inch loaf pan or a 10-inch cake pan with plastic wrap (or use two smaller pans, if you like). Pour the mixture into the lined pan. Chill for several hours.

TOQUE TIP

Always whip cream in a cool or cold bowl. In warm weather, put the bowl in the freezer for a minute or two or put ice cubes in the bowl to chill it.

Chocolate-Almond Parfait

This recipe is virtually identical to the Strawberry Frozen Parfait, except that we add a chocolate-hazelnut spread (which is widely available in stores, under the name Nutella).

Tools: *Skillet, aluminum foil, medium pot, food processor (optional), electric mixer (optional), 9 x 5 x 3-inch loaf pan or a 10-inch cake pan, plastic wrap*

Preparation time: *20 minutes*

Cooking/Freezing time: *2 hours 30 minutes (30 minutes cooking and 2 hours freezing)*

Yield: *8 to 10 servings*

$1^3/_4$ cups ($10^1/_2$ ounces) sugar

juice of 1 lemon (2 tablespoons)

1 cup (4 ounces) whole blanched almonds

$2^1/_2$ cups (20 ounces) heavy cream

$^3/_4$ cup (6 ounces) chocolate-hazelnut spread

5 eggs, separated

$^1/_4$ teaspoon cream of tartar

(continued)

1 Place 1 cup (6 ounces) sugar and the lemon juice in a wide skillet over high heat. Stir regularly until the mixture caramelizes. When it becomes liquid and turns golden-brown, add the whole almonds. Stir. The mixture will stick together and solidify in the pan at first, but let it cook — it will loosen. Stir with a wooden spoon until all almonds are coated with caramel. Remove from heat.

2 Line a baking sheet with aluminum foil and spread out the almonds 1 layer thick with a wooden spoon. (You'll need a second spoon to scrape the stuck sugar and nuts from the wooden spoon.)

Try to separate about a dozen almonds so that they don't stick to the other almonds — you'll use this dozen as a decorative garnish. If you can't wrestle any almonds free from the bunch, place the clusters back on a sheet in a 350° oven until the sugar melts. Stir the almonds around to separate. Remove from oven and let the sugar solidify again.

3 In a pot, bring $\frac{1}{2}$ cup (4 ounces) heavy cream to a boil. Put the chocolate-hazelnut spread in a separate bowl. Pour the hot cream over the chocolate-hazelnut spread and stir.

4 Chop the caramelized almonds (except the dozen single ones) in a food processor (or by hand with a large, heavy knife). Add the chopped almonds to the warm chocolate-hazelnut cream mixture and stir.

5 Place the egg yolks in a large bowl and add $\frac{1}{2}$ cup (3 ounces) sugar. Bring a medium pot of water to a boil and place the bowl snugly over the pot. Whisk until the egg mixture becomes thick and frothy. Continue whisking until the mixture becomes pale yellow and forms stiff peaks.

6 Add the almond mixture to the egg yolk mixture. Stir well. Set aside.

7 In a bowl, combine the egg whites and cream of tartar with an electric mixer or whisk. After the egg whites have tripled in volume, add $\frac{1}{4}$ cup ($1\frac{1}{2}$ ounces) sugar in a slow drizzle while mixing. Continue mixing until the whites reach stiff peaks.

8 Whisk the egg white mixture into the hazelnut-cream mixture, all at once.

9 Whip 2 cups (16 ounces) heavy cream to soft peaks. Fold gently into the egg-white-and-hazelnut-cream mixture.

10 Line a 9 x 5 x 3-inch loaf pan or a 10-inch cake pan with plastic wrap. Place the individual caramelized almonds that you separated from the mix over the bottom of the cake pan in a decorative pattern. Pour the parfait mixture into the lined pan. Freeze for 2 hours minimum.

Ribbon stage

The professional term for the correct thickness of the egg mixture in the Chocolate-Almond-Parfait is *ribbon stage* — the mixture makes ribbonlike strips when you ladle it out and pour it back on top of itself. If you have trouble with that concept, here's a more user-friendly term: *old latex.* After latex paint has sat in a damp garage for about six months, a thick, shiny crust forms on top. Open the can and toss out the crust without getting paint all over you. What's left at the bottom of the can is what fancy-pants chefs call the ribbon stage.

Cherry and Pistachio Parfait (Nougat Glacé)

This classic French dessert is among the most colorful parfaits when sliced (see photo). The term *nougat glacé* refers to iced nougat, which is white meringue with almonds and pistachios. In France, you can find candy bars made of nougat — this recipe is the ice cream version of that candy bar.

Tools: *Two medium pots, slotted spoon, aluminum foil, small saucer, double boiler, electric mixer (optional), 9 x 5 x 3-inch loaf pan or a 10-inch cake pan, plastic wrap*

Preparation time: *20 minutes*

Cooking/Freezing time: *3 hours (1 hour cooking and 2 hours freezing)*

Yield: *8 to 10 servings*

1 navel orange

4 cups (32 ounces) water

3¼ cups (19½ ounces) sugar

15-ounce can sour cherries

5 eggs, separated

¼ teaspoon cream of tartar

2 cups (16 ounces) heavy cream

½ cup (2 ounces) shelled green pistachios, coarsely chopped

1 Slice the orange, widthwise, into eight equal pieces. Plunge the slices into boiling water for 30 seconds. Remove the orange slices with a slotted spoon, discard the water, and repeat the process, which removes bitter oils in the skin.

2 In a pot, combine the water and 2 cups (12 ounces) sugar and bring to a boil. Immerse the orange slices and reduce heat to simmer. To keep the oranges from bobbing out of the sugar water and drying out, place a square of aluminum foil over the top of them and then place a small saucer on top of that to hold down the foil. Simmer for 1 hour or until soft.

(continued)

3 In a separate pot, combine the cherries, their packing juice, and ¹/₂ cup (3 ounces) sugar. Simmer for 30 minutes or until reduced by three-fourths.

4 Place the egg yolks in a large bowl and add ¹/₄ cup (1¹/₂ ounces) sugar. Whisk over a double boiler until the mixture becomes thick and frothy. (Here's a test to determine whether it's thick enough: Set the bowl aside for 5 minutes. If water starts to seep out of the egg mixture, or if it starts to separate, it's not cooked and whisked enough.)

5 Drain the cherries. Drain the candied oranges. Fold the cherries into the egg yolk mixture.

6 Chop all the orange except for 1 slice. Add the chopped oranges to the mixture.

7 In a bowl, combine the egg whites and cream of tartar and whip with a whisk or an electric mixer. After the egg whites triple in volume, add ¹/₂ cup (3 ounces) sugar in a slow drizzle while mixing. Continue mixing until the whites reach stiff peaks.

8 Whisk the egg whites into the egg yolk mixture, all at once.

9 Whip the heavy cream to soft peaks. Fold gently into the mixture.

10 Line a 9 x 5 x 3-inch loaf pan or a 10-inch cake pan with plastic wrap. Place the reserved orange slice in the center of the pan. Pour the parfait mixture into the lined pan. Freeze for at least 2 hours.

Frozen Soufflés

Frozen soufflés are a lighter version of frozen parfaits. Soufflés also have a different presentation when served in individual *ramekins* (soufflé dishes). The dishes have a paper collar around the rim to allow the frozen soufflé mixture to rise high above the lip of the ramekin (see the sidebar "Making a paper collar for your ramekin," later in this chapter). Frozen souffles are particularly festive, and you can decorate them with confectioners' sugar or cocoa powder by using stencils.

Frozen soufflés are lightened with an Italian meringue — a cooked meringue with a marshmallow texture. (For more on different types of meringues and their uses, see Chapter 8.)

You can store all these frozen desserts in the freezer for a month, covered with plastic wrap. However, it's inconceivable that you would have the will-power to let them linger so long!

TOQUE TIP

Making a paper collar for your ramekin

You want a frozen soufflé to rise above the lip of the ramekin to mimic a hot soufflé. To do so, make a paper collar that's attached to the rim of the dish. This collar holds the ice cream mixture in place while it freezes.

To make a paper collar for each ramekin:

1. Cut a 3-inch-high piece of parchment paper long enough to go around the ramekin. Tape it to the outside rim of the ramekin.

2. Pour the frozen soufflé mixture into the ramekin so that the mixture reaches to the top of the paper collar. (See the following figure.)

3. Freeze for several hours.

4. Before serving, gently remove the collar; sift some confectioners' sugar over the frozen soufflé.

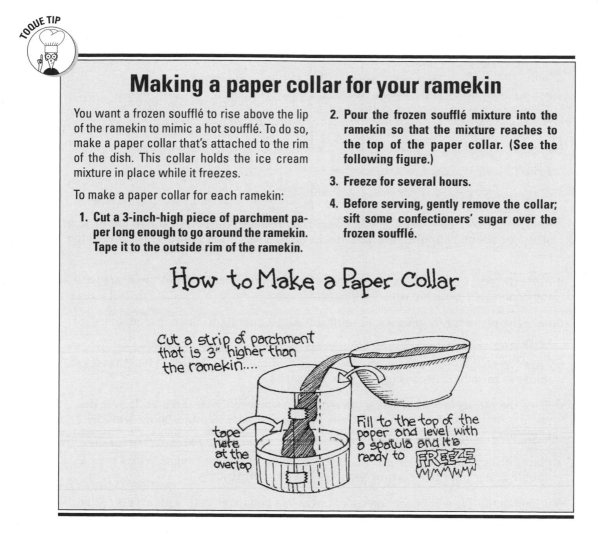

How to Make a Paper Collar

Cut a strip of parchment that is 3" higher than the ramekin....

tape here at the overlap

Fill to the top of the paper and level with a spatula and it's ready to FREEZE

Blackberry Tea and Pear Frozen Soufflé

Now *this* recipe is a great way to use tea. You can try all kinds of flavored teas or even mix flavors.

Tools: *Medium pot, aluminum foil, electric mixer (optional), 9 x 5 x 3-inch loaf pan or a 10-inch cake pan, plastic wrap*

Preparation time: *20 minutes*

Cooking/Freezing time: *2 hours 45 minutes (45 minutes cooking and 2 hours freezing)*

Yield: *8 to 10 servings*

(continued)

2 cups (16 ounces) water

3 blackberry tea bags (or any tea you like)

4 Bartlett or Anjou pears, peeled, stems removed (slice off a little of the base so that the pears can stand up)

1 egg, beaten

1 cup (6 ounces) plus 1 tablespoon sugar

$^1/_2$ cup (4 ounces) raisins

2 tablespoons whiskey (optional)

5 eggs, separated

$^1/_4$ teaspoon cream of tartar

2 cups (16 ounces) heavy cream, very cold

1 Preheat oven to 400°.

2 Boil 1 cup (8 ounces) water and immerse the tea bags. Turn off heat and let the bags steep for about 3 minutes. Discard the tea bags. Reduce the liquid by half over high flame.

3 Place the pears on a baking sheet covered with aluminum foil. Coat the pears with the beaten egg. Sprinkle with 1 tablespoon sugar.

4 Bake the pears for 45 minutes, or until soft. Use a spatula to remove from oven; let cool.

5 After the cooked pears have cooled, slice them from top to bottom (lengthwise) as thinly as possible, discarding the core and seeds.

6 Place the raisins in a bowl. Bring the remaining water to a boil and pour it over the raisins. Steep for 10 minutes and strain. (Optional: Soak in 2 tablespoons whiskey of choice.)

7 Place the egg yolks in a large bowl and add $^1/_2$ cup (3 ounces) sugar. Whisk over a double boiler until the mixture becomes thick and frothy.

8 Combine the egg whites and cream of tartar in a bowl and whip with a whisk or an electric mixer. After the egg whites triple in volume, add $^1/_2$ cup (3 ounces) sugar in a slow drizzle while mixing. Continue mixing until the whites reach stiff peaks.

9 Whisk the egg whites into the egg yolk mixture, all at once.

10 Whip the chilled heavy cream to soft peaks. Fold gently into the mixture.

11 Line a 9 x 5 x 3-inch loaf pan or a 10-inch cake pan with plastic wrap. Cover the bottom of the loaf pan with overlapping pear slices and the softened raisins. Pour the parfait mixture into the lined pan. Freeze for at least 2 hours.

Note: If the peeled pears are to stand for more than a few minutes, coat them with fresh lemon juice to prevent them from discoloring.

Toasted Coconut Frozen Soufflé

This frozen soufflé has a nice crunchy sensation from the toasted coconut.

Tools: *Food processor (optional), small pot, electric mixer (optional), 9 x 5 x 3-inch loaf pan or a 10-inch cake pan, plastic wrap*

Preparation time: *20 minutes*

Cooking/Freezing time: *2 hours 20 minutes (20 minutes cooking and 2 hours freezing)*

Yield: *8 to 10 servings*

1 cup (8 ounces) pitted dates

1 cup (8 ounces) mixed dried fruits (available in most supermarkets)

2 cups (8 ounces) shredded sweetened coconut

5 eggs, separated

³/₄ cup (4¹/₂ ounces) sugar

¹/₄ teaspoon cream of tartar

2 cups (16 ounces) heavy cream, very cold

1 Preheat oven to 325°.

2 With a large knife or in a food processor, chop the dates and mixed fruits.

3 In a food processor or by hand with a sharp knife, chop all but about ¹/₃ cup (1¹/₂ ounces) of the coconut. Set aside the reserved coconut. Spread the chopped coconut on a cookie sheet and bake, stirring frequently, for about 20 minutes or until the coconut is brown.

4 Place the egg yolks in a large bowl and add ¹/₂ cup (3 ounces) sugar. Place the bowl over a smaller pot holding boiling water and whisk until the mixture becomes thick and frothy.

5 Stir in the chopped dates, dried fruits, and toasted coconut.

6 Combine the egg whites and cream of tartar in a bowl and whip with a whisk or an electric mixer. After the egg whites triple in volume, add ¹/₄ cup (1¹/₂ ounces) sugar in a slow drizzle while mixing. Continue mixing until the whites reach stiff peaks.

7 Whisk the egg whites into the egg yolk mixture, all at once.

8 Whip the heavy cream to soft peaks. Fold gently into the mixture.

9 Line a 9 x 5 x 3-inch loaf pan or a 10-inch cake pan with plastic wrap. Cover the bottom of the loaf pan with the reserved coconut. Pour the soufflé mixture into the lined pan. Freeze for at least 2 hours.

Milk Chocolate and Mandarin Orange Frozen Soufflé

Chocolate and mandarins have a lovely affinity for each other. Orange sections work in place of the mandarins, too.

Tools: *Two medium pots, electric mixer (optional), 9 x 5 x 3-inch loaf pan or a 10-inch cake pan, plastic wrap*

Preparation time: *20 minutes*

Cooking/Freezing time: *2 hours 30 minutes (30 minutes cooking and 2 hours freezing)*

Yield: *8 to 10 servings*

8-ounce can mandarin oranges	*2 tablespoons butter*
1 cup (6 ounces) sugar	*3 1/2 cups (28 ounces) heavy cream*
8-ounce block of milk chocolate, chopped into morsel size	*5 eggs, separated*
	1/4 teaspoon cream of tartar

1 Place the mandarin oranges and packing liquid in a pot along with 1/4 cup (1 1/2 ounces) sugar. Bring to a boil and reduce by three-fourths.

2 Place the chocolate in a steel bowl and place the bowl over a pot of boiling water. Turn off the heat and let the steam melt the chocolate. Stir in 2 tablespoons butter. Remove from heat and set aside.

3 In a separate pot, boil 1/2 cup (4 ounces) heavy cream. Stir it into the milk chocolate.

4 Place the egg yolks in a large bowl and add 1/2 cup (3 ounces) sugar. Whisk over a double boiler until the mixture becomes thick and frothy.

5 In a bowl, combine the egg whites and cream of tartar and whip with a whisk or an electric mixer. After the egg whites triple in volume, add 1/4 cup (1 1/2 ounces) sugar in a slow drizzle while mixing. Continue mixing until the whites reach stiff peaks.

6 Whisk the egg white mixture into the egg yolk mixture, all at once.

7 Whip the remaining heavy cream to soft peaks. Fold gently into the mixture.

8 Line a 9 x 5 x 3-inch loaf pan or a 10-inch cake pan with plastic wrap. Cover the bottom of the loaf pan with the mandarin oranges and syrup. Pour the soufflé mixture into the lined pan. Freeze for at least 2 hours.

Part VI

Special Desserts for Special Occasions

The 5th Wave   By Rich Tennant

"We're currently in a state of weightlessness. Amazingly, everything has begun floating *except* Doug's fruitcake."

In this part . . .

You say that the Chicago Bulls fan club is coming over for dinner? Or worse, your extended family? Part VI can bail you out of such situations — at least as far as dessert goes.

Cooking for a mob requires the proper utensils and the ability to extrapolate ingredients — that's math talk for multiplying recipes by two or four. This part also gives you some winning ideas for celebratory desserts for occasions like birthdays, graduations, weddings, and surviving the line at the motor vehicle bureau.

Finally, Chapter 15 covers the wedding cake. This one is so good you shouldn't wait around for someone to tie the knot — just go for it and put normal folks in sweaters and slacks on top.

Chapter 14

You Invited How Many?! Desserts for a Mob — and Then Some

. . . .

In This Chapter

▶ Creating the amazingly expandable

▶ Buying and preparing rhubarb

▶ Making clafoutis, tarts, and chocolate desserts for invading hoards

. . . .

> **Recipes in This Chapter**
>
> ▶ Rhubarb-Almond Clafouti
> ▶ Sour Cherry Clafouti
> ▶ Pine Nut Tart
> ▶ Fruit Cobbler
> ▶ Baked Chocolate Pillows
> ▶ Chocolate Teardrops

*W*hile developing the recipes for this book, we used to invite friends and neighbors over to help sample the goods on Saturday nights. We'd have maybe five or six guests in mind at the beginning of the week, but by week's end, we'd have individually mentioned the dinner party to so many people that the guest list resembled a small-town phone directory.

Fortunately, desserts are easier to expand exponentially than, say, Dover sole. That is, with a little fast footwork and the right recipes, you can invite all the people you want without worry.

Recipes that fall into this category include cobblers, custards, puddings, tarts (make the pastry in bulk ahead of time), and even cakes. Dishes that can be made ahead and held for a day (including all the preceding) are life-savers, too.

We chose the recipes in this chapter because they multiply easily — that is, as long as you have enough pans to hold them.

Thinking Ahead Before Lowering the Drawbridge

When confronted with an advancing division of hungry, chanting diners, always think of dessert ingredients that are in season and widely available. That may mean rhubarb, strawberries, blueberries, melons, whatever. Thinking seasonally assures both an ample supply and the most concentrated flavor.

Moreover, don't get too fancy under such emergency conditions. Although making an eight-fruit compote might be just dandy under normal conditions, don't make your life more challenging than it already is when preparing for a mob. Find three perfect fruits and go for it.

If you'd like to spend less time in the kitchen on the day of the event, choose a dessert that you can finish a day or more ahead of time — like ice creams, sorbets, custard puddings, and certain very dense, rich cakes. Although pies and tarts are best served the same day, you can make the fillings in advance and bake them at the last minute.

Two of this chapter's recipes can be prepared ahead of time. The Baked Chocolate Pillows can be stored in muffin tins (even the aluminum foil kind) and taken right from the freezer to bake and serve warm. Chocolate Teardrops are great for mobs because they're original and can be made ahead ad infinitum!

For any of the recipes in this chapter, you can multiply all ingredients by two, three, or more to increase the yield. Always overestimate the amount you need, just to make sure that you don't run out.

Expanding certain recipes requires a slight adjustment in cooking times. For example, if you're tripling a custard or cobbler recipe and cooking it in a flat sheet pan with sides, the baking time only needs to be increased by 20 percent (this is just a general rule). Always keep an eye on the dessert when you get close to the finish.

Some calculations are obvious: If a recipe calls for boiling milk, for example, tripling the quantity takes longer — at least twice as long.

Clafouti

Clafouti is a fancy French term for a custard-rich tart that originated in Limousin, a French region famous for its cherries. Essentially, a clafouti is a fruit tart that has an egg custard mixture poured over it before baking. When the custard sets around the fruit, you have a wonderfully puffed and silken creation.

In one part of Brittany, cooks make a clafouti with no crust; in other areas, cooks add a crust, as we have done here. The traditional French clafouti is made with fresh cherries. We give you that recipe as well as a delicious summery version using rhubarb, which has a nice tart essence.

This clafouti recipe calls for a *short dough* (similar to a pâte brisée), which essentially means a dough made with a certain proportion of butter, flour, and eggs so that it's very easy to roll out. In this short dough recipe, you start by adding just one-third of the flour to the mix, instead of adding all the flour at once; this method lets you incorporate the flour with the butter mixture without overworking the glutens in the dough. Overworking glutens makes a crust tough.

Rhubarb-Almond Clafouti

This clafouti is an unusual kind of tart that you can start preparing beforehand and then assemble — in large quantities, if necessary — the day of the dinner. You make this dessert in three steps: Make the dough shell, make the flan filling, and poach the rhubarb. You need about 15 stalks of rhubarb for 1 tart.

You can use this recipe's basic vanilla Flan Filling as the foundation for all kinds of fruit tarts. It gives the tarts a silken texture and more substance and is especially delicious when the fruits bleed some juices into it.

Keep in mind that rhubarb is best when poached first to soften its texture. Instead of rhubarb, you can use 8 ripe pears (cored and quartered), or 2 pounds of sour cherries (see following recipe), apricots, plums (all pitted and halved), figs (halved), or blueberries (cleaned and stems removed). These fruits are not poached; rather they're combined in the tart crust mixture and cooked together. They cook by themselves in the flan.

Tools: *Electric mixer (optional), plastic wrap, scissors, aluminum foil, navy beans, sieve, cutting board, rolling pin, two 9-inch pie plates or 12 x 16-inch sheet pan, large pot, slotted spoon, colander*

Preparation time: *45 minutes*

Baking time: *1 hour 20 minutes*

Yield: *10 to 12 servings*

(continued)

Rhubarb

Rhubarb — which is actually a vegetable, not a fruit, although it's used as a fruit in tarts, pies, and dessert soups — has thick, cylindrical stalks and, when ripe, is pinkish to dark red. When buying fresh rhubarb, look for crisp, straight stalks — the brighter red, the better.

Warning: Never eat the leaves at the top of a fresh rhubarb plant and never eat a rhubarb's roots. Both substances are toxic.

You usually poach or stew rhubarb, as in the Rhubarb-Almond Clafouti recipe. Rhubarb's slightly sour flavor requires the addition of some sugar.

$^1/_2$ *cup (4 ounces or 1 stick) butter, sliced into 8 pieces, cold*

$^3/_4$ *cup (3 ounces) confectioners' sugar*

2 cups (8 ounces) cake flour

6 eggs

$^1/_2$-*inch pat butter, for greasing the pan(s)*

2 pounds navy beans or white beans, for holding down pie shell during prebaking

3 egg yolks

$1^1/_2$ *cups (9 ounces) sugar*

$1^1/_2$ *cup (6 ounces) blanched almonds, chopped fine*

3 tablespoons flour

1 vanilla bean, split lengthwise, or 1 teaspoon vanilla extract

1 cup (8 ounces) heavy cream

1 cup (8 ounces) milk

8 cups (64 ounces) cold water

15 stalks fresh rhubarb, with leaves and bases removed, cut into 1-inch pieces

Clafouti Dough

1 Preheat oven to 400°.

2 Place the butter in a bowl and mix or whisk until smooth. Add the confectioners' sugar. Mix for a minute more.

3 Add the cake flour. While you're mixing, slowly add the eggs. Mix together until smooth. (If mixing by hand, you need a wooden spoon at this point, or you can lay the dough out on a lightly floured surface and work by hand.)

4 Scoop the dough onto a sheet of plastic wrap. Lightly flour your hands and press the dough into a rough oval no more than 1 inch thick. (This process helps the dough cool faster and roll out easier.) Cover with another sheet of plastic wrap and refrigerate for 1 to 2 hours.

5 When the dough is cool, remove from the plastic wrap and place on a lightly floured cutting board. Cut the dough in half. Sprinkle with flour. Place the other half in plastic wrap and return to the refrigerator until you're finished with the first half. (This step assumes you're making 2 clafoutis in 9-inch pie plates. If you make this in 1 large baking sheet with low sides, 12 inches x 16 inches or larger, roll out the whole dough at once.)

6 Using a rolling pin, gently roll the dough half out, working from the center toward the edges. Maintain equal pressure on both ends of the rolling pin to assure even thickness. Roll it out into a round about $^1/_4$ inch thick and about 11 inches in diameter. (This size gives you enough to overlap the pie plate ring.) If using a single baking sheet with low sides, roll out the dough a little larger than the dimensions of the buttered baking sheet and lay it over the top. Press the dough into the sides with your fingers, trim any excess dough hanging over the edge, and crimp the rim with your fingers to make a decorative pattern.

7 Butter two 9 or 10-inch pie plates. Place the rolling pin on one edge of the dough. Lift the edge of the dough onto the rolling pin. Then roll back the rolling pin to pick up all the dough — it's sort of like rolling up a carpet with a giant rolling pin inside. Then you roll it back out over one of the pie plates.

8 Lift the edges of the dough that are hanging over the edge so that gravity lowers the center of the dough into the bottom of the plate. With your fingers, press the dough into the corners of the ring. The lip of the ring should have about an inch or two overlap.

9 Using scissors, cut off the ragged edges of the overhanging dough. Use your fingers to crimp the dough on the lip of the ring into fluted or crimped edges all around. Refrigerate while rolling out the other half of the dough.

10 Cover the dough in both pie plates with aluminum foil and fill with navy beans to hold the dough in place while you prebake. Bake for 15 minutes or until the dough browns around the edges. Remove the foil and the beans. (If using one 12 x 16-inch baking sheet, cook for 20 minutes and watch the crust carefully — it should be golden.)

Custard Filling for Clafouti

1 Mix together the egg yolks, $^1/_2$ cup (3 ounces) sugar, almonds, flour, and vanilla extract (not the vanilla bean yet).

2 Boil the heavy cream, milk, and vanilla bean (if using) and allow to cool for 5 minutes. Slowly add the hot cream to the egg mixture while stirring and then strain through a sieve. Set aside.

Poached Rhubarb Filling

1 In a large pot, bring the water and 1 cup (6 ounces) sugar to a boil. Plunge the rhubarb into the boiling water and reduce heat to simmer for 5 minutes.

(continued)

2 With a slotted spoon, carefully transfer the rhubarb to a colander, taking care not to break the rhubarb pieces. Allow to cool.

Assembly

1 Fill the prebaked pie shells with the poached rhubarb filling. Spread the rhubarb filling over the dough carefully so that the surface is flat. (Or spread them over a 12 x 16-inch baking sheet with low sides.)

2 Spread the custard over the rhubarb so that the filling is about $1/4$ inch below the edge of the pie shells — if it's any higher, it may run over the edge during baking. (If using a baking sheet, do not fill it all the way to the top — if you have leftover custard, pour it into ovenproof molds or dishes and bake at 350° until firm. The time depends on amount of custard mix in the dish.)

3 Bake for 1 hour at or until the flan mixture is set and not at all liquid. (A baking sheet takes about 10 minutes longer.) Let cool. Refrigerate for at least an hour before serving.

Sour Cherry Clafouti

This is the original version of the clafouti, which you can make with either regular cherries or sour cherries. For this recipe, you need to make the Clafouti Dough and Custard Filling in the preceding recipe.

Tools: No special tools

Preparation time: 15 minutes (not including clafouti dough and custard)

Baking time: 1 hour

clafouti dough, enough to make two 9-inch tart pans or a 12 x 16-inch baking pan

2 pounds ripe, fresh sour cherries, pitted (or three 12-ounce cans sour cherries, drained)

custard filling for clafouti dough

1 Preheat oven to 400°.

2 Make the clafouti dough and prebake as in the preceding recipe.

3 Fill the prebaked pie shells with the pitted cherries (or spread them over a 12 x 16-inch baking sheet with low sides).

4 Spread the custard over the cherries so that the filling is about $1/4$ inch below the edge of the pie shells — if it's any higher, it may run over the edge during baking. (If using a baking sheet, don't fill all the way to the top — if you have leftover custard, pour it into ovenproof molds or dishes and place back in the oven at 350° until firm — time depends on amount of custard mix in the dish.)

5 Bake for 1 hour or until the flan mixture is set and not at all liquid. (A baking sheet takes about 10 minutes longer.) Let cool. Refrigerate for at least an hour before serving.

Tarts and Cobblers

Tarts and cobblers generally hold up well refrigerated, so you can make them a day or two in advance and you can make double or triple portions.

Pine Nut Tart

Here's something that will be new to your guests: a crunchy, molasses-accented tart made with toasted pine nuts. The runny filling mixture can be poured easily into as many tart shells as you need.

You can make this tart with equivalent amounts of chopped pecans, walnuts, or black walnuts. If you really want to impart a rich sensation, add some macadamia nuts to the mix.

Glazing means to coat something — usually nuts or fruit — in melted sugar or honey, sometimes with other flavors added. Glazing the pine nuts in this recipe gives them an attractive shine and a sweet flavor.

Tools: *Large pan, 12 x 16-inch baking dish*

Preparation time: *40 minutes (not including the clafouti dough)*

Baking time: *40 minutes*

Yield: *12 servings*

clafouti dough, enough to make two 9-inch tart pans or a 12 x 16-inch baking pan with low sides

2 tablespoons honey

3 tablespoons butter

1 sprig fresh rosemary

2 cups (8 ounces) pine nuts

4 eggs

³/₄ cup (5 ounces) brown sugar

¹/₂ cup (3¹/₂ ounces) light corn syrup

¹/₂ cup (3¹/₂ ounces) molasses

¹/₄ teaspoon salt

1 vanilla bean, split lengthwise and all seeds scraped out, or 1 teaspoon vanilla extract

¹/₄ cup (2 ounces) whiskey (optional)

(continued)

Glazed Pine Nuts

1 In a large pan, melt the honey and butter.

2 Add the rosemary and pine nuts. Stir over medium heat for 10 minutes, until caramelized and golden-brown. With a fork, remove the rosemary sprig and discard. Set aside pine nut mixture.

Pine Nut Filling

In a bowl, whisk together the remaining ingredients.

Assembly

1 Preheat oven to 400°.

2 Add the glazed pine nuts to the pine nut filling and mix to distribute well.

3 Pour this mixture into the prebaked tart shell and bake for 40 minutes or until well set. Serve warm (not hot) or at room temperature.

Fruit Cobbler

This New England classic is a quick and delicious way to make the best of the season's fresh fruit.

Tools: *12 x 14-inch baking dish*

Preparation time: *20 minutes*

Baking time: *35 minutes*

1 1/2 cups (6 ounces) flour

2 teaspoons baking powder

1/4 teaspoon salt

1/2 cup (4 ounces or 1 stick) butter

1/2 cup (3 1/2 ounces) light brown sugar

3/4 cup (6 ounces) heavy cream

1/2-inch pat butter, for greasing the dish

4 cups (32 ounces) fruit of choice: apples, pears, peaches, rhubarb, nectarines, raspberries, blueberries, apricots, or plums

1/2 cup (3 ounces) sugar

Fruit Cobbler

1 Preheat oven to 375°.

2 Place the flour, baking powder, salt, and butter chopped into nickel-size pieces into a bowl, pour the brown sugar over the top, and stir well until ingredients are blended.

3 Pour in the heavy cream and mix until mixture is moist. Set aside.

Assembly

1 Butter the baking dish and place chopped fruits evenly on the bottom. Sprinkle the sugar over the fruits.

2 Sprinkle the cobbler mixture over the top and bake for 35 minutes until the top is golden-brown. Serve hot with your favorite ice cream.

Two Chocolate Crowd-Pleasers

The following two desserts are very different in every respect except that they're based on chocolate. The chocolate pillows, made in muffin tins, are soft and luscious. The teardrops, on the other hand, are crispy and intensely flavored. Both are good bets for a crowd because you can make them in large quantities with little extra effort.

Baked Chocolate Pillows

This easy-to-assemble party dessert, a sure crowd-pleaser, is essentially a flourless chocolate cake cooked in muffin tins. You can garnish the pillows with whipped cream (flavored, if you like), crème anglaise, or countless other sweets. The little cakes are called pillows because of their puffed, pillow-like shape when unmolded.

You can prepare these pillows several days ahead of time. After you pour the batter into buttered muffin tins in Step 6, place the tins in the freezer instead of baking right away. You can bake them right from the freezer in a 400° oven for 8 minutes. When finished, they should be soft and moist in the center. Serve immediately.

(continued)

The yield in this recipe is for 24 small muffin-sized chocolate pillows. To double that amount, you should make two separate batches because, even if you have a standup kitchen mixer, you'll have too much batter to mix at once.

You can serve these muffins with Hot Chocolate Fudge Sauce for Profiteroles (see Chapter 4).

Tools: *Two 12-cup muffin tins, medium pot, electric mixer (optional)*

Preparation time: *20 minutes*

Baking time: *10 minutes*

Yield: *24 muffin-size cakes*

$^1/_2$ *-inch pat of butter, for greasing muffin tins*

9 ounces bittersweet chocolate, chopped

4 tablespoons butter

8 eggs, separated

$^1/_2$ *cup (3 $^1/_2$ ounces) brown sugar, sifted but not packed*

1 Preheat oven to 400°. Grease the muffin tins.

2 In a large bowl set over a pot of boiling water, melt the chocolate and butter and stir to combine. Set aside — keep warm but not too hot.

3 Whisk the egg whites until they form soft peaks. Add the brown sugar and continue whisking until stiff peaks form.

4 In a large, separate bowl, whisk the egg yolks until they're bright yellow and smooth, and blend into the melted chocolate mixture. Immediately fold in the egg whites, one-third at a time. Fold just until incorporated.

5 Use a whisk to deliberately overmix the batter, which makes the batter fall slightly and gives it a shiny appearance.

6 Pour the mixture into well-buttered muffin tins (fill each section three-fourths full). Bake for 6 to 8 minutes or until the pillows start to puff up out of their cups and an inserted toothpick comes out clean. To test for doneness, touch the top of a muffin — it should be slightly resilient.

7 When the pillows are done, invert the muffin tin over a cookie sheet gently. Tap the muffin tin lightly to make the chocolate pillows fall out. Serve immediately.

Chocolate Teardrops

This recipe is a bit fancy, meant to wow your guests. It takes some work, but you can do a lot of it beforehand. The little chocolate teardrops hold for a week or so in a cool place (not refrigerated).

You curl the chocolate into teardrops by using smooth, thick paper, such as parchment. Or you can use plastic notebook dividers, which are even better because you can wash and reuse them.

Tools: *30 strips (2 x 12 inches each) of parchment paper, plastic cutting board (optional), medium pot*

Preparation time: *15 minutes (not including garnishes)*

Cooking time: *15 minutes*

Yield: *24 teardrops*

32 ounces bittersweet chocolate, chopped

2 cups (16 ounces) cubed (about thumb size) fresh fruit of choice: strawberries, mangoes, papayas, kiwi, apricots, pears, or pineapples

1 cup (8 ounces) water or white wine

$^1/_4$ cup ($1^1/_2$ ounces) sugar or honey (especially flavored honey, like acacia, lavender, or orange blossom)

3 stems fresh mint (optional)

juice of 1 lemon

grated zest of 1 lemon

1 cinnamon stick

4 cups (32 ounces) heavy cream, well chilled

$^1/_2$ cup (2 ounces) confectioners' sugar

2 teaspoons vanilla extract, or 2 teaspoons almond extract

Teardrops

1 In a large bowl placed atop a pot of hot (but not boiling) water, melt two-thirds of the chocolate pieces, stirring occasionally. (Boiling water would burn the chocolate.)

2 After this first batch of chocolate has melted, add the remaining chocolate and stir.

3 Leave the bowl over the hot water to keep it warm and liquid, stirring periodically.

4 Place 4 or 5 strips of parchment paper one at a time on a flat, nonpourous work surface that you can clean easily (so that you can scrape off and reuse all the chocolate that drips onto the surface). A plastic cutting board works well.

5 Make sure that the chocolate is thick but liquid. (If it's too liquid, then it's too hot and needs to cool somewhat.) Dribble enough chocolate on each strip to cover the strip end to end. Then use a spatula to spread the chocolate evenly over the strip.

(continued)

6 Lift a parchment strip and set it on its edge while bringing the 2 ends together. Pinch the 2 ends so that the strips form a curve, or a teardrop.

7 Place the teardrops on a flat cookie sheet and refrigerate. When they're cold and well set, gently peel the paper off. Leave the chocolates in the refrigerator until you're ready to assemble them (with the homemade fruit marinade and whipped cream).

Homemade Fruit Marinade

1 Combine the cubed fruits in a bowl.

2 Bring to a boil the water, sugar, mint, lemon juice and zest, and cinnamon stick. Remove from heat and let cool slightly. Remove the cinnamon stick. Pour over the fruit. Stir and let sit overnight.

Whipped Cream

In a large mixing bowl, combine the heavy cream, confectioners' sugar, and vanilla. Whisk until the cream forms stiff peaks.

Assembly

1 Place the cold chocolate teardrops on chilled dessert plates. Then, using a table-spoon, fill each teardrop's cavity just to the top (not overflowing) with the whipped cream.

2 Place 2 tablespoons fruit marinade on top of each teardrop.

Chapter 15

Why Not Make Your Own Wedding Cake?

. . . .

In This Chapter

▶ Counting down to the wedding day

▶ Setting up your tools and ingredients

▶ Making the cake over the course of a couple of days

▶ Adding your personal touch with cake decorations

▶ Cutting the cake

. . . .

*I*f you think of a wedding cake as a "Moby spongecake" with lots of stuff all over it, the whole thing sounds less intimidating. And that *is* basically the essence of a wedding cake. The biggest challenge is the sheer size of the cake — you become part baker, part architect. But the task isn't such a big deal as long as you set up everything you need ahead of time and follow the instructions.

This chapter gives you a foolproof three-day plan for making your own wedding cake. We break it up over three days to make the task easier (it won't tie up one whole day of your life) and the cake better (a wedding cake is better after it's rested for a day).

Unlike some fabulous-looking commercial cakes that are primarily meant as showcases, the wedding cake in this chapter not only looks great (see photo) but also tastes great. Ours is a real dig-in dessert — after all, you burn lots of calories doing the bunny hop.

Ready, Set, I Do!: Preparing for the Big Day

A wedding cake is a lot like a marriage: if you have the patience and will to deal with potential pitfalls, chances are you'll succeed.

For a wedding cake, this means reading over the entire procedure to make sure that you feel comfortable with it. (If it contains a technique that you don't feel confident about, you may want to look it up in this book and practice in advance.) Also, you need a game plan so that you can organize all the equipment and ingredients beforehand. Nothing's worse than lurching around the kitchen looking for a spatula while your cake burns.

The following sections cover what you should do well in advance all the way up to what you do on the Big Day.

Several weeks before the wedding: Gathering tools

Long before crunch time, make sure that you have all the necessary equipment. Check out the tools list in the recipe later in this chapter. Here are some of the items you should specifically be thinking about:

✔ **Fancy cake decorations, such as little bride and groom figures:** Visit some cake supply stores (ask your local baker) or any bakery that specializes in wedding cakes. If you can't find what you want, try the mail-order sources listed in Appendix C. (You may want to place your order up to several months in advance to be sure that it arrives on time.)

Top five reasons to make your own wedding cake

Following are the five top reasons why you should even think of such a foolish project as making your own wedding cake:

✔ Doing it yourself — or having family or friends do it — instead of buying the cake saves hundreds of after-tax dollars that you can spend on overpriced cocktails and lunches at your honeymoon hotel's poolside restaurant.

✔ If you do it yourself, you'll know how to make a wedding cake when your kid gets married — and thus save hundreds of after-tax dollars that you can use for paying off college loans.

✔ It takes your mind off all the other wedding tensions.

✔ Any relatives who dare arrive too early for the wedding can be put to work.

✔ It's a hoot!

✔ **Cake molds:** You need a 14-inch round cake mold, a 10-inch cake mold, and an 8-inch cake mold (for the three tiers of the cake). Again, try some cake supply stores or mail-order. *Note:* As long as your cake molds are within an inch or two of these sizes, the amounts and instructions shown in this chapter's recipe will work fine for you.

✔ **Drinking straws or dowels:** You can get drinking straws at grocery stores or get thin (1/8 inch thick) wooden dowels at art shops or lumber stores. You need 16 of them, and they should be at least 10 inches long.

✔ **Cardboard or wood base for each of the top two cake tiers:** You need two sturdy (cardboard, posterboard, or wood) circular bases, one with a 10-inch diameter and one with an 8-inch diameter. You can buy these bases at a cake supply store, or you can buy the cardboard or posterboard at an art shop and make them yourself.

✔ **Serving platter:** The ideal serving platter is a 16-inch-diameter flat plate. If you don't have a platter, you can make a 14-inch-diameter cardboard base — be sure to use very thick cardboard — and cover it with aluminum foil (see Chapter 9).

The three-day plan

We suggest that you give yourself several hours on each of the two days before the wedding (as well as on the day of the wedding itself) to complete the task of making your wedding cake. Although you'd probably have the time to do it all in one day, it would be grueling. Also, the cake should rest overnight refrigerated to firm up sufficiently, anyway.

Day 1

Assemble all ingredients. See the recipe later in this chapter for the list of what you need.

Here's a very important step that you may not have thought about: Clean out your refrigerator so that you'll be able to fit your monstrous work-in-progress inside. Each layer of the cake is about 4 inches high and needs to be stored separately before assembly — you can't stack the cakes in the refrigerator before assembly, or they may sink under their own weight.

Then after you assemble and decorate the cake (on the wedding day), it could be 12 inches high or taller; you'll probably need to remove a shelf from the refrigerator to store the cake until the wedding. Be sure to include your serving platter when calculating how much space you need.

Traditional or contemporary: Wedding cake styles

You need to decide what style of wedding cake you want — that is, traditional or more contemporary.

✔ **English-style (traditional):** This cake is actually a dense fruit cake that's covered with marzipan and weighs as much as a St. Bernard.

✔ **American-style (contemporary):** This much lighter cake is made with a vanilla sponge cake and covered with white frosting and other decorations.

In this chapter, we give you a recipe for an American-style wedding cake.

Day 2

The day before the wedding is when you make all the cake ingredients (sponge cake, buttercream, and fruit compote), awaiting final assembly.

Actually, you *can* make the sponge cake a week or two in advance and freeze it until Day 2, when you apply the icing. You can do the initial preparation — the icing application — as early as two days before the wedding.

Day 3 (wedding day morning)

The first thing you do on this day is buy some fresh flowers for decorating the cake. (We recommend smaller flowers like wildflowers, pansies, roses, bachelor buttons, freesia, or orchids.) Then you tackle the very rewarding task of putting the whole cake together, when you finally see the true fruits of all your labor.

Wedding Cake

This contemporary-style wedding cake has a lovely yellow-gold appearance (it comes from the egg yolks) and a moist, semisweet flavor (see photo). The garnish is a highly whipped, light buttercream. As for decoration, we opted for a rather traditional style. We show you how to make decorative flowers with buttercream as well as how to make different kinds of filigrees and curlicues. If you want to get fancier — say, little Eiffel Towers or Harley Davidson Sportsters — you can use these same pastry bag techniques to go off on your own.

This cake's buttercream is slightly unconventional. Most wedding cakes use vegetable shortening or butter and egg whites, combinations that have little flavor. This recipe calls for a stirred custard made with egg yolks and combines it with an Italian meringue (see Chapter 8 for more about meringues) and butter — a much tastier garnish.

Note: You need to make two batches of the Lemon-Vanilla Sponge Cake — one batch fills the 14-inch cake mold, and the second batch is divided between the 10-inch mold and the 8-inch mold. (Even if your cake molds are an inch or two different in size, this amount of batter works.)

Tools: Electric mixer, 3 round cake molds (14 inch, 10 inch, and 8 inch), strainer, candy thermometer (with 260° capacity), serving platter (16-inch flat plate or 14-inch cardboard base covered with aluminum foil), 2 round cardboard bases (10 inch and 8 inch), pastry bag (at least 10 inches long) with star tip (#5 or smaller) and special tip for making roses, sixteen 10-inch wooden barbecue (shish kebab) skewers, drinking straws, or dowels ($^1/_8$ inch thick), cake decorations: fresh flowers

Preparation time: 6 to 8 hours

Cooking time: 1 hour for the spongecake; 45 minutes for the buttercream

Yield: 3-tier wedding cake (the bottom 2 tiers yield 50 servings, and the top is traditionally reserved for the couple's first anniversary)

Lemon-Vanilla Sponge Cake

Note: You need to make two batches of this recipe, so the total ingredients you need are double the amounts shown.

$^1/_2$-inch pat of butter, for greasing cake mold

10 eggs, room temperature

$1^1/_3$ cups (8 ounces) sugar

1 teaspoon vanilla extract

zest of 2 lemons

juice of 2 lemons (4 tablespoons)

2 cups (8 ounces) cake flour, sifted

1 Preheat oven to 400° and butter the 14 inch mold. (On your second run through this recipe, butter the 10-inch and 8-inch molds.)

2 In a large bowl, combine the eggs, sugar, vanilla, lemon zest, and lemon juice. Whisk on high speed for 10 minutes, or until the mixture is frothy.

3 Fold in the sifted cake flour. Pour the batter into the buttered cake mold. (On your second run through this recipe, divide the batter between the 10-inch and 8-inch molds.)

4 Bake for 30 minutes, or until a toothpick inserted in the center of the cake comes out clean and dry. Remove the cake from the oven and let it sit for at least 30 minutes before you unmold it.

5 To unmold the cake, run a knife around the perimeter of the cake mold and flip the mold onto a mesh cooling rack or directly onto parchment paper. Tap the mold until the cake falls out. Let the cake cool upside down.

6 After the cake has thoroughly cooled, wrap it in plastic wrap and freeze for at least 1 hour or more. (Freezing makes the cake much easier to cut.)

(continued)

Cutting sponge cake into three horizontal layers

Here's how you cut a cake into three horizontal layers:

1. **Using a long serrated knife, make a 1-inch-deep horizontal cut a third of the way down the side of the cake.**

2. **Saw evenly (1 inch deep) horizontally around the entire cake.**

3. **Continue sawing around the cake, cutting deeper and deeper each time, until you've cut an even third off the top of the cake. Remove this top layer.**

4. **Make a 1-inch-deep cut halfway down the side of the remaining cake and repeat Steps 2 and 3. Now you should have three even layers.**

7 Remove the cake from the freezer. At this point, cakes tend to have a slight dome on top. Use a serrated knife to cut off the dome so that the top of the cake is level.

8 Slice the cake into thirds horizontally, as described in the sidebar "Cutting sponge cake into three horizontal layers."

9 Assemble all the same ingredients and repeat Steps 1 through 8 to make the other 2 tiers of the cake (remember that a single batch of this batter fills both the 10-inch and 8-inch molds).

Buttercream

8 eggs, separated

2 cups (16 ounces) milk

2 1/2 cups (15 ounces) sugar

1 teaspoon vanilla extract (preferably the clear type rather than the dark type, if you can find it)

1/2 cup (4 ounces) water

6 cups (48 ounces) butter, room temperature

1 In a bowl, whisk the egg yolks until well blended — about 1 minute.

2 In a medium pot, bring the milk, 1 cup (6 ounces) sugar, and vanilla extract to a boil. Slowly pour the hot milk mixture over the egg yolks while whisking by hand or with a mixer. Return the milk-egg mixture (the custard) to the pot.

3 Return the pot to medium heat, whisking continually for about 2 minutes. Strain the custard and transfer to another bowl. Cover and chill.

4 Clean the bowl very well (meringue needs a spotless, dry bowl to rise) and place the egg whites in it. Whisk at medium-high speed until frothy (about 7 to 10 minutes), adding 2 tablespoons sugar at midpoint.

5 Combine the remaining sugar and water in a medium pot. Bring to a boil. Immerse thermometer so that it touches the bottom and heats to 254°.

6 While continuing to whisk, pour the hot sugar mixture over the egg whites — try not to hit the turning whisk, or the hot sugar could splatter. After you've incorporated the sugar, continue whisking at medium speed for 2 minutes to cool the meringue.

7 Whisk to cool the meringue while adding the butter, a tablespoon at a time. Continue whisking until all the butter is incorporated.

8 If using an electric mixer, reduce to slow speed and gradually pour in the chilled custard while whisking. By hand, continue moderate whisking.

9 Continue whisking until the mixture is smooth and shiny — about 5 minutes.

10 Set aside at room temperature. If you won't be using the buttercream for several hours, be sure to refrigerate it.

If you do refrigerate, you need to whisk it again for about 15 minutes at medium speed before using it. Don't worry if the mixture looks broken, like cottage cheese; it eventually combines and regains its smooth texture.

The Wedding Cake Filling: Apricot and Blueberry Compote

4 cups (32 ounces) water

2 cups (12 ounces) sugar

20 apricots, halved and pits removed (skins on)

11 cups (88 ounces) blueberries, washed and drained, stems removed

1 In a pot, bring 2 cups (16 ounces) water and 1 cup (6 ounces) sugar to a boil. Add the apricots and simmer for 10 minutes. Remove and set aside.

2 In a separate pot, bring 2 cups (16 ounces) water and 1 cup (6 ounces) sugar to a boil. Add the blueberries and simmer for 10 minutes. Remove and set aside.

Initial Cake Assembly (Day before Wedding)

At this point, you should have 3 sponge cakes, each divided into 3 equal layers horizontally, along with the buttercream and the fruit filling. You now assemble all 3 cakes simultaneously (but you don't put them together into a single cake until the next day).

Note: *You can complete this initial assembly as early as 2 days before the wedding, rather than the day before.*

(continued)

1 Place the bottom layer of the largest sponge cake on the serving tray (or its cardboard base, if you don't have a serving tray). Place the bottom layers of the medium cake and the small cake on their respective cardboard bases.

2 Place the star tip in the pastry bag and fill the bag halfway with buttercream. (See illustrated pastry bag instructions in Chapter 4.)

3 Squeeze a line of buttercream around the perimeter of the large cake.

4 Spoon $1/4$ of the apricot compote onto the center of the cake, using the buttercream that's around the perimeter as a boundary to prevent the compote from oozing Spread out the apricot compote as smoothly as possible.

5 Repeat Steps 3 and 4 with the base layers of the other 2 cakes.

6 Place the middle layer for each cake on top of its base layer, being careful to center it exactly.

7 Squeeze a line of buttercream around the perimeter of each middle layer. (You should still have plenty of buttercream left over after this step.)

8 Spoon enough of the blueberry fruit inside the buttercream perimeter to cover the cake and smooth it over with the back of a spoon or a spatula. Then spoon some of the blueberry juice over the fruit to moisten each cake.

9 Place each cake's top layer on top of the middle layers — upside down so that the flatter surface is on top.

10 Place large tablespoons full of buttercream onto the top of each cake. Using a long, thin spatula, spread the buttercream back and forth over the surface to smooth it all over. Don't be too worried about appearances yet — just flex your icing-technique chops. Right now, you're applying the first layer of icing; the second layer will cover more blemishes. You should have plenty of icing left for that.

> *Toque Tip:* Try not to bring up crumbs from the surface of the cake as you run the spatula over it — any crumbs will show through the icing. Every so often, dip the spatula in hot water to heat it; then dry it off and continue spreading. (A warm spatula makes the icing easier to apply.)

11 Now apply some buttercream all over the sides of the cake and smooth it out. You should have more than half the buttercream left — place the remaining buttercream in a bowl, cover with plastic wrap, and refrigerate.

12 Refrigerate the cakes overnight lightly covered with plastic wrap (or over 2 nights, if you're doing this step 2 days ahead of time) so that the buttercream can get firm.

Final Cake Assembly (Wedding Day)

At this point, your three cakes — garnished with buttercream and chilled sufficiently — are ready for you to apply the final buttercream decoration and stack into 1 magnificent cake! Make sure that you have more than a foot of vertical space in your refrigerator available to store the assembled cake — that is, unless you serve it immediately.

1 Remove the cakes from the refrigerator and place on a flat working surface.

2 Let the cold buttercream sit for about 10 minutes to warm up. Then whip on medium speed for about 15 minutes to bring it back to a creamy consistency. (At first, it'll look like a mess, sort of like cottage cheese, but don't worry — as you continue to whip, it will come together.)

3 With a spatula, spread some buttercream over any bare spots, crumbs, or other imperfections on the cake. Focus on just the biggest spots for now — you cover up the rest when you use the pastry bag in Step 10. (See Figure 15-1.)

4 Using a knife or a skewer, sketch an 8-inch-diameter circle in the center of the largest cake's surface (leaving about a 3-inch space between the circle and the cake's edge, all around the cake). Place one skewer close to the edge of the cake anywhere around the rim and carefully plunge it straight down to the bottom of the cake.

5 Carefully pull the skewer straight up out of the cake. The buttercream residue on the wood tells you how deep the cake is. With a serrated knife or large scissors, cut 8 skewers, drinking straws, or dowels to be as long as the depth of the cake.

6 Plunge the skewers into the cake, placing them evenly around the cake a little inside the perimeter of the circle you sketched. (See Figure 15-1.)

7 Add the second story to the cake: With a large spatula, lift the edge of the middle (10 inch) cake's cardboard base so that you can get one hand under the base. Using both hands, pick up the cake and carefully place it symmetrically on top of the large cake, right in the center. (Stand up and look down at the big cake as you lower the middle cake to get it centered correctly.)

Toque Tip: Don't panic if your cake looks a little lopsided at this point — that is, one side is lower than the other or if the center sags. Lopsided cakes happen all the time. Rotate the cake until you get the most vertical assembly possible.

8 Strengthen the middle layer with skewers so that it can support the top layer: Repeat Steps 4 through 6, this time making a 6-inch-diameter circle and carefully plunging this second batch of 8 skewers, drinking straws, or dowels all the way down to the base of the bottom cake.

9 Add the final tier to the cake: Repeat Step 7 to place the smallest cake on top of the middle layer.

(continued)

10 With all this lifting and moving around, some of the cake is probably showing through the icing, particularly at the base of each cake. (That's one reason for the remaining buttercream.) Put a star tip in your pastry bag and fill the bag halfway with buttercream. Squeeze a line of buttercream all the way around the base of the middle cake to conceal the cardboard base. (See Figure 15-1.) You can use a straight line or a squiggly line — just be sure to use one or the other design consistently for each cake tier.

11 Repeat the process around the base of the largest cake and then around the base of the top cake.

12 Now comes the fun part (as if the rest of this process hasn't been fun!): Decorating the cake. See the next section for details. And then check out "Photo Finish: Cutting the Cake" for the final stage of your crowning achievement.

The Fun Part: Decorating the Cake

Cake decoration is an individual choice. As with any other skill, cake decorating takes a little practice — start off modestly and gain some confidence. Try some of the following suggestions:

- **Making rosettes:** Using a pastry bag and star tip with buttercream, make a little open circle in a clockwise motion on a practice plate until you can reproduce the same rosette over and over. Then apply to the cake.

- **Buttercream star points:** With the star tip, squeeze a little dab of buttercream onto the cake and quickly pull the bag away, perpendicular to the cake, to create a star effect. Practice first on a plate; then apply to the cake.

- **Adding fresh flowers:** Wherever you see imperfections in the cake — a bare spot, a place where the icing did not come out as you liked, an icing rose that resembles Ernest Borgnine — you can cover it with fresh flowers. Small flowers work best: violets, anemones, bleeding hearts, little roses, tulips, and daffodils. Wildflowers are also nice, but they don't last very long, so put them on at the last minute.

- It should go without saying, but the flowers you use to decorate the cake are not edible — only eat the buttercream flowers!

How to Build a Wedding Cake

1. Start with 3 different sizes of cake rings. These will be the layers of your wedding cake!

2. Frosting the Cake

First, lay a layer flat in front of you.

Smooth the buttercream across the top of the cake.

Then, holding the spatula perpendicular to the top of the cake, smooth the buttercream around the sides.

3. Stacking the Cake

For the 2 lower layers:
Stick about 10 drinking straws into the center of the cake and snip at the frosting height. Put them where the next layer covers them only!

☆ This will keep the layer above from crushing the layer underneath it!

4. Decorating the Cake

Figure 15-1:
How to
build a
wedding
cake.

Once the cakes have been stacked, finish decorating. (DON'T DO IT BEFORE OR YOU MAY MESS UP THE LAYERS WHILE STACKING!) Using your star tip, make long letter 'U's around the top of each layer...

Photo Finish: Cutting the Cake

At many weddings, the bride and groom cut the first piece of cake, and then the cake returns to the kitchen to be sliced. If you decide to do the cutting yourself right there in the dining room, you want to look as if you know what you're doing.

Use a sharp, 8 to 10-inch knife and dip it in hot water occasionally for best results. (Don't dry off the knife.)

1. **Using a sturdy spatula and a few hands, remove the top tier of cake and freeze it (wrapped well, of course) for the couple to have as a first-anniversary treat.**

2. **Remove the middle tier, along with its cardboard base, and set it on a cutting board.**

3. **From the bottom (largest) cake, cut out one rectangular piece (not a wedge) roughly $3^1/_2$ inches deep and 1 inch wide.**

4. **Run a knife around the inside of the cuts — you should have roughly 20 pieces; cut around the skewers that support the cake.**

5. **Repeat Step 3 on the remaining bottom cake, following the same dimensions.**

   This step should yield about 15 pieces.

6. **From the middle layer, cut 1-inch-wide wedges all around to yield about 15 servings.**

   Now you have about 50 pieces total. If you cut the top layer, you could get another 10 to 12 pieces.

Variations

Many people these days prefer chocolate wedding cakes to the traditional vanilla sponge cake. To convert this chapter's recipe to a chocolate cake, just substitute the Classic Chocolate Mousse Layer Cake in Chapter 9 for the Lemon-Vanilla Sponge Cake recipe shown in this chapter. That recipe is also a 10-egg cake, so you follow the recipe twice, just as you do for the Lemon-Vanilla Sponge Cake, to fill all three cake molds.

You can also vary the filling. If you don't want to make your own filling, you can just buy quality preserves in the flavor you prefer.

Chapter 16

Holiday Desserts

In This Chapter

▶ Building a gingerbread house with an 8 percent mortgage

▶ Making the classic pound cake

▶ Creating candied fruits

▶ Preparing holiday cookies

▶ Making macaroons

▶ Making cookies with kids

▶ Decorating desserts

*T*he holidays are high season for a dessert cook. This chapter runs you through a range of great options, from fruit cake and gingerbread houses, to decorative cookies.

Life of the Party

Face it, having ambitious friends who invite you to dinner and say, "Don't bring anything, we're under control" is always best. However, a lot of friends think that a pot-luck deal, where everyone brings a dish, is great fun. So what do you do in those cases? Lugging over a casserole that weighs as much as a St. Bernard puppy may be more than you want to tackle. Besides, you may get stuck with the leftovers. Salads and side dishes are easy, but when is the last time you heard guests say, "Wow! Could you give me the recipe for that salad?"

If you're going to accept the pot-luck challenge during holidays or other occasions and want to impress the crowd, why not make a dessert? After all, aren't appetizers and main courses only excuses to get to desserts, anyway? (For great entertaining ideas, check out *Entertaining For Dummies* by Suzanne Williamson and Linda Smith [IDG Books Worldwide, Inc.])

If you want to be a local hero, follow the directions for the foolproof sweets in this and other chapters. The kinds of simple desserts you find in this chapter are made particularly festive by piped-on icings and other decorations. You can make gingerbread, cookies, pound cakes, and macaroons in advance and then carry them to the party without fear of back spasms. What's more, they taste great.

Family Projects That Are More Fun Than Lawn Mowing

Certain desserts lend themselves to a team effort, like constructing gingerbread houses, making holiday cookies, and making fruitcakes to give away as gifts. In this section, you find out how to make all three.

Gingerbread houses

Gingerbread has a noble pedigree, dating back to the Middle Ages. Fair ladies of the court were said to make rather dense, sweet gingerbread cakes for the dashing knights who were about to thrust into tournament competition. No one knows whether the knights consumed the cakes before battle (unlikely, given the hour they just spent putting on layers of metal headgear) or whether they held on to the gingerbread as their secret weapon. (An old-fashioned, dense, honey-laced gingerbread brick, deftly tossed, could probably ground an unsuspecting knight at 30 paces.) Today's gingerbreads are inferior as weapons, but they do have the advantage of possessing moistness and a nice sharp flavor.

Transporting your desserts

Transporting cakes with frosting is a delicate process. We recommend placing them in a sturdy box with low sides (like a shirt box). If the frosting is soft, it's probably better not to cover the cake box at all.

You should remove a cake from the refrigerator at the last minute. Secure the serving plate to be transported in the box with tape so that it doesn't slide into the side of the box.

You should transport cookies, pound cakes, and other sturdy desserts in a box, first covered with plastic wrap.

Transport stacked cakes, such as large wedding cakes, decorated in individual layers but assembled on site. Bring a few decorating tools and frosting to do repair work and finishing touches once the cake is in place.

Quick breads

The consistency of quick breads is softer and more moist than any other bread. In fact, quick breads are not really breads at all, but are more like a small cake, such as muffins. They're called quick because the baking powder rises without any waiting as for yeast breads. Yeast breads must sit in a warm humid place until the yeast produces CO_2 (which makes the fluffy holes in yeast-risen bread). Quick breads usually are sweeter than yeast breads.

For these gingerbread recipes, we recommend fresh ginger, which is available in supermarket produce sections. (Dried ginger can work, but the flavor is not as pure.) Fresh ginger gives a deeper and richer essence to your desserts. If you decide to use powdered ginger, the quantity is the same as for fresh.

If you're using fresh ginger, break the ginger into individual pieces so that it's easy to handle. First, cut off the little nubbly ends and then peel the ginger root with a potato peeler to remove the skin, placing a plate or bowl underneath to catch the juices. If the recipe calls for grated ginger, grate on the fine side of the grater. Don't worry about the stringy pieces; they blend into the batter. Be sure to save all the ginger juice that drips out and add it to the batter for extra flavor.

The following gingerbread recipe is called a *quick bread* because it's made with baking powder rather than other leavening agents, such as yeast or beaten eggs. The best known quick bread is banana bread. To find out more about quick breads, see the sidebar called "Quick breads."

Gingerbread

This astonishingly simple and delicious recipe allows you to stride into a party with cool confidence. The gingerbread recipe here is a traditional, soft cake that is served with whipped cream. Just don't eat it all on the way to the party.

Tools: *Double boiler, sifter, two 10-inch round cake pans or three $5^{1}/_{4}$ x $3^{1}/_{4}$-inch terrine molds, cooling rack*

Preparation time: *30 minutes*

Baking time: *50 minutes*

Yield: *8 servings*

(continued)

¹/₂ cup (4 ounces or 1 stick) butter

¹/₂ cup (2 ounces) lightly packed brown sugar

¹/₂ cup (4 ounces) dark molasses

¹/₂ cup (4 ounces) water

¹/₂ cup (4 ounces) honey

1³/₄ cups (7 ounces) cake flour, sifted

1 tablespoon baking powder

1 teaspoon cinnamon

¹/₄ teaspoon salt

1 tablespoon ground freshly grated ginger, or 1 tablespoon powdered ginger

2 eggs

¹/₂-inch pat of butter, for greasing the pans

3 tablespoons confectioners' sugar

1 cup (8 ounces) heavy cream, chilled

1 Preheat oven to 350°.

2 Over a double boiler, with the water boiling, melt the butter, brown sugar, molasses, water, and honey. Stir occasionally until the ingredients melt. Remove from heat once the butter is melted.

3 In a large mixing bowl, combine the flour, baking powder, cinnamon, and salt.

4 Sift the flour mixture into a second bowl by passing it through a flour sifter or by shaking it through a metal strainer. Set aside.

5 After the butter mixture has melted, add the ginger and blend together. Whisk in the two eggs. (Be careful: If this mixture gets too hot, it cooks the eggs.)

6 Gradually pour the flour mixture into the warm butter mixture, whisking constantly until thoroughly mixed. Set aside.

7 Butter two 10-inch cake pans or three small 5¹/₄ x 3¹/₄-inch terrine molds.

8 Fill the molds with the batter to about half capacity. Place in the preheated oven. Bake for 50 minutes, or until it's dark brown on the top and the cake springs back to the touch (or until an inserted toothpick comes out clean). Cool on a cake rack.

9 In a bowl, combine the confectioners' sugar with the chilled cream and whip until it forms stiff peaks. Serve on the side with a slice of gingerbread cake.

Double boilers

A double boiler (see figure) is nothing more than a pot with a little water in it, holding a second pot that fits snugly atop it. If you don't have a double boiler, you can improvise with two pots or with a snug-fitting metal bowl on top a pot of boiling water.

Use a double boiler when you want to limit the amount of heat that food is exposed to. Because steam reaches 212° and no higher, you can gently heat delicate sauces in the top of a double boiler. Even though the burner is on high, a double boiler can reach only to a certain degree of gentle heat because the steam does the cooking.

double boiler

Gingerbread House with Royal Icing

Gingerbread houses are a centuries-old holiday tradition, but few of today's home cooks know how to make them from scratch (see photo). Although a gingerbread house takes time and patience, if you follow the steps carefully, you'll be considered a regular culinary I.M. Pei around the house. The only potential drawback may be that your newfound reputation as a gingerbread house maker finds you making a dozen or more houses every holiday for awestruck kids.

For the stencils, use the ones in the back of this book.

The dough in this recipe makes a brittle, cookielike substance, which is perfect for constructing a gingerbread house.

(continued)

Tools: *Sifter, plastic wrap, parchment paper, electric mixer (optional), stencils, cardboard, pizza cutter (optional)*

Preparation time: *2 hours and an additional 30 minutes to cut stencils out of cardboard from samples in the back of the book*

Baking time: *25 minutes*

Yield: *One 8 x 6 x 9-inch house (or 6 servings)*

1¹/₈ cups (10 ounces or 2¹/₄ sticks) butter	pinch of salt
1 cup (7 ounces) light brown sugar (soft, not granular)	1 teaspoon cinnamon
	1 teaspoon baking powder
¹/₈ cup (1 ounce) molasses	2 cups (12 ounces) confectioners' sugar
1 teaspoon grated ginger, or 1 teaspoon dry ginger	1 egg white
2 eggs	juice of 1 lemon
2¹/₂ cups (10 ounces) cake flour	gum drops, Life Savers, and jelly beans (for house decoration)
2¹/₂ cups (10 ounces) flour	

1 Preheat oven to 325°.

2 Cream the butter and brown sugar until soft. (If mixing by hand, allow butter to soften more and stir sugar and butter with a stiff whisk.) Scrape the bowl if batter sticks to the side. The mixture should have no lumps.

3 All at once, add the molasses, ginger, and eggs to the brown sugar/butter mixture, mixing together until smooth.

4 Sift together the flours, salt, cinnamon, and baking powder into a bowl. Add to the egg mixture and blend.

5 In a bowl, blend the ingredients. If mixing by hand, blend well using a wooden spoon. In both cases, stop occasionally to scrape out the bottom of the bowl, where flour tends to stick. Blend until smooth.

If using an electric mixer, finish kneading by hand in that bowl. Continue until the dough becomes smooth. (This process is necessary because most home mixers can't handle such firm dough. Some dry parts will not be incorporated at the bottom of the bowl.) Turn the bowl over onto the table and fold the dough over onto itself to mix this flour mixture into the rest of the dough. Continue kneading in this way until the dough is smooth and even in color.

Essential Skill: The term *working the dough* refers to pushing it down with your hands, turning it, folding it onto itself and repeating the process. This working action, called *kneading,* makes the dough form into a homogenous mixture.

6 Cut the dough in half and work each half piece into a rough 1 inch thick oval. Lay each oval on plastic wrap, cover with another sheet, and refrigerate for 1 hour.

7 Line a baking sheet with parchment paper. Make a sticky glue by blending together about a teaspoon of flour with a teaspoon of water and stirring thoroughly. Use this combination to glue down the edges of the parchment paper to the baking sheet — this homemade glue process is much faster than running all over the house, turning drawers upside down and looking for Elmer's Glue.

8 Roll out one half of the dough into a thin layer — about cookie thickness — about 15 x 15 inches.

9 Lay one part of your gingerbread stencil over the dough. Using a pizza cutter or a sharp knife, cut around the stencil. (Don't drag your knife, but rather cut down firmly into the dough to get a cleaner cut.) If your stencil has windows, cut those out, too. Use a spatula to transfer the stenciled dough to the parchment paper on the baking sheet. Repeat this process with the rest of the stencils.

10 Bake for 25 minutes or until edges become slightly brownish and the gingerbread's surface is no longer shiny. Let cool for 10 minutes.

Royal Icing

Combine the confectioners' sugar, egg white, and lemon juice in a mixing bowl. Blend for a minute, scraping the beaters and the bowl. (Whisking takes about 10 minutes.)

Assembly

1 When the gingerbread is cool, cut a flat base for the house out of stiff cardboard that's about 2 inches wider and longer than the house itself. Using a narrow metal spatula or the back of a spoon, cover the cardboard base with a thick layer of icing (about 1/4 inch thick).

2 Take one of the side walls and insert it into the icing to form one side of the house. While someone holds that wall upright (we told you it was a family project), place the back wall perpendicular to it.

While holding them in place, place some icing along the joint where they meet. Smooth that over with a spatula so it serves as a "glue" to hold the two walls together. Don't be afraid to overdo it with icing because it will look like snow when you're finished. Repeat with other two walls. (See Figure 16-1.)

3 Build up snow drifts of icing around the house. (These drifts double as glue to hold up the walls of the house.)

4 Glue the two remaining rectangles, or the "roof," onto the top.

5 Add snow drifts to the front and sides of the house, using a narrow spatula or back of a spoon. Also add snow to the edges of the roof and the top.

6 While the icing is still wet and sticky, decorate the house with colored gum drops, jelly beans, and Life Savers.

How to Build a Gingerbread House

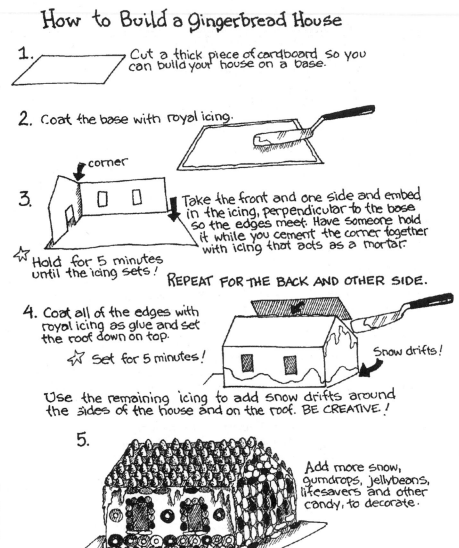

1. Cut a thick piece of cardboard so you can build your house on a base.

2. Coat the base with royal icing.

corner

3. Take the front and one side and embed in the icing, perpendicular to the base so the edges meet. Have someone hold it while you cement the corner together with icing that acts as a mortar.

☆ Hold for 5 minutes until the icing sets!

REPEAT FOR THE BACK AND OTHER SIDE.

4. Coat all of the edges with royal icing as glue and set the roof down on top.

☆ Set for 5 minutes!

Snow drifts!

Use the remaining icing to add snow drifts around the sides of the house and on the roof. BE CREATIVE!

5. Add more snow, gumdrops, jellybeans, lifesavers and other candy, to decorate.

Figure 16-1:
Building a
gingerbread
house.

ESSENTIAL SKILL

How to sift flour

Because flour tends to clump together, you need to pass it through a fine mesh to separate it. You can sift with either a regular wire mesh strainer or with a special sifter that has a rotating metal bar that breaks up the flour before it passes through the wire. (See Chapter 2 for more equipment information.)

✔ **With a strainer:** Hold a strainer over a bowl with one hand. Pour flour into the strainer. Shake the strainer back and forth, tapping with your free hand.

✔ **With a sifter:** Hold the sifter over a bowl. Add flour. Crank the handle, and the flour will pass through the mesh.

Pound cake solutions

Although pound cake may not be considered a holiday dessert, it's the basis for one of the most traditional holiday sweets, the fruit cake. A moist, firm homemade pound cake produces a great fruit cake.

The name *pound cake* (shown weighing in in Figure 16-2) comes from its simple composition: one pound of flour, one pound of sugar, one pound of eggs, and one pound of butter.

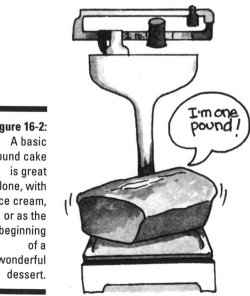

Figure 16-2: A basic pound cake is great alone, with ice cream, or as the beginning of a wonderful dessert.

I'm one pound!

Basic Pound Cake

Cake flour is especially important in this pound cake recipe (see photo) because the texture should be soft and melt in the mouth. You also can create a lovely citrus flavor in this pound cake by adding the zest of 1 orange and zest of 1 lemon to the batter during the last mixing.

Tools: *Strainer, electric mixer (optional), six 6 x 3 x 3-inch loaf pans (foil version available in supermarkets) or three 8-inch cake molds*

Preparation time: *20 minutes*

Baking time: *30 to 50 minutes, depending on size of loaf pan*

Yield: *Six 6 x 3 x 3-inch-wide mini-cakes or three 8-inch round cakes*

4 cups (16 ounces) cake flour	4$^1/_2$ cups (16 ounces) confectioners' sugar
$^1/_2$ teaspoon salt	1 vanilla bean, split lengthwise, or 1 teaspoon vanilla extract
2 teaspoons baking powder	
2 cups (4 sticks) butter	9 large eggs

1 Over a large bowl, sift together the flour, salt, and baking powder. Set aside.

2 Cream together the butter and sugar. (If mixing by hand, allow butter to soften more and stir the sugar and butter.) If using a vanilla bean, cut open to expose the flavorful seeds inside and add here. If vanilla extract is used, also add until the ingredients are well-blended.

Blending the sugar and butter is important because you don't want lumps of butter in the batter; the batter must be completely smooth. Any lumps will be difficult to remove later.

3 If you use an electric kitchen mixer, turn machine on low and slowly raise bowl to avoid making the flour fly about. Begin adding the eggs slowly, allowing them to drop in one by one. After all the eggs are in, stop the mixer and scrape down sides of bowl and then continue mixing until well blended.

If you're blending by hand, with a whisk, or with an electric handheld mixer, use room temperature butter. When the butter and sugar are smooth, switch to a wooden spoon to blend in the flour — the mixture gets very dense at this stage.

4 Pour batter into buttered loaf pans or the three 8-inch round cake molds.

5 Bake for about 30 minutes or until an inserted toothpick comes out clean.

Tea Cake

To paraphrase a line from Mark Twain, a fruit cake (or tea cake) is essentially a pound cake with a college education. In its simplest incarnation, tea cake is easy to make. Tea cake is based on the same principle as pound cake — a pound of sugar, a pound of flour, a pound of butter, and a pound of eggs. The difference is that tea cake includes lots of other goodies. In this recipe, for example, we add candied orange peel, candied lemon rind, cognac-steeped raisins, and candied cherries (recipes for which you can find in the following section). You can soak fruits in any liqueur you like, or in fruit juice or flavored teas to soften them (see photo).

Tools: *Sifter, electric mixer (optional), mini-loaf pans, three 8-inch pans, or two 8 x 4 x 5-inch loaf pans (foil version available in supermarket)*

Preparation time: *90 minutes, including preparation of the candied fruits*

Baking time: *30 to 60 minutes, depending on size of loaf pan*

Yield: *Six mini-loaves, three 8-inch loaves, or two 8 x 4 x 5-inch loaves*

4 cups (16 ounces) cake flour

2 teaspoons baking powder

2 cups butter (16 ounces or 4 sticks), room temperature

2 cups (8 ounces) confectioners' sugar

6 large eggs

1/2 teaspoon salt

1/4 cup (2 ounces) milk

1/2 cup (4 ounces) honey

1 vanilla bean, split lengthwise, or 1 teaspoon vanilla extract

1/2 cup (4 ounces) candied orange peel

1/2 cup (4 ounces) candied lemon peel

1/2 cup (2 ounces) cognac-steeped raisins and prunes

1/2 cup (4 ounces) candied cherries

1 Preheat oven to 375°.

2 Over a large bowl, sift together the flour and baking powder. (Use a sifter or a wire strainer.) Set aside.

3 Cream together the butter and sugar with an electric mixer. (If mixing by hand, allow butter to soften more and stir sugar and butter with a stiff whisk.) Scrape the bowl if batter sticks to the side. Be sure that no lumps are in the batter.

4 Add roughly half the eggs, and the salt, milk, honey, and vanilla to the bowl. Add the flour mixture. Mix well. Add remaining eggs and mix until smooth. With a mixer, mix for 5 minutes at low setting; if mixing by hand, mix about 5 minutes until very smooth. (Use room temperature butter if mixing by hand so that it's easier to work.)

5 Stir in the candied fruit, drained: orange peel, lemon peel, raisins, prunes, and cherries.

(continued)

6 Pour the batter into 6 buttered loaf pans about 6 x 3 x 3 inches. Bake for about 30 minutes. (If you're using a larger loaf pan, bake for 1 hour and then test with a toothpick. The 8-inch round pan needs to bake about 45 minutes.) Let the cakes rest in their loaf pans for 10 minutes before removing; pound cakes are very fragile and need time to solidify. After the cakes have solidified in the loaf pans, gently move the cakes to a rack to cool.

Strudels

This dessert, which comes from the snow-capped ski resorts of Austria, is a perfect warm finish to a hearty winter meal.

Strudels are sort of a renegade in the pastry world. Strudel dough is different from most other doughs because you encourage the development of gluten, which causes elasticity — in most pastries, you try to minimize gluten to keep them tender and light. But this dough gets its magical texture from its elasticity and thinness.

At its best, very thin strudel dough is flaky, but also firm to the bite. It's very different from puff pastry (see Chapter 4). To make a great strudel dough, you use high-gluten flour so that it becomes as flexible as possible. In the supermarket, buy bread flour or even all-purpose flour. Both have enough gluten, and we overwork the dough to make it more pliant.

The rolling and stretching technique is similar to that of pizza dough, but more exaggerated. Resting the dough between stretches is important, too, because it gives the glutens a chance to flex their muscles.

The absorption rate of water by flour varies according to flour types and the weather. In the following recipe, we call for approximately 1 cup (between 6 and 8 ounces) water, which should be fine, but you are the ultimate judge. You want a rubbery dough that is smooth and thin. If the dough is too wet, add a little flour. If it crumbles and breaks when you roll, add a little water.

The tricky part is when you stretch the strudel — you don't want to puncture it when it becomes paper thin. Remove all hand and wrist jewelry and turn rings stone side into palm when stretching. Use the back of fingers and hands to stretch it. And be sure to place the stretched dough over a dry towel on the table so that you can roll it up easily.

Cheese and Cherry Strudel

This barely see-through pastry is popular in Austria, Germany, and Eastern Europe (see photo). You can roll strudels around all sorts of delicious things — most commonly fruit, various sweet creams, and nuts.

Tools: *Plastic wrap, rolling pin, electric mixer (optional), pan, 14-inch baking sheet, parchment paper, pastry brush*

Preparation time: *45 minutes*

Baking time: *35 minutes*

Yield: *8 servings*

2 cups (8 ounces) plus 4 tablespoons flour

1 teaspoon salt

2 tablespoons salad oil

1 cup (8 ounces) warm water

2 cups (16 ounces) farmer cheese or ricotta

$1/2$ cup (3 ounces) sugar

$1/2$ cup (4 ounces) heavy cream

zest of 1 lemon, grated

3 eggs

2 cups (16 ounces) sour cherries, pitted, or 1 16-ounce can sour cherries, drained

2 tablespoons butter, melted

2 tablespoons confectioners' sugar

Strudel Dough

1 Place 2 cups (8 ounces) flour in a large bowl. Add the salt, oil, and water little by little, mixing constantly until a ball of dough has formed.

2 Continue kneading the dough and folding it over on itself, reshaping it until it becomes a smooth and elastic dough ball.

3 Continue working the dough in this manner for 5 minutes (to develop the elasticity).

4 Cover well in plastic wrap and refrigerate for 1 hour.

5 Remove from the refrigerator and roll out the dough on a floured surface as thin as possible.

6 Slide your hands under the dough and lift it gently, thus allowing the weight of the dough to stretch it out. You should hold the dough above the table and move it around on your hands so that each part of the circle of dough is stretched out as thinly as possible.

(continued)

7 When the dough reaches paper thinness, set it on a kitchen towel or on a flat surface.

Cheese Filling

1 Blend the cheese and ¹/₂ cup (3 ounces) sugar. Sift 4 tablespoons flour and whisk into the cheese mixture.

2 Add the heavy cream, lemon zest, and eggs. Beat well to combine.

3 Keep cool until needed.

Assembly

1 Preheat oven to 400°.

2 Lay a dry towel over a flat surface and sprinkle lightly with flour.

3 Stretch strudel dough and place on top of the towel and place a 3 ¹/₂-inch wide strip of the cheese filling on it. Sprinkle the cherries on top of the filling.

4 Roll the strudel by rolling the towel and pushing the strudel forward until the filling has 3 layers of strudel dough around it. At this point, you can cut off the edges of strudel, leaving only the thin layers of the center.

5 Line a baking sheet with parchment paper. Transfer the strudel to the baking sheet by lifting the four corners of the towel and gently slide the strudel onto the parchment paper.

6 Lightly brush the strudel with 2 tablespoons melted butter. Sprinkle with confectioners' sugar. Bake for 35 minutes or until the strudel becomes crispy and golden-brown.

Candied fruit

Our simple procedure for making candied fruit yields a far superior result to the store-bought version, whose flavors are dulled by preservatives. Home-made candied fruit is also more frugal because it uses citrus rinds that would normally be thrown away.

Candied fruit lasts a long time when refrigerated in its cooking syrup and can be used for many holiday recipes, including cookies, puddings, and sauces.

Instead of using liqueur, you also can use flavored teas to soak the fruit. Follow the same instructions in each recipe.

Candied Orange Slices

The technique for preparing candied lemon slices is exactly the same as for candied orange slices. You can use the slices as a garnish for almost any dessert.

Tools: *2 medium pots, slotted spoon*

Preparation time: *30 minutes*

Cooking time: *2 hours*

Yield: *1 cup (8 ounces)*

4 navel oranges or 6 lemons, sliced widthwise into ¹/₈-inch pieces.

3 cups (24 ounces) water

2 ¹/₂ cups (15 ounces) sugar

1 Bring a pot of water to a boil and drop in all the orange slices for about 30 seconds. Remove the slices with a slotted spoon and set aside for 3 minutes. Repeat the process with the same slices two more times, changing the water and bringing fresh water to a boil each time. This *blanching,* as it is called, removes the bitter acids from the peel.

2 In another pot, combine the water with the 2 cups (12 ounces) sugar. After the mixture begins to boil, lower the heat to simmer. Drop the orange slices in and simmer uncovered for
2 hours. Add more water as it evaporates.

3 Drain the orange slices into a bowl and let the slices cool. Discard cooking liquid.

4 Dredge the orange slices in the ¹/₂ cup (3 ounces) sugar and set on a platter for about 45 minutes to an hour. (*Dredging* means to drag through something, like flour or sugar, to coat lightly.)

Brandied Cherries

These sweetened and brandy-soaked cherries are made specifically for fruit cake batter. They can be made in advance and stored in a jar or covered container, refrigerated, for a week — much longer, and the cherries get too soft.

(continued)

Tools: *Large shallow pan*

Preparation time: *30 minutes*

Cooking time: *15 minutes*

Yield: *1 pound of cherries*

¹/₂ cup (4 ounces) water

¹/₄ cup (1¹/₂ ounces) sugar

*2 cups (16 ounces) pitted cherries —
half white, half sour, or Bing*

*1¹/₄ cups (10 ounces) brandy or cognac
(optional)*

1 In a large, shallow pan (a big fry pan will do), combine the water and sugar. Bring to a boil, lower the heat to simmer, and then add the cherries.

2 Simmer about 15 minutes. Drain well, sprinkle with brandy to taste, and allow to cool for 15 minutes.

Brandied Prunes and Raisins

Dried prunes and raisins are often associated with fruit cake and plum pudding, the ultimate Christmas desserts. Traditionally, these fruits were used in cakes because of their long shelf life.

For a variation, try soaking dried cranberries with Triple Sec or vodka; dried cherries with cognac or Chambord; or dried apricots in Grand Marnier.

Tools: *No special tools*

Preparation time: *10 minutes*

Cooking time: *30 minutes (plus 2 hours for fruit to marinate)*

Yield: *1¹/₂ cups (12 ounces)*

2 cups (16 ounces) water

¹/₂ cup (4 ounces) golden raisins

¹/₂ cup (4 ounces) dark raisins

*¹/₂ cup (4 ounces) pitted dried
prunes, chopped*

*²/₃ cup (5 ounces) brandy, rum,
Calvados, whisky, or tea*

1 Boil the water. Place the raisins in a bowl and the prunes in another bowl. Cover each bowl with boiling water and let sit for 5 minutes to soften the raisins and prunes.

2 Drain well and pack tightly in an airtight container. Cover the raisins and prunes with the liqueur, seal the container, and store in refrigerator for at least 2 hours.

Chocolate-Dipped Orange Slices

Here is something else you can do with candied orange slices. You can serve chocolate-dipped orange slices as a dessert garnish or as an after-dessert tidbit with coffee. You need to have made the Candied Orange Slices in the earlier recipe and have dried them overnight.

Tools: *Wax paper, double boiler or pot*

Preparation time: *30 minutes (not including the Candied Orange Slices)*

Baking time: *2 hours*

Yield: *8 servings*

Candied Orange Slices

4 ounces bittersweet chocolate (in block form), coarsely chopped.

1 Take the candied orange slices, drain, and set them out to dry on wax paper overnight.

2 Peel off the membrane and white pith, leaving just the fruit. Cut these fruit slices into strips.

3 In a double boiler or a pot set into a slightly larger pot holding very hot water (not boiling), add the chocolate, and let it melt.

4 Dip the candied orange strips halfway into the chocolate and lay out on wax paper in a cool place to dry (about half an hour).

Cookies: Surefire Favorites

Cookies are often the first homemade dessert attempted by home cooks. They're perfect for the holidays because they can be made in large batches and easily transported. Cookies also have a long shelf life when stored in an airtight container. And the variations are endless. Cookies also are good desserts to make with children.

Following are tips to remember when baking all types of cookies:

> ✔ **Parchment paper can be a substitute for buttering a cookie sheet.**
> Aside from being a cleaner way to cook, parchment paper also transfers heat well without sticking or catching fire.

✔ **When creaming butter or mixing batter in a mixer, stop occasionally and scrape the sides of the work bowl with a plastic spatula.** This process removes large lumps that cling to the sides.

✔ **Use a large melon baller — or an ice cream scoop for larger cookies — to form balls of dough.** Cold cookie dough is hard, so you need something strong to portion it — also, these scoops yield equal-sized cookies.

✔ **When grinding nuts in a food processor, always add 1 tablespoon confectioners' sugar per pound of nuts.** Adding confectioners' sugar minimizes the seepage of oil from the nuts, which can make batters heavy.

TOQUE TIP

When you remove dough from the refrigerator, whether a flat piece or a ball, always test the dough to see whether it's too cold to roll. Press the heel of your hand on the dough. If you don't make an indentation, the dough is still too cold to work with.

Anise Drop Cookies

Anise, the licorice-flavored seed associated with Mediterranean cooking, has been a vital element in dessert-making for centuries. The ancient Romans had a zeal for anise that was almost indecent. When Quintus Fabius Cunctator, a leading general, won a big battle, he traditionally gave his plebes hard candies flavored with anise. (His gesture was hardly magnanimous, considering many of the plebes were bleeding and missing limbs, but they were grateful for small favors.)

Today, anise is widely used in cakes and cookies. Anise drop cookies are so named because they supposedly can drop from a four-foot counter without breaking — but we have no source to verify this rumor.

When you make these cookies, you can place a raisin or two atop each cookie before baking. If you have an impish sense of humor — and you must if you bought this book — arrange the raisins so that the cookie resembles your most vain family member.

Tools: _Electric mixer (optional), sifter, parchment paper_

Preparation time: _30 minutes_

Baking time: _15 minutes_

Yield: _32 cookies_

¹/₂ cup (4 ounces or 1 stick) butter, cut into 8 pieces and left at room temperature

¹/₄ cup (2 ounces) molasses

1 cup (4 ounces) lightly packed brown sugar

1 egg

1 teaspoon grated ginger, or 1 teaspoon powdered ginger

1¹/₃ cups (5 ounces) cake flour, sifted

¹/₄ teaspoon salt

¹/₂ teaspoon baking powder

1 teaspoon cinnamon

¹/₂ teaspoon freshly grated nutmeg, or ¹/₂ teaspoon powdered nutmeg

pinch of ground clove

2 tablespoons Sambuca or other anise liqueur, or 1 tablespoon anise seeds

1 Preheat oven to 350°.

2 With an electric mixer, cream together the butter, molasses, and brown sugar. (If mixing by hand, allow butter to soften a bit more and then blend sugar and butter with a stiff whisk.) Scrape the bowl of the mixer if the batter sticks to the side. The batter should have no lumps.

3 Add the egg and grated ginger. Blend. Combine the dry ingredients — cake flour, salt, baking powder, cinnamon, nutmeg, and clove — and then sift into another bowl. Add the Sambuca and stir.

4 Line a cookie sheet with parchment paper. Use a tablespoon to scoop out a little less than a tablespoon of batter per cookie. Arrange in rows on the sheet, about 16 per sheet. (The cookies spread in the oven, so don't crowd them.) Repeat with another sheet. Bake both sheets for 15 minutes or until the edges turn slightly brown.

Chocolate Chip Cookies

The key to great chocolate cookies is using the best quality bittersweet chocolate that you can find — buy a block of chocolate and make your own chips. As far as texture goes, you have two schools of thought: the crunchy and the chewy. We tell you how to do both.

For extra flavor and a different texture, add different kinds of nuts, like almonds or pecans. Or use milk chocolate or white chocolate instead of bittersweet chocolate.

Tools: *Sifter, ice cream scoop (optional), parchment paper (optional)*

Preparation time: *30 minutes*

Baking time: *15 minutes*

Yield: *50 cookies*

(continued)

$1^1/_2$ cups (12 ounces or 3 sticks) butter, room temperature

$1^1/_4$ cups ($7^1/_2$ ounces) sugar

$1^1/_4$ cups (9 ounces) packed brown sugar

3 eggs

$^1/_3$ cup (3 ounces) milk

2 teaspoons vanilla extract (we break our rule here about always using beans for convenience)

$1^1/_2$ teaspoons salt

$1^1/_2$ teaspoons baking soda

5 cups (20 ounces) cake flour

1 pound bittersweet chocolate (block), cut up into small, chip-like pieces (they don't have to be uniform at this point)

1 cup (4 ounces) chopped walnuts

3 tablespoons molasses for chewy cookies (optional)

1 Preheat oven to 375°.

2 In a bowl, stir together the softened butter with white and brown sugars until creamy.

3 Add the eggs, milk, vanilla, and salt. Stir to combine.

4 In a bowl, sift together the baking soda and the cake flour. Add to the batter and stir well. When well blended, add the chopped chocolates and chopped nuts. (For chewy cookies, add the molasses here.)

5 Using an ice cream scoop, wooden spoon, or large metal spoon, scoop out a golf ball-sized portion onto a parchment-covered cookie sheet (or buttered sheet if you don't have parchment paper). Continue until all the dough is used. Leave about 4 inches between each cookie because they expand while cooking. You'll need 3 or 4 cookie sheets. If you don't have that many, bake them in batches.

6 Bake for about 12 to 15 minutes or until browned around the edges and dry in the center. (Bake less if you want a chewier consistency.)

Christmas Nut Cookies

The sweet, rich flavor of nuts makes for a memorable holiday cookie. And the cookies can be made inside of an hour — if you don't stop to sip eggnog along the way.

Tools: Food processor (optional), sifter, melon baller (optional), cookie sheet, plastic wrap

Preparation time: 20 to 30 minutes, plus 2 hours refrigeration

Baking time: 15 minutes

Yield: About 5 dozen cookies

8 ounces skinned sliced almonds

8 ounces chopped pecans

8 ounces chopped walnuts

3 cups (24 ounces or 6 sticks) butter, cut into tablespoon-size pieces, room temperature

1 cup (4 ounces) packed light

brown sugar

4 cups (16 ounces) cake flour

$^1/_2$ teaspoon salt

$^1/_2$-inch pat of butter, for greasing the cookie sheet

$1^1/_2$ tablespoons confectioners' sugar

1 Preheat oven to 350°.

2 In a food processor, grind the nuts to a coarse bread crumb consistency. (If you don't have a food processor, chop the nuts coarsely on a cutting board.)

3 With an electric mixer on low speed, cream the butter. Add the brown sugar and blend until smooth, scraping the bowl occasionally. (By hand or with a handheld mixer, place a large mixing bowl over another bowl filled with hot water. Combine butter and brown sugar and whisk or beat until smooth.)

4 Add the flour, salt, and nuts to the butter mixture. Blend briefly.

5 Remove from the bowl, cover in plastic wrap, and chill in the refrigerator for 2 hours. After the dough cools, coat your hands with a little flour and form the dough into small balls (the size of a chocolate truffle) or a large marble. Bake on a buttered cookie sheet or bake on parchment baking paper on cookie sheet at 350° for 12 minutes. The cookies should be browned around the edges and crumbly textured. Be careful when picking them up because they fall apart easily.

6 Remove cookie sheet from the oven and set on a flat surface. Sprinkle the cookies generously with confectioners' sugar. (You may want to shake the sugar through a strainer to distribute it more evenly.) A glaze forms on the cookies as heat from the cookies melts the sugar.

Christmas Cookies

This cookie recipe is simple and quick to make. Because the dough is like putty, kids can easily roll it out without tearing it. It also is easy to use with cookie cutters. And because these cookies are flat, they're well-suited to decorating.

(By the way, you can eat these cookies before Christmas, but if you do, your tree will look pretty lame!)

(continued)

Tools: *Rolling pin, cutter shapes, plastic wrap, parchment paper, pastry bag*

Preparation time: *45 minutes*

Baking time: *15 minutes*

Yield: *12 to 16 cookies, depending on size of cookie cutters*

$^1/_2$ cup (4 ounces or 1 stick) butter, cut into tablespoons, room temperature

2 $^3/_4$ cups (11 ounces) confectioners' sugar

$^1/_4$ cup (2 ounces) cold water

1 egg

zest of 1 orange

2 cups (8 ounces) cake flour

pinch of salt

1 egg white

2 teaspoons lemon juice

food coloring

1 Preheat the oven to 350°.

2 Cream the butter and $^3/_4$ cup (3 ounces) confectioners' sugar with a mixer or by hand until smooth. Add the water, egg, and the orange rind. Blend well. Add the flour and salt. Blend.

3 Spread the dough over a sheet of plastic wrap. The dough should be about an inch thick all around. Cover with another sheet and place in the freezer for 15 minutes. Meanwhile, make the icing. (See instructions for icing.)

4 On a floured surface, roll out the cookie dough ($^1/_4$ inch thick). Using cookie cutters or the rim of a glass, cut out cookies. Use something pointy, like a chopstick or a cocktail stirrer, to make a hole near the edge of the cookie so that you can run a string or a ribbon through it and hang it on a tree. Lay parchment paper over a baking sheet. With a flat spatula, place the cookie dough on the parchment. Bake for 12 minutes.

5 Remove from the oven and allow cookies to cool on a rack or a cool sheet pan.

Royal Icing

1 Combine the remaining 2 cups (8 ounces) confectioners' sugar, egg white, and 2 teaspoons lemon juice in a mixing bowl. Blend for a minute, scraping the beaters and the bowl. (Whisking takes about 10 minutes.)

2 Divide the icing into 3 different bowls and add food coloring of choice to each bowl.

3 Use a pastry bag with a pencil-point tip. Fill with colored icing and draw the icing on the cookie (see Figure 16-3).

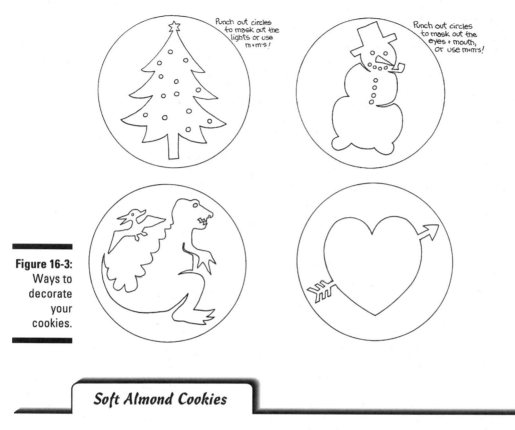

Punch out circles to mask out the lights or use m+m's!

Punch out circles to mask out the eyes + mouth, or use m+m's!

Figure 16-3:
Ways to
decorate
your
cookies.

Soft Almond Cookies

You can freshen up your holiday cookie selection with these fruit-topped almond cookies (see photo). They even add color to the Christmas cookie plate.

Tools: *Electric mixer (optional), sieve, cupcake pan or muffin tin*

Preparation time: *25 minutes*

Baking time: *15 minutes*

Yield: *24 small cookies*

$^1/_2$ *cup (3 ounces) honey*

$^1/_2$ *cup (3 ounces) sugar*

3 eggs

$^1/_2$ *cup (2 ounces) almonds, chopped fine*

$^1/_2$ *cup (4 ounces) yogurt*

$^1/_2$ *cup (4 ounces) melted butter*

2 teaspoons vanilla extract

$^1/_2$ *teaspoon baking powder*

2 cups (8 ounces) flour

2 tablespoons apricot jam

1 mango, sliced

2 cups (16 ounces) blueberries

(continued)

1 Preheat oven to 400°.

2 In a mixing bowl, mix the honey, sugar, eggs, and almonds.

3 Add the yogurt, melted butter, and vanilla to the honey mixture.

4 Sift the baking powder and flour together and add to the mixture.

5 Bake in a small cupcake pan or muffin tin for 12 minutes.

6 Remove the cookies from the pan or tin. Spread the apricot jam on top of the cookies. Add the mango slices and blueberries over the jam. Set the cookies upright on a plate and refrigerate for 15 minutes before serving.

Coconut Macaroons

Macaroons have two definitions: The American version is an almond-flour-and-egg-white cookie, flavored with shredded coconut. The French macaroon is usually almond flavored but has two halves and a center filled with buttercream or another flavored cream. We describe the easier-to-make American macaroons.

We like these American macaroons for their chewy texture and slightly crunchy coconut flavor. They're nothing more than a Swiss meringue (cooked egg whites and sugar) and shredded coconut. Stored in an airtight container at room temperature, they last about 10 days.

Swiss meringue, the second part of the recipe, is a special kind of meringue specifically used for coconut macaroons. This type of meringue, which is cooked, has more substance and thickness than the uncooked French-style meringue. You use this meringue when you want a more mouth-filling, luxurious dessert. This recipe has the addition of vanilla for extra flavor and an egg yolk (for color).

Tools: *Parchment paper*

Preparation time: *20 minutes*

Baking time: *15 minutes*

Yield: *About 50 cookies*

8 egg whites

1 cup (6 ounces) sugar

1 vanilla bean, split lengthwise, or 2 teaspoons vanilla extract

1 egg

2 tablespoons flour, sifted

2 cups (12 ounces) sweetened shredded coconut

1 tablespoon apricot or peach jam

1 Preheat oven to 375°.

2 To prepare the Swiss meringue, put the egg whites and sugar in a bowl and place over a pot of boiling water. Whisk until the mixture is thick and frothy and sticks to the whisk as it drops. This process takes about 10 to 15 minutes.

3 Add the vanilla and whisk well. (Use the meringue right away. Have all your other ingredients and tools ready to go.)

4 Add the egg, sifted flour, shredded coconut, and jam to the Swiss meringue. (Pass the jam through a sieve if chunky.) Stir well. Remove from heat and take out the vanilla bean.

5 Using a tablespoon and your finger dipped in hot water from time to time, arrange the batter in little cookie shapes on buttered parchment-lined baking sheets. (Use a dab of the batter to glue the parchment to the baking sheet.)

6 Bake for 15 minutes or until browned on the peaks and white around the edge. The macaroons should have a shiny, crusty surface.

WHAT IF?

On egg whites

You should keep certain tips in mind whenever you're using egg whites in a recipe.

✔ **Your work bowl must be obsessively clean.** If not, the egg whites won't whip correctly.

✔ **No yolks or other objects (nails, newspaper) should be in the whites.** Yolks in particular prevent the frothing of whites.

✔ **Egg whites should be at room temperature to achieve more volume when whipping up meringue.**

✔ **Older egg whites — a week or more in the refrigerator — froth up better than fresh ones.**

✔ **Use lemon juice or cream of tartar to get the best results when whipping.** Cream of tartar breaks down the whites and promotes the frothing. It also makes the airholes of the meringue smaller and thus the meringue has better body. Add these only after the whites have become a little frothy. For more tips on eggs and meringues, see Chapters 6 and 8.

Truffles

Don't confuse chocolate truffles with chocolate kisses, which is like comparing a Mercedes to a Honda Civic. The real chocolate truffle is dusted with cocoa powder so that it resembles its namesake, the glorious black truffle (a fungus) of Périgord in France. The real chocolate truffle is a multisensational treat.

Chocolate tends to burn if melted over boiling water. Use hot water from the tap or water that is short of simmering. (For more tips on working with chocolate, see Chapter 20.)

You can flavor your chocolate truffles with any number of liquors: rum, brandy, Cognac, eau-de-vie, Sambuca, or just about any flavored drink you like. We haven't tried martinis, so if you do, drop us a note.

Chocolate Truffles

These truffles, which make fabulous and elegant gifts, are made with nothing more than chocolate, heavy cream, butter, and the liqueur of your choice. After you master the technique for rolling them, you'll be the most popular party guest in the neighborhood.

If you want, you can omit the alcohol; if you do so, you don't need to substitute another liquid.

To see how these truffles turn out, check out the photos — you can see the normal chocolate truffles described here and chocolate truffles dressed up with chocolate shavings.

Tools: *Double boiler, medium pot, wax paper*

Preparation time: *1 hour 30 minutes*

Cooking time: *15 minutes*

Yield: *36 truffles*

12 ounces chopped bittersweet chocolate

1 cup (8 ounces) heavy cream

$^1/_4$ cup (2 ounces or $^1/_2$ stick) butter, softened but not melted, cut into tablespoon-size pieces

1 tablespoon Grand Marnier or another liqueur of choice

$^3/_4$ cup (3 ounces) cocoa powder

1 In a double boiler over hot (but not boiling) water, melt 8 ounces of the chocolate pieces, which takes about 15 minutes. Remove from heat. Meanwhile, in a separate pot, bring the cream to a boil.

2 Pour the boiled heavy cream into the chocolate bowl and stir with a wooden spoon, not a whisk. Let sit until the mixture is room temperature and smooth. Then add the soft butter and continue stirring until well blended.

3 Add the Grand Marnier or liqueur of your choice. Let the mixture sit at room temperature for 40 minutes or until chocolate becomes smooth and firm like frosting, stirring occasionally.

4 Using a pastry bag with a #5 tip, squeeze the mixture onto wax paper, making individual chocolate truffles — about the size of large candy kisses. Refrigerate for 30 minutes.

5 Remove the chocolates from the refrigerator and roll them one by one between your palms until they're roughly rounded.

6 Melt the remaining 4 ounces of chopped bittersweet chocolate over a double boiler and pour it into a large, wide bowl. Sift the cocoa powder into another bowl.

7 Use a fork to lift one of the chocolate truffles and dip it into the melted chocolate, rolling it all around. Remove the truffle with the fork and roll in the cocoa powder, coating it all over. Place on a baking sheet lined with wax paper. Chill for a minimum of 30 minutes.

Homemade pastry bag

What if you don't have a pastry bag? Flexibility is the hallmark of a creative cook. If you don't have a certain piece of equipment or an ingredient, don't give up too quickly. Use your ingenuity to solve the problem.

For example, if you're trying to make the Chocolate Truffles recipe in this section and you don't have a pastry bag, try the following steps:

1. **Fill a plastic sandwich bag or a food storage bag halfway with chocolate.**

2. **Twist the bag from the open top and force the soft chocolate into one corner of the bag.**

3. **Using sharp scissors, cut a small hole out of the tip — about the size of a pencil eraser.**

Voilà! Instant pastry bag.

Other Great Holiday Recipes

Great holiday recipes aren't limited to those listed in this chapter. Some recipes you may want to work up for the holidays include

- ✔ English Trifle (Chapter 11)
- ✔ Fallen Chocolate Soufflé, (Chapter 11)
- ✔ Lemon-Lime Charlotte with Mousse Filling (Chapter 10)
- ✔ Pineapple Upside-Down Cake (Chapter 11)
- ✔ Cherry and Pistachio Parfait (Chapter 13)
- ✔ Mamie Eisenhower Cheesecake with Graham Cracker Crust (Chapter 11)
- ✔ Mom's Apple Pie (Chapter 3)
- ✔ Traditional Bread Puddings (Chapter 7)

Chapter 17

Sweets without Sinning: Great Reduced-Fat Desserts

In This Chapter

▶ Have your cake and wear a bathing suit, too

▶ Creating miracles with angel food cake

▶ Quick frozen fruit desserts

▶ Making a lowfat dessert that looks high-fat

▶ How to give a rich dessert a healthful twist

▶ Making exhilarating fruit soups

▶ Creating lean and mean dessert crêpes

About ten years ago, we had a lunch interview with Malcolm Forbes at a midtown-Manhattan French restaurant called La Réserve. As expected, the ebullient publisher had endless opinions on every subject, from the economy of China to motorcycles to journalism and, yes, dessert.

When presenting the dessert menu, the waiter said, "We also have a lovely lowfat selection today made with seasonal fruits."

Mr. Forbes didn't miss a beat with his response: "You know," he replied, "lowfat dessert is sort of like being ten years old and getting clothes for Christmas."

Well, maybe Malcolm Forbes never had a *good* lowfat dessert — or he may have had a lowfat dessert that was so exceptionally good, he didn't realize that it was lowfat. In this chapter, you can find out how to create great desserts that are good for you. We introduce some simple techniques for making light, refreshing desserts in minutes. And we also show you how to make lowfat creations that look so enticing that they would please any publishing mogul at your table.

Miracles with Angel Food Cake

Angel food cake is a traditional American cake that is made with whipped egg whites (no egg yolks), sugar, and vanilla. The absence of egg yolks, which most cakes contain, makes it lowfat. Its fluffy texture is an excellent match for all kinds of fruit compotes, ice cream, and custards — although the latter two combinations, of course, would jack up anyone's cholesterol count.

Note that we use cake flour, not all-purpose flour, in our angel food cake recipe. Cake flour has a lower gluten content, which is desirable when you want to make a light, airy cake. (Gluten is a protein in flour that, when moistened, becomes elastic — for example, gluten makes certain breads chewy.) In fact, this angel food cake recipe is *so* light that you may want to run a string through the center and tie each end to a table leg to keep it from floating away like a hot-air balloon.

Is guilt part of the fun?

The travel writer and novelist Paul Theroux once said that anticipation is 50 percent of the pleasure in travel. In the same way, it could be said that guilt is 50 percent of the payoff in eating rich desserts. Doing something you shouldn't do — or at least that you believe you shouldn't do — could well have a delicious aftertaste all its own.

When we were putting together this chapter on guilt-free, lowfat desserts that don't taste like lowfat desserts, we started to worry about this phenomenon. "Where is the guilt factor?" we asked. "What if people don't like these desserts because they have nothing to feel guilty about?"

After a few days of hand wringing, we came up with a solution. The point here is that if you are eating guilt-free desserts and still want to feel guilty, here are some reasons you can feel guilty:

✔ Another year goes by, and you still haven't read a single Charles Dickens book.

✔ The health club officials mailed back your sneakers so that they could offer your locker to someone else.

✔ You still can't play the piano.

✔ That tin can you threw into the "organic only" recycling bag will remain in the earth, intact, for at least 100 years.

✔ You listen to the local public radio station every day on the way to work but have never once contributed to the annual fund drive.

✔ Your dinner guests last week praised your culinary prowess, even though you served store-bought spaghetti sauce.

Although you can use any high-sided ($2^1/_2$ inches high, minimum) cake mold to make angel food cake, the pan designed specifically for angel food has a tube in the center (see Chapter 2) that helps egg whites rise exceptionally high in the oven. The tube also gives angel food cake that characteristic doughnut shape.

Angel Food Cake with Orange Glaze

This recipe contains a great twist on conventional angel food cake: a glazing of fresh orange juice. We suggest that you serve this angel food cake with a plum compote (see following recipe and photo), but many other types of seasonal fruits and berries work fine, too.

The orange glaze can be used on all sorts of desserts, including pound cakes, tea cakes, sponge cake, muffins, and cupcakes.

Tools: *Copper bowl, electric mixer (optional), sifter, angel food cake pan, medium saucepan*

Preparation time: *25 minutes*

Baking time: *40 minutes*

Yield: *8 to 10 servings*

12 egg whites (absolutely clean, no spots of yolk)

$^1/_8$ teaspoon cream of tartar, if not using copper bowl

$1^1/_4$ cups ($7 ^1/_2$ ounces) sugar

$^3/_4$ cup (3 ounces) cake flour

zest of 1 navel orange

juice of 3 medium oranges (1 cup or 8 ounces)

3 tablespoons confectioners' sugar

Cake

1 Preheat oven to 400°.

2 In a very clean bowl (copper is best), whisk the egg whites, cream of tartar (not necessary if using copper bowl), and a pinch of the sugar. When the whites are getting fluffy (and reach about halfway up the bowl), gradually add the remaining sugar and whip until stiff peaks form.

3 Sift in the cake flour while folding with a spatula. Add the orange zest and continue folding.

4 Pour the batter into the angel food cake pan. Bake for 35 minutes.

(continued)

Orange Glaze

Place the orange juice and confectioners' sugar in a pot and bring to a boil, stirring occasionally. Pour over cake when hot.

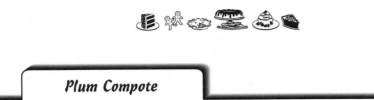

Plum Compote

This embarrassingly simple plum dessert can be an accompaniment to the angel food cake — adding a lovely color to the plate and a fresh, summery flavor. You can serve this compote with all sorts of cake, over ice cream, or even by itself with whipped cream.

Tools: *Heavy-bottomed pot*

Preparation time: *10 minutes*

Cooking time: *20 minutes (plus 1 hour refrigeration)*

Yield: *Enough for a 9-inch cake*

¹/₂ cup (3 ounces) sugar

¹/₂ cup (4 ounces) water

1 vanilla bean, split lengthwise, or 1 teaspoon vanilla extract

12 ripe medium to large plums, pits removed, quartered

1 In a pot, combine the sugar, water, and vanilla in a heavy-bottomed pot. Bring to a boil.

2 Place the plums in the pot (not aluminum — it may react with the acidity of the plums). Cook over low heat, stirring occasionally, until the fruits soften and break down — about 20 minutes. Remove from heat to cool. Refrigerate for an hour or more. Remove the vanilla bean before serving. Serve with the angel food cake.

Quick and Easy Fruit Ice (Granité)

Nothing's better on a summer day than a fresh fruit ice. You don't need an ice cream machine to make these ices (called *granités* in French), either. An ordinary kitchen blender can purée fruits just fine.

The flavorings you can add to fruit ices are endless — fresh mint, vanilla, cinnamon, fresh herbs, and the like. You can find additional recipes for granité in Chapter 12.

Quick No-Fat Calvados Ice (Granité)

This recipe calls for firm apples, specifically Granny Smith or Golden Delicious. You can even substitute pears. This ice is wonderful served over the Granny Smith Apple Gratin (see recipe later in this chapter).

In this recipe, we add a dash of Calvados, an apple-based brandy, which gives the ice an extra flavor boost.

To avoid the apples discoloring, don't let them sit out for more than 15 minutes after they're peeled.

Tools: *Blender or juicer, 8 x 10-inch baking sheet or 2 to 3 ice cube trays, medium pot*

Preparation time: *30 minutes*

Freezing time: *2 hours*

Yield: *8 to 10 servings*

4 tablespoons sugar

$^1/_2$ cup (4 ounces) water

4 medium apples peeled, cored, and quartered lengthwise just before using

1 500 mg vitamin C tablet, crushed

1 tablespoon apple brandy (optional)

1 In a medium pot, bring the sugar and water to a boil. Stir to dissolve the sugar. Remove from heat and let cool for 15 minutes.

2 In a blender, combine about $^2/_3$ of the sugar water, as much of the apples as you can fit into the blender, and the vitamin C. Purée well. Pour contents into a large mixing bowl and repeat the purée with the rest of the apples and sugar water. Transfer to the same bowl and stir.

3 Stir the apple brandy into the apple purée. Pour the purée into an 8 x 10-inch baking sheet with shallow sides or 2 or 3 ice cube trays (with dividers removed).

4 Freeze for 30 minutes. Remove from freezer and use a fork to scrape the frozen surface — if the ice is still mushy, return to the freezer until solid. (This breaks up the solid ice into little shards of ice, which is the proper texture for granite.) Continue scraping deeper and deeper until you get to the bottom. Return to freezer for another 30 minutes.

(continued)

5 Remove from freezer after 30 minutes and repeat scraping in Step 4. Then return to the freezer again and repeat Step 4 yet again. By now, the ice should be all shards of flavored ice that melt instantly on the tongue. Make sure that there are no big chunks of ice — if so, break them down into shards with a fork.

6 Serve in a chilled glass garnished with fresh mint, or atop a dessert such as the Granny Smith Apple Gratin (see recipe later in this chapter).

Apples: A Lowfat Gift from Nature

Apples seem custom-made for dessert-making. They have a crisp texture that you can use in many ways, they have lots of juice to make ices, they purée well, they make great fruit compotes — and they are ridiculously healthful.

In this chapter, we give you a triple whammy of apple desserts: a luxurious-looking (but lowfat) apple gratin, a cooling apple ice (see preceding section), and an addictive little garnish called apple chips.

Different apples have different flavors and texture, making certain varieties better for particular desserts. The recipes for apple gratin and apple chips call for a crisp, very fresh, firm apple that holds its shape and texture when cooked — Granny Smith, Golden Delicious, Matsuto, and Macintosh all work well.

Granny Smith Apple Gratin

This recipe may sound like a fancy restaurant dessert, but it's little more than apples grated and blended with egg whites and then popped under the broiler. We suggest serving with some Quick No-Fat Calvados Ice (see preceding recipe) on the side, and crispy Apple Chips (see following recipe).

Tools: *Grater*

Preparation time: *10 minutes*

Baking time: *10 minutes*

Yield: *6 to 8 servings*

10 medium Granny Smith apples,
peeled and cored

3 tablespoons confectioners' sugar

juice of 2 limes (2 tablespoons)

1 500 mg vitamin C tablet, crushed

1 vanilla bean, split lengthwise,
or 1 teaspoon vanilla extract

1 tablespoon flour

1 egg white

3 tablespoons granulated brown sugar

1 Grate the apples over the large holes of a hand grater into a bowl. Stir in the confectioners' sugar, lime juice, vitamin C, seeds from the inside of the split vanilla bean, flour, and egg white.

2 Pour the mixture into a towel and twist the towel at both ends. Twist hard to remove excess juice. Set aside.

3 Mold the grated apples into the size of small hamburger and place on a baking sheet — you should have about 8 portions. Sprinkle with brown sugar. Broil just until browned on top.

4 Remove from broiler and turn the oven down to 400°. When the oven reaches that temperature, return the patties to the oven and bake for 10 minutes.

5 Remove the warm gratin to a plate. You can serve the gratin with Quick No-Fat Calvados Ice (see recipe earlier in chapter) next to it and garnish with Apple Chips (see following recipe).

Crispy Apple Chips

These simple and healthful apple chips make great garnishes for all sorts of desserts. You can store the chips in an airtight plastic container or plastic wrap.

Tools: *Medium pot, mandoline (optional), parchment paper*

Preparation time: *20 minutes*

Baking time: *1 hour*

Yield: *About 40 chips*

4 tablespoons sugar

1 cup (8 ounces) water

2 medium Granny Smith apples

1 tablespoon fresh lemon juice

salad oil, for greasing parchment paper

(continued)

1 Preheat oven to 250°.

2 In a medium pot, combine the sugar and water. Bring to a boil, stirring occasionally. Set aside to cool to room temperature.

3 Core the apples as neatly as possible. Halve them lengthwise. Place each half, cut side down, on a cutting board. And, with a sharp, large knife, slice the apple as thinly as you can. (Or use a mandoline (optional) — see instructions in the "Using a mandoline" sidebar.) Discard the core and seeds.

4 Line a baking sheet with parchment paper. Brush the parchment paper with salad oil. Soak the apple slices in the sugar water for 10 minutes. Remove with a slotted spoon, drain, and place on the baking sheet. Bake the chips until crispy, about an hour.

Making Three Notoriously High-Fat Desserts Guilt-Free

Baked meringue with ice cream is a classic French dessert combination called *vacherin*. The classic version is a multi-layered concoction containing hazelnut ice cream, chocolate ganache (made with chocolate, butter, and cream), and sponge cake.

We've taken the concept of a vacherin — that is, a meringue-based layered dessert — and given it a lowfat twist. Instead of all that chocolate, butter, and ice cream, this recipe substitutes fresh mangoes and fruit sorbet. (You can make your own sorbet from Chapter 12 or buy a quality commercial one). The meringue gives the dessert crunch, and the fruits are wonderfully refreshing.

Using a mandoline

Be exceptionally careful when using a mandoline (see mandoline description in Chapter 2). Although a mandoline has a protective guard, you can still scrape or cut your finger.

1. Place the fruit on top of the mandoline. Slide it down the mandoline.

Make sure the mandoline is on the thinnest setting.

2. Run the fruit over the blade repeatedly.

The fruit slices fall below.

Meringue is based on egg whites, which have no fat. Of course, meringue requires sugar, so you have to take that. But if you're watching your saturated fat, the Baked Meringue with Fresh Mango Filling recipe is a dandy. (See Chapter 8 for more information on meringues.)

In humid weather, meringues may become sticky in the middle. After halving them, just scoop away the gummy interior with a dry spoon.

Baked Meringue with Fresh Mango Filling

The crunchy baked mango is a perfect base for the tropical mango flavor (papaya works just as well). In lowfat cooking, you can sometimes use texture as a substitute for richness — that is, the interesting texture of this dessert diverts one's thoughts from the ice cream that could have been in there.

The sweet and faintly citric filling is very easy to make. You also can substitute equal amounts of papaya, bananas, 2 cups (16 ounces) strawberries, or blueberries.

Try serving a scoop of your favorite sorbet next to each vacherin.

Tools: *Electric mixer (optional), parchment paper, serrated knife*

Preparation time: *30 minutes*

Baking time: *90 minutes*

Yield: *12 servings*

6 egg whites	*4 tablespoons brown sugar*
pinch of cream of tartar	*juice of 2 lemons (3 tablespoons)*
$1/_2$ cup (3 ounces) sugar	*1 pint fruit sorbet*
$1/_2$ cup (2 ounces) confectioners' sugar	
4 ripe mangoes, peeled, flesh cut away from the pit and cut into nickel-size pieces	

Baked Meringue

1 Preheat oven to 250°.

2 With an electric mixer or whisk, whip the egg whites and cream of tartar until frothy. Slowly add the sugar while whisking until smooth and full-bodied. Then increase mixing speed until stiff peaks form, creating a meringue.

3 Immediately scoop the meringue into a bowl and fold in the confectioners' sugar.

(continued)

4 Cover a baking sheet with parchment paper. Using a wet tablespoon, scoop out some meringue and place on the parchment paper — use the back of the spoon to mold the meringue into dome shapes. You should be able to form about 12 meringues.

5 Bake for 90 minutes. To test, remove one meringue and set out on the counter to cool slightly. When cool, it should be crispy, crunchy, and dry. If it's still gummy inside, bake the whole batch of meringues for another 20 minutes.

Mango Filling

In a bowl, toss the mangoes, brown sugar, and lemon juice.

Assembly

1 With a serrated knife, slice the meringues in half widthwise. Some of the brittle meringues may break. Save the pieces and reconstruct the meringue on the serving plate.

2 Place the bottom half of a meringue dome in the center of a serving plate. Scoop 2 tablespoons of mango filling on top. Scoop some fruit sorbet on top. (See Chapter 12 or buy commercial sorbet.) Place the top of the meringue dome on the sorbet. (If you have to reassemble the meringue pieces, just place them together where they cracked before adding the mango or sorbet. They will hold the cracked meringue in place.)

3 Repeat Steps 1 and 2 with remaining meringues.

Sweet Corn Crêpes

These sweet crêpes have dozens of uses. Serve with ice cream, fruit, dessert sauces like crème anglaise, or even sweet yogurt. We've used a half-and-half mix of corn flour, which gives this dessert an earthy texture, and cake flour, which keeps the crêpes exceptionally light. You can substitute cornmeal for the corn flour. These corn crêpes are ideal when served with the Baked Fruits with Vanilla and Rum (see Chapter 19).

Tools: *Sieve, 8-inch crêpe pan or 8-inch nonstick fry pan, pastry brush, ladle*

Preparation time: *30 minutes*

Cooking time: *30 minutes*

Yield: *About 20 crêpes*

¹/₂ cup (2 ounces) cake flour

¹/₂ cup (2 ounces) corn flour or cornmeal

6 tablespoons sugar

pinch of salt

1 cup (8 ounces) skim milk or soy milk

3 egg whites

3 tablespoons safflower or corn oil

zest of 1 lemon (1 tablespoon)

2 tablespoons Cointreau, an orange-flavored liqueur (optional)

vegetable oil, for greasing the pan

1 In a bowl, sift together the cake flour, corn flour, 3 tablespoons sugar, and salt.

2 While mixing (by hand with a whisk is best), slowly add the milk. Then whisk in the egg whites, followed by the safflower or corn oil. (If lumps appear in the batter, try to break them up with a whisk — if you can't, press the batter through a sieve with a rubber spatula.) When the batter is smooth, add the lemon zest and Cointreau (optional).

3 Prepare a crêpe pan or an 8-inch nonstick fry pan by brushing it with vegetable oil.

4 Heat the crêpe pan over medium setting for about a minute.

5 Ladle some batter onto the middle of the pan and immediately start swirling the pan to distribute the batter over the surface. All the while, keep the ladle over the center of the pan as the remaining batter pours out — you want the batter to always land in the center of the pan for even distribution. Pour the batter so that it's very thin on the pan. Remember to move the *pan,* not the ladle.

6 Cook the crêpe for about 30 seconds, or until it's brown around the edge and dry in the center. Using a thin spatula, flip the crêpe quickly and cook for about 15 seconds. Remove the crêpe to a warm plate. Sprinkle the crêpe with the remaining sugar.

7 Repeat Steps 5 and 6 with the remaining batter. Before dipping your ladle into the batter to make another crêpe, remember to stir up the corn flour that sinks to the bottom of the bowl. After the first few crêpes, you shouldn't have to add more oil to the pan. Be careful not to let the pan get too hot — it will sizzle too much, and the batter will cook immediately upon hitting the pan rather than swirl around.

Lowfat Cheese-Filled Phyllo Napoleon

Usually, any dessert involving phyllo and cheese is sure to derail your New Year's resolution to "eat lowfat." This recipe, however, makes a flaky and cheesy napoleon that won't bust your beltline. (Take a look at this dessert in the color section of this book.)

Tools: *Pastry brush, parchment paper, pizza cutter (optional), strainer*

Preparation time: *30 minutes*

Baking time: *20 minutes*

Yield: *4 servings*

1 package phyllo leaves	*1 packet unflavored gelatin*
2 tablespoons salad oil	*1 cup (8 ounces) lowfat yogurt*
2 tablespoons confectioners' sugar	*¹/₂ cup (3 ounces) sugar*
1 cup (8 ounces) ricotta cheese or fromage blanc	

1 Preheat oven to 325°.

2 Lay out 4 phyllo leaves. Brush the leaves with salad oil and sprinkle with confectioners' sugar. Lay one of the phyllo leaves on top of another one. Repeat with the other 2 leaves, pressing down lightly.

3 Line a cookie sheet with parchment paper. With a pizza cutter or paring knife, trim the edges of the phyllo sheets and cut the sheets into 4 x 4 x 4-inch triangles. (You should have 12 triangles.) Discard the edges. Place the triangles of phyllo leaves onto the cookie sheet and bake for 20 minutes until golden-brown. Set aside.

4 Push the ricotta cheese through the strainer and set aside.

5 Sprinkle gelatin over the yogurt and allow to set 5 minutes.

6 Warm the yogurt mixture with the sugar in a pan over low heat, stirring constantly until the gelatin dissolves.

7 While still warm, whisk into the ricotta mixture. Refrigerate for 30 minutes until firm.

Assembly

1 Place one of the phyllo triangles on a serving plate and spoon 2 tablespoons of the ricotta mixture on top. Place another phyllo triangle on top of the first triangle and repeat. Then place the third phyllo leaf on top to make a single serving and repeat with the other leaves. (You should have 4 phyllo stacks with cheese filling.) Serve with your favorite sorbet or baked fruit.

Slurp Your Dessert

Dessert soups are terrific light punctuations to any meal, particularly in warm weather. The basic technique for making rhubarb soup works for many fruits besides rhubarb. Always get the ripest fruit you can find. For extra flavor, we added star anise, an anise-flavored spice that's widely available in produce shops and gourmet groceries.

Star anise (the name comes from its star shape) is a member of the magnolia family and has a strong licorice flavor that comes from the seeds inside. In desserts, it's added to all kinds of boiled liquids, such as soups and syrups. You remove the star anise before serving.

Rhubarb-Vanilla Soup

You can substitute sliced peaches or nectarines for the rhubarb in this recipe — follow the same directions. Add a crushed vitamin C tablet to keep the colors vibrant.

You can garnish this soup with your favorite sorbet.

Tools: *Medium saucepan*

Preparation time: *30 minutes*

Cooking time: *10 minutes*

Yield: *10 servings*

4 cups (32 ounces) water

³/₄ cup (4¹/₂ ounces) sugar

1 vanilla bean, split lengthwise, or 1 teaspoon vanilla extract

2 ripe plums, halved and pitted

2 cups (16 ounces) cherries

2 star anise

juice of 1 lemon (2 tablespoons)

15 stalks rhubarb, cut into 1-inch-long strips (about 4 cups)

1 In a large pot, combine the water, sugar, vanilla bean, plums, cherries, star anise, and lemon juice. Bring to a boil. Reduce to simmer.

2 Add the rhubarb and simmer 5 minutes.

3 Remove from heat and chill.

Part VII
The Part of Tens

In this part . . .

So you left work at 5:45 p.m. and have six people coming over to dinner at 7? What do you do first? Cancel. But what if they don't answer? Just check out this part, where you can find good quick dessert ideas.

Moreover, we also give you some neat little tricks to turn an everyday dessert into a fantasy on a plate. Okay, how about something that looks a whole lot better than it did when you pulled it out of the fridge?

Chapter 18

Ten Ways to Make Your Dessert Creations Look Great

Diners devour great desserts with their eyes before picking up a fork. With just a little effort, you can make any dessert look magical. In this chapter we give you ten or so techniques to make your desserts shine.

Decorate Your Desserts with Writing

Make a cone with parchment paper, fill it with an icing, and then write happy birthday or any message on cakes and other desserts. You also can make stars or other decorative patterns.

To make the cone, simply cut a triangular sheet of parchment, fold it in two, and then bring the three corners together to form a cone (see Figure 18-1).

If you want, you can fill the cone with melted chocolate for inscription writing:

1. **Melt 3 ounces bittersweet chocolate over low heat.**

   (Make sure that no water gets in the chocolate.)

2. **Pour the chocolate into the cone, filling it halfway.**

3. **Close the back of the cone by folding the top flaps several times.**

4. **Snip the pointed tip of the cone to allow the chocolate to ooze out (just a tiny bit from the tip to make a pencil-point hole).**

5. **Use the cone as a writing pen.**

   Write an inscription or just make zigzag patterns across the dessert plate for a jazzy look.

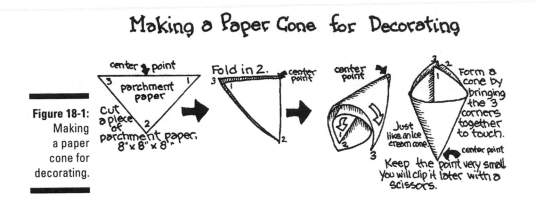

Figure 18-1:
Making
a paper
cone for
decorating.

You can also write on white chocolate. Melt 4 ounces white chocolate and 2 tablespoons confectioners' sugar. Using a thin metal spatula, spread the chocolate evenly over a sheet of parchment paper and place it in the refrigerator until it sets. Peel the chocolate off the parchment and use it as a sheet for writing messages with melted dark chocolate and a parchment cone. (See previous steps for parchment assembly and chocolate sauce.)

Frost Your Cookies with Royal Icing

Royal icing, a versatile creation, is a mixture of $2\frac{1}{4}$ cups (9 ounces) confectioners' sugar and 2 egg whites. You can ice cookies with this frosting or put it into a parchment cone to write (see preceding section). For the Royal Icing recipe, see Chapter 16.

Make Shapes with Cookie Patterns

Use the cookie patterns in Chapter 16 to cut out decorative shapes (or make your own). To make a design on your dessert or dessert plate, simply place the stencil on it and then sprinkle confectioners' sugar or cocoa over the stencil.

Top Off Your Desserts with Chocolate Curls

You can sprinkle fluffy chocolate curls over a piece of cake or on a plate. Simply set a slab of chocolate on a table or counter, placing one end against a wall. Using a large, sharp knife, scrape, away from you, across the top, to form chocolate curls. Be careful when pressing the knife firmly across the surface of the chocolate.

Or, if you want to get really fancy, using a razor knife, cut thin sheets of plastic into leaf shapes (trace over real leaves, if you want) and paint over the stencils with melted bittersweet chocolate. Refrigerate. When cool, peel off the leaf stencils to make chocolate leaf shapes for the top of your cake or dessert plate.

Grow Caramel Flowers

If you have extra caramel from one of the recipes, pour it right from the warming pot onto a piece of aluminum foil to imitate flower patterns or random abstract shapes and lines. The caramel hardens when you leave it on the kitchen counter to cool. You can lay the caramel decorations on a plate or stand them upright in ice cream.

Make Puff Pastry Twists

If you have some leftover puff pastry dough (see Chapter 3), cut it into strips 1 inch wide and 6 inches long. Generously sprinkle the strips with confectioners' sugar and then twist them into candy cane shapes. Bake at 400° for 10 minutes.

You can use the puff pastry twists to decorate dessert plates or to place on top of cakes.

Frost Your Cake with Italian Meringue

Make the Italian meringue from the recipe in Chapter 8 and use it as a frosting for your cake. Then sift confectioners' sugar over the top and pass it under a hot broiler for 30 seconds until it develops a golden-brown crust.

Frost Your Fruits

Take small fruits, such as raspberries, red currants, blueberries, gooseberries, grapes, or strawberries, and wash them. Dry well with paper towels. Whisk 2 egg whites in a bowl for 2 minutes or until frothy, dip the fruits into the whites with a slotted spoon, and transfer to aluminum foil to let the excess egg whites drain off. Then sprinkle 2 tablespoons sugar over a plate. Roll the fruits — the sugar will adhere.

Shake off the excess sugar and set aside on a cake cooling rack or plate to dry. This quick frosting lasts, refrigerated, for up to ten hours. Garnish any dessert with these frosted fruits.

Decorate with Caramel

When you're feeling really confident, try these special techniques to jazz up your desserts. Both use caramel to make your desserts extra special.

Angel Hair Spun Sugar

This has to be one of the craziest recipes in this book. Keep in mind that making angel hair out of spun sugar isn't the kind of thing you do while waiting for the laundry to dry. Although the recipe takes uninterrupted concentration and patience, we offer it just in case you really want to show off.

Tools: Medium pot, cardboard or newspaper, parchment paper or aluminum foil

Preparation time: 15 minutes

Cooking time: 10 minutes

Yield: 6 to 8 servings

3 cups (18 ounces) sugar   3 tablespoons corn syrup

juice of ¹/₂ large lemon (2 tablespoons)

1 Place all ingredients in a pot over high heat. Bring to a boil. Place the candy thermometer in the pot. Continue boiling until the liquid reaches exactly 340°.

2 While the caramel is heating, stir occasionally. (You don't want to whip the caramel — that is, lift it up out of the pan and drop it back down — because doing so incorporates air into it.) When the caramel mixture becomes brownish and liquid, do not stir it any more. Instead, rotate the pot to move the melted sugar around rather than stir it.

3 As soon as the caramel reaches 340°, remove from heat and dip the bottom of the pot into a bowl of cold water to cool it. (Make sure that absolutely no water touches the caramel because that can cause dangerous splatters.)

Warning: Sugar burns at 340°. Make sure that this scalding substance doesn't touch your skin.

4 Place 2 large metal bowls about a foot apart (place cardboard or newspapers between the 2 bowls). Take 3 forks in 1 hand and dip the tines into the caramel mixture (see Figure 18-2).

5 Test the caramel's consistency by lifting the forks and rapidly waving them side to side over some newspaper to see whether that creates thin strands, like angel hair. If the strands are thin and stretch out very long (a foot or more), you can begin. Don't worry if some of the caramel sticks to the newspaper because you only want the dangling angel hair that doesn't touch the ground.

6 Wave the forks back and forth over the bowls. Strands of sugar, called angel hair, should stick to the tops of each bowl and dangle between the 2. When you have a good sized batch of angel hair, reach under the middle of the stands and remove them (they cool quickly) and set batches of them aside in clusters, about the size of a baseball, on parchment paper or aluminum foil.

7 Repeat Steps 4 through 6.

8 If you have leftover caramel, reheat it to a runny consistency and pour it over parchment paper to form various shaped candies: trees, houses, dogs, Ford Explorers, or whatever.

Figure 18-2:
Creating
decorative
angel hair
spun sugar.

Edible Caramel Plate

For a dessert that's truly good to the last bite, use caramel to make an edible plate.

Tools: *Medium pot, cake mold*

Preparation time: *15 minutes*

Cooking time: *10 minutes*

Yield: *6 to 8 servings*

2 tablespoons salad oil

3 cups (18 ounces) sugar

juice of ¹/₂ large lemon (2 tablespoons)

3 tablespoons corn syrup

1 Use the salad oil to grease the cake mold.

2 Place remaining ingredients in a pot over high heat. Bring to a boil. Place the candy thermo-meter in the pot. Continue boiling until the liquid reaches exactly 340°.

3 While the caramel is heating, stir occasionally. When the caramel mixture becomes brownish and liquid, do not stir it any more. Instead, rotate the pot to move the melted sugar around rather than stir it.

4 As soon as the caramel reaches 340°, remove from heat and dip the bottom of the pot into a bowl of cold water to cool it.

Chapter 19

Ten Desserts You Can Make in 30 Minutes or Less

T his chapter is devoted to those home cooks who are always pressed for time — who isn't? These near-instant treats use just a few ingredients and require just a little preparation time.

Baked Fruits with Vanilla and Rum

You make this quick recipe in an aluminum foil packet. When you open the packets at the table, the aromas of fruits and vanilla fill the room.

You use 6 different fruits, in any combination you like: apples, pears, plums, apricots, bananas, pineapples, mangoes, papayas, cherries, or any kind of berries.

Tools: *Two 12 x 24-inch sheets of aluminum foil*

Preparation time: *10 minutes*

Baking time: *20 minutes*

Yield: *6 servings*

6 different ripe fruits (2 cups — 16 ounces — of each, washed and stems removed)

2 tablespoons sugar

2 tablespoons rum, or 2 tablespoons orange juice

1 vanilla bean, split lengthwise, or 1 teaspoon vanilla extract

(continued)

1 Preheat oven to 400°.

2 Core the fruits and cut lengthwise into about 2-inch thick pieces. Place on a double sheet of aluminum foil measuring 12 x 24 inches.

3 Sprinkle the fruits with the sugar and rum. Add the vanilla bean (or sprinkle the vanilla extract over the fruit).

4 Enclose the fruit tightly in aluminum foil. Bake for 20 minutes. Open the foil at the table and then transfer the fruit to dessert plates (leave vanilla bean on the foil). Serve with ice cream.

Bananas Foster

What a terrific way to elevate the humble banana to an eye-popping desssert. This recipe is a classic tropical dessert that restaurants often prepare tableside. We recommend baby bananas for this recipe because of their size and flavor. You can substitute other liqueurs for the rum.

Tools: *8-inch skillet*

Preparation time: *10 minutes*

Cooking time: *15 minutes*

Yield: *5 servings*

³/₄ cup (4 ¹/₂ ounces) sugar

juice of 1 lemon (1 tablespoon)

¹/₄ cup (2 ounces or ¹/₂ stick) butter

¹/₄ cup (2 ounces) rum

¹/₄ cup (2 ounces) water

5 whole ripe bananas, halved

1 Place the sugar in a skillet with the lemon juice and heat until it turns into a brown caramel (about 5 minutes). Add the butter slowly and stir. Then add the rum and water. Stir together and bring to a boil. When the mixture boils, add the banana halves.

2 Reduce to medium heat and cook for 1 minute. Immediately spoon onto the serving platter. Serve hot with vanilla ice cream.

Strawberries Marinated in Red Wine with Mint

This easy marinade provides its own sauce of a vivid crimson color. A pale-colored plate shows off the contrast in colors. The dry red wine adds a lovely tart edge that is counterbalanced by the mint and sugar.

Tools: *Pot*

Preparation time: *10 minutes*

Cooking time: *10 minutes (plus 2 hours refrigeration)*

Yield: *4 servings*

2 cups (16 ounces) dry red wine

$^1/_2$ cup (3 ounces) sugar

10 to 12 fresh mint leaves, maximum

length $^1/_2$ inch

2 cups (16 ounces) ripe strawberries, hulled and washed

1 In a pot, bring to a boil the red wine, sugar, and mint leaves. Remove from heat and let sit 15 minutes to cool.

2 Slice the strawberries and add to the chilled wine mixture. Cover and marinate, refrigerated, for 2 hours. Serve chilled with either cookies, ice cream, or sorbet.

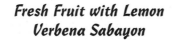

Fresh Fruit with Lemon Verbena Sabayon

Lemon verbena is a sweet, lemon herb found in some supermarket produce sections, farmers' markets, and specialty food shops.

For a variation, place the berries in an ovenproof baking dish (4 inches in diameter). Spoon the sabayon sauce over the berries. Glaze under a broiler for 30 seconds or until the sabayon sauce turns golden-brown. (Optional: Garnish with ice cream or sorbet.)

Tools: *Medium pot*

Preparation time: *10 minutes*

Cooking time: *10 minutes*

Yield: *4 servings*

(continued)

5 egg yolks

$^1/_3$ cup (2 ounces) sugar

$^1/_2$ cup (4 ounces) white wine or orange juice

6 or 7 fresh lemon verbena leaves, maximum length 1 inch

2 cups (16 ounces) fresh blueberries or raspberries, washed and stems removed

1 Boil a pot of water.

2 Place a mixing bowl over the pot holding boiling water. Place all ingredients, except the berries, in the bowl. Immediately begin whisking, continuing until the mixture is yellow, frothy, and thickened (about 5 minutes).

3 Place the berries in a dessert bowl. Spoon the warm sabayon sauce over the top. Serve immediately.

Jamaican Pineapple Fruit Soup

After you taste this soup, you'll never throw away pineapple skins again. You can serve this soup with your favorite sorbet (see Chapter 12) and a pound cake (see Chapter 16).

Tools: *Medium pot, sieve*

Preparation time: *10 minutes*

Cooking time: *20 minutes*

Yield: *10 to 12 servings*

1 pineapple, skin removed (washed and reserved)

2 cups (16 ounces) water

$^3/_4$ cup (4 $^1/_2$ ounces) sugar

12 mint leaves

ice cubes, enough for a bowl

1 apple (Granny Smith or Golden Delicious)

1 pear (Bartlett, Anjou, or Bosc)

1 banana

2 cups (16 ounces) raspberries

2 cups (16 ounces) blueberries

1 Skin the pineapple, reserving skin (see Chapter 5). Quarter the pineapple from top to bottom, leaving core exposed. Cut off the hard central core. Discard core but save the ripe pineapple. Cut the pineapple skin into 4-inch squares. Place the skin in a pot with the water, sugar, and mint leaves. Bring to a boil, reduce to simmer, and cook for 5 minutes. Remove from heat, cover, and place the pot in a bowl filled with ice for 45 minutes. When chilled, strain into a soup tureen or big bowl.

(continued)

2 Cut the pineapple flesh into 1-inch cubes. Peel and core the apple and pear and cut into the same-sized cubes. Cut the banana into 8 pieces. Add all to the soup. Wash the berries and add to the soup. Refrigerate for 1 hour. Serve chilled.

Instant Chocolate Mousse

Even though it's quick, this chocolate mousse has a terrific, smooth texture. Be sure to keep the whipped cream soft and the melted chocolate very warm to the touch.

Tools: *Double boiler (optional)*

Preparation time: *15 minutes*

Cooking time: *5 minutes*

Yield: *8 servings*

4 cups (32 ounces) heavy cream, very cold	*10 ounces bittersweet chocolate, cut into small cubes*

1 In a bowl, whip the cream to very soft peaks. (Keep the cream loose, but not liquid.) Refrigerate.

2 Place the chocolate in a pot and place the pot over a slightly larger pot holding very hot (but not boiling) water. Melt the chocolate while stirring. While the chocolate is very warm, whisk it rapidly into the whipped cream to make an instant chocolate mousse. (The chocolate needs to be warm to the touch so that it doesn't get stiff when it hits the cold whipped cream.) Serve immediately.

10-Minute Strawberry Chiffon Mousse

This recipe works best with fresh summer strawberries, but you can make it year-round.

Tools: *No special tools*

Preparation time: *10 minutes*

Baking time: *10 minutes*

Yield: *6 to 8 servings*

(continued)

¹/₂ cup (2 ounces) sliced almonds

2 cups (16 ounces) heavy cream, very cold

2 cups (16 ounces) strawberries, washed, hulled, and cut into ¹/₄ -inch cubes

4 tablespoons rock sugar or 12 sugar cubes

1 Preheat oven to 350°.

2 Place the sliced almonds on an unbuttered cookie sheet and bake 10 minutes or until golden-brown. Cool to room temperature.

3 In a bowl, whip the cream until it forms stiff peaks and gently fold the strawberries and sugar into it. (Do not overmix the cream, or it will get too watery.) Sprinkle the browned almond slices over the top and serve immediately.

Tapioca Whipped Cream

Tapioca gives this whipped cream an interesting texture. You also can add the following items to the milk to make this a dessert for grown-ups: 1 cinnamon stick, ¹/₄ cup (1 ounce) coconut, or ¹/₄ teaspoon saffron.

Tools: *Medium pot*

Preparation time: *10 minutes*

Cooking time: *15 minutes*

Yield: *4 to 6 servings*

1 tablespoon tapioca (quick cooking)

2 cups (16 ounces) milk

2 tablespoons sugar

2 eggs

1 vanilla bean, split lengthwise, or 1 teaspoon vanilla extract

1 cup (8 ounces) heavy cream, whipped

1 In a pot, soak the tapioca in milk (and any of the optional flavorings) for 5 minutes. Add the sugar, eggs, and vanilla bean to the pot.

2 Place on medium heat and stir constantly for about 5 minutes. Reduce to simmer and cook, stirring, until slightly thickened. Remove from heat and cool to room temperature.

3 Remove the vanilla bean, fold the whipped cream into the tapioca, and serve chilled. Garnish with your favorite seasonal fruits.

Quick Dessert Pancake

Based on a regional dessert from Brittany, France, this dessert is one you can prepare for surprise guests in winter time. This pancake puffs up as it comes out of the oven so try to bring it to the table as soon as possible.

Tools: *9-inch cake pan*

Preparation time: *10 minutes*

Baking time: *30 minutes*

Yield: *6 servings*

¹/₂-pat of butter, for greasing the cake mold

¹/₂ cup (2 ounces) flour

¹/₂ cup (3 ounces) sugar

¹/₂ teaspoon baking powder

5 eggs

2 cups (16 ounces) warm milk

1 tablespoon rum

1 teaspoon vanilla extract

1 cup (4 ounces) raisins, dried prunes, dried apricots, or dried pears (or any combination), chopped into dime-size pieces

1 Preheat oven to 400°. Grease the cake pan with the butter.

2 In a bowl, whisk together the flour, sugar, baking powder, and eggs. Slowly pour in the warm milk while stirring. Then add the rum and vanilla extract.

3 Gently fold in the dried fruit. Slowly pour into the cake pan. Bake for 25 minutes or until golden-brown. Serve immediately in the pan in which it was cooked (so that it doesn't collapse) with your favorite ice cream.

Chapter 20

Ten Things You May Want to Know about Chocolate

. . . .

. . . .

*I*n this chapter, we cover ten or so things that you may want to know when working with chocolate.

What Exactly Is Chocolate, Anyway?

Knowing just exactly what chocolate is can be helpful. The cacao tree is one of the oldest plants on earth, and it grows its seed pods on the trunk of the tree. Inside these pods, which vary in color from an almost fluorescent red to vibrant green, are the seeds that become the cocoa beans and eventually chocolate.

The beans are harvested and then fermented like wine, which improves their flavor. They're then set in the sun to dry; this process is called *curing*. The beans are roasted when they arrive at the chocolate factory, and then they're crushed into a paste. The two elements of this paste are cocoa butter and chocolate liquor.

The word *liquor* here doesn't refer to any alcohol content (the paste has none), but is merely the term for the thick brown paste. This paste is then recombined with the cocoa butter along with vanilla and lecithin for stability in a long mixing process called *conching*. Milk chocolate is made by adding milk powder to this mixture.

Use Good Quality Chocolate

When you use a good quality chocolate, you end up using less of it to achieve a rich flavor — so in the end, quality chocolate doesn't cost any more than the cheaper brands.

Good quality chocolate is sold in bar form and is usually divided into easily breakable sections, which make measuring easy because most chocolate recipes are given in ounces. You just divide the ounces by the number of segments the chocolate bar has and that gives you the weight of each segment.

Bar chocolate melts to a smoother texture than morsels. Morsels have an ingredient that prevents them from melting because they're primarily used for chocolate chip cookies.

Melt Chocolate with Another Ingredient

If you're blending chocolate with other ingredients, the recipe may ask you to melt the chocolate with butter or another ingredient. That way, the chocolate is more easily combined because it's already diluted during the melting process. For example, whipped cream added to melted chocolate cools the chocolate immediately. The cream's cold temperature makes the melted chocolate firm up into block chocolate.

Make Brownies to Enjoy Chocolate at Its Best

What's the best way to enjoy chocolate? There are many, but brownies must be one of the best.

Chocolate Brownies

This recipe is our favorite for chocolate brownies.

Tools: *9 x 12-inch baking dish, electric mixer (optional)*

Preparation time: *20 minutes*

Baking time: *30 minutes*

Yield: *12 brownies, 3 x 3 inches each*

(continued)

¹/₂-inch pat of butter, for greasing the baking dish

8 ounces bittersweet dark chocolate, chopped into small, dime-size pieces

³/₄ cup (6 ounces or 1¹/₂ sticks) butter

4 eggs

2³/₄ cups (16¹/₂ ounces) sugar

1 vanilla bean, split lengthwise, or 1 teaspoon vanilla extract

¹/₂ teaspoon salt

1¹/₂ cups (6 ounces) flour

1¹/₂ cups (6 ounces) walnuts or pecans, chopped

1 Preheat oven to 350°. Grease a 9 x 12-inch baking dish.

2 Set aside ¹/₃ of the chocolate pieces and place the other ²/₃ of the chocolate and all the butter into a metal bowl. Place the metal bowl over another bowl of very hot tap water to melt. Set aside and keep warm.

3 Place the eggs, sugar, vanilla, and salt in a mixing bowl and beat until frothy.

4 Stir in the melted chocolate mixture and then gently fold in the flour, nuts, and remaining chocolate pieces until well blended.

5 Pour into a baking dish and spread evenly. Bake for 30 minutes. The center should still be soft.

6 Remove from oven and let cool for 1 hour. Cut into 3 x 3-inch pieces.

Tempering Chocolate

The word *tempering* is often used when talking about melted chocolate. When chocolate is melted, the cocoa paste and cocoa butter separate again (like oil and water). If the chocolate is to be used in its pure state, it must be *tempered,* or brought back to its well-blended condition (like when it's purchased in a block).

Tempering is done by bringing the melted chocolate up to a specific temperature (120°), lowering it (to 80°), and then raising it by two more degrees. Whew!!! (If you want to try it, a chocolate thermometer is helpful.)

You then can spread the tempered chocolate onto a piece of wax paper and refrigerate it. You end up with a giant sheet of thin brittle chocolate, which you can use to decorate your cakes.

Storing Chocolate

Storing chocolate is a no-brainer. Keep it well wrapped in a cool, dry place — not the fridge — and it will keep for months.

Chocolate sometimes develops a white color on the outside of the bar after long periods. The white color is the cocoa butter that becomes visible on the surface of the chocolate. Don't worry if that happens — just melt the chocolate and remix it together.

A Chocolate Favorite for a Cold Day

Chocolate is a perfect cold-weather pick-me-up. Hot chocolate can even be a dessert in itself.

Quick Hot Chocolate

Try this quick hot chocolate. For a change of pace, try these optional flavorings: 1 orange rind, 3 sprigs of mint, or 1 tablespoon ground coffee.

Tools: *Pot, strainer*

Preparation time: *5 minutes*

Cooking time: *5 minutes*

Yield: *2 servings*

¹/₂ cup (4 ounces) milk

¹/₂ cup (4 ounces) heavy cream

2 ounces bittersweet chocolate, chopped into dime-size pieces

1 tablespoon whipped cream

1 Boil the milk and heavy cream together and remove from heat. Add the optional flavorings, if desired, and cover the pot. Allow to steep for 3 minutes.

2 If using the optional flavorings, strain from milk. Pour the still hot milk mixture over the chocolate pieces. Stir until the chocolate pieces are melted and serve hot with a tablespoon of whipped cream on top.

Chopping Chocolate

The best way to chop chocolate is with a large serrated chef's knife. This type of knife breaks the chocolate into small pieces and makes the melting process quicker and easier. Less heat is required to melt the small pieces, and thus you don't take the risk of burning them.

Don't Boil Chocolate

Never boil chocolate or let it go over 140°. The chocolate scorches and becomes grainy and bitter.

Cleaning Up Chocolate

Don't worry, it's not you — chocolate is always messy. To clean up chocolate, allow the chocolate to cool and harden. Then scrape the chocolate off counters and bowls with a spatula. Use a towel soaked in very hot water to finish wiping up the counters.

Decorating with Chocolate

Try using pure melted chocolate to decorate a plate or write an inscription such as "Happy Birthday" or "Congratulations." (See Chapter 18 for instructions.) Be sure to practice on another plate or piece of paper first. When you're comfortable, you can put your decoration on the finished cake or dessert. Remember, you only get one chance, so plan your spacing well.

More Chocolate Recipes to Try

Following are two delicious chocolate recipes that can pick up your spirits on any occasions.

Chocolate Tart

This small chocolate tart gives more bang for the buck than most chocolate desserts. It's compact and dense, yet smooth and creamy.

Tools: *Plastic wrap, pot, rolling pin, tart ring*

Preparation time: *30 minutes*

Baking time: *15 minutes*

Yield: *9-inch tart*

1 ³/₄ cups (7 ounces) flour

³/₄ cup (6 ounces or 1¹/₂ sticks) butter, room temperature

¹/₂ cup (2 ounces) confectioners' sugar

¹/₄ cup (1 ounce) cocoa powder

2 eggs

12 ounces bittersweet chocolate, chopped into dime-size pieces

2 cups (16 ounces) heavy cream

¹/₂-inch pat of butter, for greasing the cookie sheet

¹/₂ cup sliced blanched almonds

Tart Dough

1 Preheat oven to 400°.

2 Mix the flour and butter in a bowl. Add the confectioners' sugar and cocoa. Mix well. Add the eggs and squeeze the ingredients by hand in the bowl until a smooth paste forms.

3 Spread the mixture out 1 inch thick on plastic wrap. Cover and refrigerate at least 30 minutes. While the tart dough is chilling, prepare the filling.

Filling

1 Place the chocolate in a bowl.

2 Place the heavy cream in a pot and bring to a boil. Slowly pour the hot cream over the chocolate while stirring with a whisk until chocolate is completely melted. Set aside at room temperature, covered, until ready to use.

Assembly

1 Remove the chilled tart dough from the refrigerator. Lightly flour the counter.

2 Using a rolling pin, gently roll out the dough, working from the center toward the edges. Maintain equal pressure on both ends of the rolling pin to assure even thickness. Roll the dough out into a round about ¹/₄ inch thick and about 13 inches in diameter. (This size gives you enough to overlap the tart ring.) If you want a quick way to measure the thickness, ¹/₄ inch is about 50 pages of a book.

3 Place the tart ring over a cookie sheet. (Butter the part of the cookie sheet that is covered with the tart ring.) Now you're ready to pick up the tart dough.

4 Place the rolling pin on one edge of the dough. Lift the edge of the dough onto the rolling pin. Then roll back the rolling pin to pick up all of the dough — it's sort of like rolling up a carpet with a giant rolling pin inside. Then you roll the dough back out over a tart ring.

5 Lift the edge of the tart dough that is hanging over the edge of the ring so that gravity lowers the center dough into the bottom of the plate. With your fingers, press the dough into the corners of the ring. The lip of the ring should have about an inch or two overlap.

6 Using scissors, cut off the ragged edges of the overhanging dough. Use your fingers to crimp the dough on the lip of the ring into fluted or crimped edges all around.

7 Poke the bottom of the dough with a fork all over. This is to prevent the dough from shrinking.

8 Bake for 15 minutes. Remove from oven and pour the chocolate filling into the chocolate tart shell and refrigerate for a minimum of 30 minutes, if serving immediately. If serving later, remove from refrigerator 2 hours prior to serving.

9 Before serving, chop the almonds and sprinkle them over the top of the tart.

Chocolate Fudge

Tools: *Candy thermometer, 8 x 8-inch pan*

Preparation time: *10 minutes*

Baking Time: *None*

Yield: *16 servings*

2 ounces bittersweet chocolate

2 cups (12 ounces) sugar

³/₄ cup (6 ounces) milk

2 tablespoons light corn syrup

1 tablespoon salad oil

¹/₈ cup (1 ounce or ¹/₄ stick) butter, cut into pieces

1 teaspoon vanilla extract

1 Place the chocolate, sugar, milk, and corn syrup in a heavy pot and set over low heat, stirring slowly. Bring to a boil and boil for 3 minutes. Using a candy thermometer, bring to 234°.

2 Remove from heat and allow to cool 10 minutes. While waiting, use the salad oil to grease the 8 x 8-inch pan. Add the butter and vanilla extract and stir until the mixture thickens. Pour into the oiled pan and when cooled to room temperature (30 minutes), cut into 2-inch squares and serve.

Part VIII
Appendixes

The 5th Wave By Rich Tennant

"Anyone for more caramel upside-down cake?"

In this part . . .

Not quite sure what it means to whisk? Then check out Appendix A, your handy guide to desserts terminology.

Appendix B lists common substitutions, abbreviations, and equivalents. And in Appendix C, you find out where to order hard-to-find equipment and ingredients.

Appendix A

Glossary of Common Dessert and Baking Terms

Almond paste: A mixture of finely ground almonds and sugar.

Bain-marie: A large open container, partially filled with hot water, that holds a smaller pan for gentle heating.

Batter: An uncooked, semiliquid mixture, usually containing beaten eggs, flour, liquid, and a leavening ingredient, such as baking soda or baking powder, that rises when cooked.

Beat: To mix ingredients briskly in a circular motion so that they become smooth and creamy. A hundred hand-beaten strokes generally equal one minute with an electric mixer (if you're the type who counts these things).

Blanch: To plunge vegetables or fruits into boiling water for less than a minute to loosen their skin or preserve their color.

Blend: To mix or combine two or more ingredients with a spoon, whisk, spatula, or electric mixer.

Bloom: A surface film that appears when chocolate hasn't been correctly stored. Sugar bloom, where moisture collects on the surface and develops a white fuzz, occurs when chocolate has been exposed to damp conditions. Fat bloom, gray-white blotches and streaks, appears when chocolate has been stored in a warm place.

Boil: To bring the temperature of a liquid to 212°, causing bubbles to break at the surface.

Cake flour: A fine white flour made from soft wheat. Used for extra light and delicate texture in cakes and pastries.

Caramelize: To heat sugar until it melts into a syrupy state that ranges from golden to dark brown in color (320° to 350° on a candy thermometer).

Charlotte: A molded dessert served either hot or cold. As a cold dessert, it's made of Bavarian cream or other cream in a special mold, usually lined with ladyfingers.

Chiffon cake: A cake that attains its light, airy texture from its batter — whipped egg whites folded into flour, egg yolks, and oil.

Clarify: To remove solids from an item, usually butter, by melting it so that the solids float to the top and at the same time sink to the bottom. You discard those solids to create clarified butter, which can be put in a very hot pan without burning.

Coagulation: The process by which proteins become firm, usually when heated. For example, a soft egg yolk hardens when cooked.

Cocoa butter: The fat found in all natural chocolate that may be removed during processing.

Cocoa powder: A dry powder that remains after the cocoa butter is removed from chocolate liquor.

Compote: Fruit cooked in a sugar syrup.

Confectioners' sugar: A fine powdered sugar cut with cornstarch that's used for cake icings or to powder cakes and cookies. Also called powdered sugar.

Coulis: A fruit or vegetable purée, used as a sauce.

Crème anglaise: A vanilla custard sauce made of milk, sugar, and egg yolks. Used with fruit combinations or steamed puddings.

Custard: A mixture consisting of eggs, milk or cream, sugar, and flavorings that thickens or sets (because of the eggs) when cooked.

Cut in: To blend fats into dry ingredients with two knives, a pastry blender, or by hand, forming a coarse, crumbly texture similar to cornmeal.

Double boiler: A nested pot where the bottom pot is filled with just enough water so that the top portion doesn't touch it. A double boiler cooks with steam that never goes above water's boiling point, 212°. A double boiler is often used to melt baking chocolate and warm egg-based sauces.

Dredge: To roll something in dry, powdery ingredients.

Dry: A product condition caused by low liquid content or a too high baking temperature.

Dust: To sprinkle or shake (through a sieve) fine, powdery ingredients (such as flour, sugar, or nuts) over a surface.

Emulsion: Achieving a uniform consistency when mixing two immiscible substances — for example, oil and vinegar.

Film: A thin covering that forms on the surface of cooked custard when exposed to air.

Fold: To combine a light mixture, such as beaten egg whites, with a heavier mixture, such as whipped cream or sugared egg yolks, by using a gentle turning motion with a spatula.

Frothy: Showing a surface of light, foamy bubbles.

Ganache: A rich cream made of sweet chocolate and heavy cream.

Garnish: A decoration either on the dessert itself or on the plate.

Gelatinization: The process by which starch granules absorb water and swell in size. References to the gelatin product pertain to unflavored gelatin, not sweetened gelatin mixes.

Génoise: A light, layered sponge cake containing eggs, sugar, melted butter, and flour.

Glaze: A shiny coating, such as a sugar syrup or fruit glaze, applied to food. Gives a shine to baked products and prevents drying.

Gluten: An elastic substance present in flours that gives structure, elasticity, and strength to baked products.

Granité: An Italian ice consisting of water, sugar, and flavoring (usually fruit juice or coffee) that is scraped repeatedly during freezing to achieve a crystallized texture.

Grate: To make thin, flakelike particles by scraping food (like lemon or fruit) against a grater.

Italian meringue: A dense and resilient meringue in which a boiled sugar syrup is slowly beaten into stiff egg whites. Used mostly for frozen soufflés.

Ladyfinger: A delicate sponge cookie that's also used in various desserts, including tiramisu and charlottes.

Leavener: A leavener simply leavens, or inflates, a cake by producing gas in the batter.

Lekvar: A special type of jam used for cake and pastry fillings such as strudels or Hamantaschen (a traditional triangular-shaped Jewish cookie served over the Purim holiday). Lekvar generally consists of a fruit (such as apricot or prune), sugar, citric acid, and pectin. The texture is thicker than regular jam, which prevents it from oozing during the baking process.

Liaison: To build or thicken a substance, such as starch, egg yolks and/or heavy cream, with another.

Macerate: To soak fruit in a liquid — usually a liqueur, wine, or sugar syrup.

Marinade: A seasoned mixture, usually a liquid, in which food is moistened and flavored before cooking.

Meringue: A thick, white foam made of whipped egg whites and sugar.

Net weight: The weight of the total contents of a can or package, minus the package.

Nougat: A candy made of caramelized sugar and almonds or other nuts. Hard nougat is used as decorative work for cakes and desserts and, when finely ground, as a confection and flavoring.

Parfait: A layered frozen dessert made of ice cream and ribboned with syrups, sauces, or fruit and nut fillings.

Pastry cream: A thick custard sauce containing eggs and starch.

Pastry flour: A low-gluten flour used for pastries and cookies.

Pâte à choux: A crisp, light pastry that, when cooked, has a hole in the center that can be filled with various sweet fillings (for example, eclairs and cream puffs).

Pâte feuilletée: French name for puff pastry. The dough is folded (or turned) many times with butter so that it rises and creates a light, layered, flaky pastry.

Petit four: A finger-food cake or pastry.

Phyllo: Crispy, flaky, paper-thin dough layers, often used in Greek and Middle Eastern desserts as well as in savory dishes.

Pipe out: To squeeze soft batter or other substance out of a cone-shaped canvas bag onto baking pans into desired forms.

Pith: The white spongy tissue between outer skin and the pulp of citrus.

Poach: To cook foods slowly in simmering liquid.

Pot de crème: A French chocolate custard made with heavy cream and chocolate, traditionally baked in a little pot or ramekin.

Praline: A hardened candy made of caramelized sugar and nuts (usually pecans, almonds, or hazelnuts).

Puff pastry: See **pâte feuilletée.**

Punching: Deflating a dough after it has risen by pulling up dough on all sides, folding it to the center, and pressing down. Punching redistributes the yeast and equalizes the temperature throughout the dough.

Purée: To mash or grind food into a paste by forcing it through a food mill or a sieve or by whirling in a food processor or a blender.

Reduce: To rapidly boil a liquid, such as wine, stock, or sauce, to evaporate water and decrease its original volume so that it thickens and concentrates in flavor.

Refresh: To cool hot food quickly, either by holding under running water or by plunging it into iced water.

Ribbon: Used to describe batters and other thick mixtures. A batter forms ribbons when a little is poured back onto their shape and the ribbons hold — meaning the batter is very thick.

Rind: The firm outer covering of fruit.

Royal icing: A simple icing of confectioners' sugar, egg whites, and lemon. Used to decorate cakes and cookies.

Sabayon: A smooth, creamy dessert sauce made with egg yolks, sugar, and kirsch or Madeira. Served warm or at room temperature over poached fruit.

Sauté: To cook food quickly in a small amount of fat, usually butter or oil, over very high heat.

Score: To make slashes across a surface, forming a crisscross pattern.

Sherbet: A frozen dessert of sugar syrup and fruit purée enriched with milk, cream, or egg whites.

Sift: To shake dry ingredients, such as flour or confectioners' sugar, through a fine mesh sifter to incorporate air and make them lighter.

Simmer: To cook gently in a liquid, just below the boiling point or just until tiny bubbles begin to break the surface (at about 185°).

Simple syrup: A syrup consisting of sugar and water in varying proportions.

Skim: To remove with a spoon the fat and bits of food that rise to the surface of a liquid.

Soft peaks: Egg whites or cream whipped to a frothy and soft state with rounded peaks.

Sorbet: A frozen mixture made of fruit juice, water, and sugar.

Soufflé: A baked dessert containing a flavored egg yolk base blended with whipped egg whites that cause it to puff up while cooking.

Sponge cake: A cake based on whipped eggs, sugar, and flour.

Spun sugar: Boiled sugar made into long, thin threads by a special technique. This mass of fine strands is used to decorate cakes.

Stabilize: To fortify a delicate substance like beaten egg whites or whipped cream with an ingredient that strengthens it.

Steam: To cook over a small amount of simmering or boiling water in a covered pan.

Steep: To soak food, usually in a hot liquid, in order to soften and/or to extract flavors.

Stiff meringue: Egg whites and sugar whipped to a light, firm mass.

Stiff peaks: Egg whites whipped until they form sharp peaks that stand on their own.

Stirring: To agitate the batter with a wooden spoon in a back and forth motion of varying intensity and length of time.

Streusel: A crumbly topping for baked goods consisting of a butter, sugar, and flour mixture.

Strudel: Refers both to a paper-thin dough and to a baked item consisting of filling that is rolled up in a sheet of strudel or phyllo dough.

Temper: To make chocolate more malleable and glossy. A quick version involves melting it to 120°, cooling it, and then reheating.

Vacherin: A large meringue shell or container that can be filled with ice cream or fruit.

Weeping: To exude liquid, as when uncooked beaten egg whites break down from standing or when meringues are tightly covered.

Well: A hole or depression in the center of dry ingredients.

Whip: To beat air into ingredients with a whisk or electric beater to make them light and fluffy.

Whisk: A handheld wire kitchen utensil, used to whip ingredients like eggs, cream, and sauces. When used as a verb, the term whisk describes the process of whipping or blending ingredients together with a wire whisk.

Zest: The pared skin (only the colored part) of citrus.

Appendix B

Common Substitutions, Abbreviations, and Equivalents

• •

*N*ext time you have have an occasion — and we all have them — when a particular ingredient can't be found, refer to this appendix. Some ingredients are almost always interchangeable. For example, you can substitute almonds for walnuts in baked breads and muffins, or light cream for half and half.

But sometimes, there is no acceptable substitution for an ingredient. Other times, the substitution is very exact and specific, or the result is disastrous. This is most often the case for baked goods where you need to follow a formula to produce a cake, soufflé, pastry, or bread with the perfect height, density, and texture.

Most of the following substitutions are for emergency situations only — when you've run out of an essential ingredient and need a very specific replacement.

The following substitutions can save your day.

For flour:

- 1 cup (250 mL) minus 2 tablespoons (30 mL) sifted all-purpose flour = 1 cup (250 mL) sifted cake flour

- 1 cup (250 mL) plus 2 tablespoons (30 mL) sifted cake flour = 1 cup (250mL) sifted all-purpose flour

- 1 cup (250 mL) sifted self-rising flour = 1 cup (250mL) sifted all-purpose flour plus $1^1/_4$ teaspoons (6 mL) baking powder and a pinch of salt

For dairy:

- 1 cup (250 mL) skim milk = 1 cup (250 mL) = water plus $^1/_4$ cup (50 mL) nonfat powdered milk *or* $^1/_2$ cup (125 mL) evaporated skim milk plus $^1/_2$ cup (125 mL) water

- 1 cup (250 mL) sour cream = 1 cup (250 mL) plain yogurt

For eggs:

- 2 egg yolks = 1 egg for thickening sauces and custards
- 4 extra-large eggs = 5 large eggs or 6 small eggs

For sweeteners:

- 1 cup (250 mL) sugar = 1 cup (250 mL) molasses (or honey) plus ¹/₂ teaspoon (2 mL) baking soda
- 1 cup (250 mL) brown sugar = 1 cup (250 mL) white sugar plus 1¹/₂ tablespoons (22 mL) molasses

Miscellaneous:

- 1 tablespoon (15 mL) crème fraîche = 1 teaspoon (5 mL) nonfat powdered milk plus 2 tablespoons heavy cream
- 1 cup (250 mL) fine bread crumbs = ³/₄ cup (175 mL) cracker crumbs
- 1 square (1 ounce/28 g) unsweetened chocolate = 3 tablespoons (45 mL) cocoa plus 1 tablespoon (15 mL) butter, margarine, or vegetable shortening
- 1 ounce (28 g) semisweet chocolate = 3 tablespoons (45 mL) cocoa plus 2 tablespoons (30 mL) butter, margarine, or vegetable shortening plus 3 tablespoons (45 mL) sugar
- 1 vanilla bean (split lengthwise to expose inner seeds) = 1 teaspoon (5 mL) pure vanilla extract

Although we spell out nonmetric measurements in this book, many cookbooks use abbreviations. Table B-1 lists common abbreviations and what they stand for.

Table B-1	Common Abbreviations
Abbreviation	*What It Stands For*
C, c	cup
g	gram
kg	kilogram
L, l	liter
lb	pound
mL, ml	milliliter
oz	ounce

Abbreviation	What It Stands For
pt	pint
t, tsp	teaspoon
T, TB, Tbl, Tbsp	tablespoon

Cookbook writers have a penchant for practical jokes. Just when you're getting the hang of cups and tablespoons, they throw you a recipe in ounces and pounds. Tables B-2 and B-3 list common equivalent measures. All measurements are for level amounts. Note that some metric measurements are approximate.

Table B-2	Conversion Secrets	
This Measurement	**Equals This Measurement**	**Equals This Metric Measurement**
Pinch or dash	$1/4$ teaspoon	0.5 mL
3 teaspoons	1 tablespoon	15 mL
2 tablespoons	1 fluid ounce	30 mL
1 jigger	$1^1/_2$ fluid ounces	45 mL
4 tablespoons	$1/4$ cup	60 mL
5 tablespoons plus 1 teaspoon	$1/3$ cup	75 mL
8 tablespoons	$1/2$ cup	125 mL
16 tablespoons	1 cup	250 mL
1 cup	8 fluid ounces	250 mL
2 cups	1 pint or 16 fluid ounces	500 mL
2 pints	1 quart or 32 fluid ounces	1 L
4 quarts	1 gallon	4 L

Table B-3	Food Equivalents	
This Measurement	*Equals This Measurement*	*Equals This Metric Measurement*
3 medium apples or bananas	approximately 1 pound	500 g
1 ounce baking chocolate	1 square	28 g
2 slices bread	1 cup fresh bread crumbs	250 mL
1 pound brown sugar	2$\frac{1}{4}$ cups packed	550 mL packed
4 tablespoons butter	$\frac{1}{2}$ stick	50 to 60 mL
8 tablespoons butter	1 stick	125 mL
4 sticks butter or margarine	1 pound	454 g
6 ounces chocolate chips	1 cup	250 mL
1 pound confectioners' sugar	4$\frac{1}{2}$ cups sifted	1.125 L sifted
1 pound granulated sugar	2 cups	500 mL
$\frac{1}{2}$ pound hard cheese (such as cheddar)	approximately 2 cups grated	500 mL grated
1 cup heavy whipping cream	2 cups whipped	500 mL whipped
1 medium lemon	3 tablespoons juice 2 to 3 teaspoons grated lemon peel or orange peel	45 mL juice, 10 to 15 mL peel
4 ounces nuts, chopped	approximately 1 cup	150 ml chopped
1 cup converted rice	4 cups cooked	1 L cooked
1 pint strawberries	approximately 2 cups, sliced	500 mL sliced
1 pound all-purpose flour	4 cups sifted	1 L sifted
5 large whole eggs	1 cup	250 mL

Table B-4 lists the common temperature conversions.

Table B-4	Temperature Conversions
°F	**°C**
250	120
275	135
300	150
325	160
350	175
375	190
400	205
425	220
450	230
475	245
500	260

Table B-5	Common Metric Conversions	
Actual Volume	*Avoirdupois Equivalent Weight*	*Convenient Metric*
Liquid Weight Equivalents		
1 teaspoon	.16 ounce	5 mL
1 tablespoon	.5 ounce	15 mL
2 tablespoons	1 ounce	30 mL
1/4 cup	2 ounces	60 mL
1/2 cup	4 ounces	120 mL
3/4 cup	6 ounces	180 mL
1 cup	8 ounces	240 mL
2 cups	1 pint	480 mL
4 cups	1 quart	1 liter
Dry Weight Equivalents		
flour sifted, 1 teaspoon	.083 ounce	3 grams
grated cheese or chopped nuts, 1 tablespoon	.25 ounce	7 grams
1/4 cup	1 ounce	30 grams
1/2 cup	2 ounces	60 grams
3/4 cup	3 ounces	85 grams
1 cup	4 ounces	115 grams
sugar, 1 teaspoon	.14 ounce	5 grams
dried beans or uncooked rice, 1 tablespoon	.42 ounce	15 grams
1/4 cup	1.68 ounce	50 grams
1/2 cup	3.36 ounces	100 grams
3/4 cup	5.04 ounces	150 grams
1 cup	6.72 ounces	200 grams
butter, 1 teaspoon	.16 ounce	5 grams
1 tablespoon	.5 ounce	15 grams
1/4 cup	2 ounces	60 grams
1/2 cup	4 ounces	115 grams
3/4 cup	6 ounces	170 grams
1 cup	8 ounces	230 grams

Mail-Order Sources for Equipment and Ingredients

● ●

Mail-Order Sources for Kitchen Equipment

These kitchenware stores carry all the dessert-making and baking equipment you need.

East Coast

Bridge Kitchenware
214 East 52nd Street
New York, NY 10022
phone 212-838-6746, fax 212-758-5387
E-mail: s.bridge@ix.netcom.com
Web site: www.Bridgekitchenware.com
Catalog available: $3 charge applicable toward first purchase. European-imported cooking utensils, bakeware, cutlery, and porcelain.

Broadway Panhandler
520 Broadway
New York, NY 10012
phone 212-966-3434, fax 212-966-9017
No catalog available. Kitchen equipment includes cookware, bakeware, pastry-making equipment, cake-decorating tools, appliances (includes ice-cream machines), cookbooks, linens, and knives.

Cooktique
9 West Railroad Avenue
Tenafly, NJ 07670
phone 201-568-7990, fax 201-568-6480
E-mail: Cooktique@msn
No catalog available. Kitchen equipment includes bakeware, cookware, gadgets, pastry-making equipment and tools. Carries specialty ingredients, such as baking chocolate (Callebaut), Dutch-processed cocoa, candied roses and violets, crystallized ginger, flavored extracts, and assorted nuts.

Dean & DeLuca, Inc.
560 Broadway
New York, NY 10012
phone 212-431-1691 or 800-221-7714 (mail-order), fax 800-781-4050
Web site: www.dean-deluca.com
Catalog available: $3 charge applicable toward first purchase. Kitchen equipment includes cookware, bakeware, pastry-making equipment, and cutting and garnishing tools.

La Cuisine–The Cook's Resource
323 Cameron Street
Alexandria, VA 22314
phone 703-836-4435 or 800-521-1176 (toll-free in Canada and U.S.),
fax 703 836-8925
E-Mail: lacusine@vmcs.com
Web site: www.vmcs.com/lacuisine
Free catalog available upon request. Kitchen equipment includes classic cookware, bakeware, and pastry-making supplies.

Lamalle Kitchenware
36 West 25th Street
New York, NY 10010
phone 212-242-0750 or 800-660-0750, fax 212-645-2996
Free catalog available upon request. Smallwares: Pots, pans, and pastry tools imported mostly from France and Italy.

New York Cake and Baking Center
56 West 22nd Street
New York, NY 10010
phone 212-675-2253, fax 212-675-7099
Catalog available: $3 charge. Bakeware, pastry-making equipment imported from France, and cake decorating items.

Zabar's
2245 Broadway
New York, NY 10024
phone 212-787-2000/2003 or 800-697-6301 (mail-order), fax 212-580-4477
Free catalog available upon request. Note: Everything in the store is available by mail-order. Kitchenware including cookware, bakeware, appliances (mixers, food processors), and pastry-making tools (pastry tips and sieves).

Midwest

The Chef's Catalog
3215 Commercial Avenue
Northbrook, IL 60062
phone 847-480-9400 or 800-338-3232 (mail-order), fax 800 967-3291
E-mail: chefscat@aol.com
Web site: www.chefscatalog.com
Free catalog available upon request. Kitchen equipment includes cookware, cutlery, bakeware, small electric appliances, ice cream machines, and limited home/living items.

Sweet Celebrations
14150 Nicollet Avenue
Burnsville, MN 55337
phone 800-328-6722, fax 612-943-1688
Free catalog available upon request. Cake decorating and candy-making tools and equipment.

Wilton Enterprises, Inc.
2240 West 75th Street
Woodbridge, IL 60517
phone 603-963-7100 or 800-772-7111 or 800-794-5755 (mail-order)
Free catalog available through mail-order division. Specialty ingredients such as flavored extracts, meringue powder, gum paste, and cake decorating items such as edible glitter, ready-to-use fondants, icing colors, and mixes.

West Coast

Jane's Cakes and Chocolates
2331 Honolulu Avenue
Montrose, CA 91020
phone 818-957-2511 or 800-262-7630 (mail-order)
Free catalog available upon request. Kitchen equipment includes bakeware, candy-making equipment, and cake decorating tools including pastry tips, bags, silver and gold dragées.

The Chef's Store
836 Traction Avenue
Los Angeles, CA 90013
phone 213-617-2963 or 888-334-CHEF (toll-free)
E-mail: chef@chefstore.com
Web site: www.chefstore.com
Catalog available Fall 1997: $5 applicable toward first purchase. Carries kitchen equipment for the professional and home baker: tableware, cookware, pastry-making tools, and equipment (pastry tips and cones).

Sur La Table
84 Pine Street
Seattle, WA 98101
phone 206-448-2244, fax: 206-448-2245
90 Central Way, Kirkland, WA 98033; phone 425-827-1311
1806 4th Street, Berkeley, CA 94710; phone 510-849-2252
77 Maiden Lane, San Francisco, CA 94108; phone 415-732-7900
Toll Free: 800-240-0853 or 800-243-0852 (Catalog)
Free catalog available upon request. Kitchen equipment and tools including bakeware, small appliances, mixers, molds, five types of ice cream machines (including hand-cranked Donvier), and crêpe pans.

National retailers

Bullocks/Macy's
P.O. Box 8098
Mason, OH 45040-8098
phone 800-622-9748 (mail-order)
Free catalog available. Kitchen equipment includes bakeware, cookware, earthenware, mixers, and pastry decorating tools.

Crate and Barrel
P.O. Box 9059
Wheeling, IL 60090
phone 800-323-5461 (mail-order)
Free catalog available. Kitchen equipment includes bakeware, cookware, and earthenware.

Williams-Sonoma
P.O. Box 7456
San Francisco, CA 94120-7456
phone 800-541-2233 (mail-order) or 800-541-1262 (customer service), fax 415-421-5153
Free catalog available at the store. Kitchen equipment, includes bakeware, cookware, earthenware, mixers, and pastry decorating tools.

Mail-Order Sources for Baking Products

California

Ghirardelli Chocolate
South Coast Plaza
3333 Bristol Street
Costa Mesa, CA 92626
phone 888-402-6282 (mail-order) or 800-877-9338 (corporate office, but you can get product info here as well), fax 714-444-1578 (mail-order)
Free catalog available upon request. Carries six types of baking chocolate including bittersweet, semisweet, milk, sweet dark, unsweetened, and white. Also have chocolate chips and ground chocolate that can be used as sweetened cocoa for either baking or hot chocolate.

Jane's Cakes and Chocolates
2331 Honolulu Avenue
Montrose, CA 91020
818-957-2511 or 800-262-7630 (mail-order)
Free catalog available upon request. Hard to find ingredients include imported baking chocolate (Callebaut), melting chocolate (Merken), superfine sugar, pastry flour, candied fruit, cake fillings, flavored extracts, candy oils, candied flowers, decorative cake ornaments, Magic Line paste colors, gum paste, meringue powder, and petal dust.

Connecticut

Hauser Chocolatier, Inc.
18 Taylor Avenue
Bethel, CT 06801
phone: 203-794-1861 or 800-5-HAUSER (toll-free mail-order number)
Free catalog available upon request. Carries Hauser's baking chocolate, available in dark, milk, and white chocolates. Also available are cocoa butter and cocoa powder.

Minnesota

Sweet Celebrations
14150 Nicollet Avenue
Burnsville, MN 55337
phone 800-328-6722, fax 612-943-1688
Free catalog available upon request. Limited specialty ingredients include flours, flavor extracts, and chocolate for candy-making.

New Jersey

Cooktique
9 West Railroad Avenue
Tenafly, NJ 07670
phone 201-568-7990, fax 201-568-6480
E-mail: Cooktique@msn
No catalog available. Kitchen equipment includes bakeware, cookware, gadgets, pastry-making equipment, and tools. Carries specialty ingredients, such as baking chocolate (Callebaut), Dutch-processed cocoa, candied roses and violets, crystallized ginger, flavored extracts, and assorted nuts.

New York

Bazzini, A.L. Co., Inc.
339 Greenwich Street
New York, NY 10013
phone 212-334-1280 or 800-228-0172 (outside NY state), fax 212-941-5840
Free catalog available upon request. Selection of fresh roasted nuts, dried fruit, specialty flours, and nougat paste.

Broadway Panhandler
520 Broadway
New York, NY 10012
phone 212-966-3434, fax 212-966-9017
No catalog available. Specialty ingredients available include dried egg whites, meringue powder, gum paste, vegetable gums and gum arabic, confectionary gloss, and confectionary solvent.

Chocolatier Magazine
45 West 34th Street, Suite 600
New York, NY 10001
phone 212-239-0855 or 815-734-1109 (customer service, subscriptions), fax 212-967-4184
E-mail: chocmag@aol.com
A good source for specific chocolate-related questions.

Dean & DeLuca, Inc.
560 Broadway
New York, NY 10012
phone 212-431-1691 or 800-221-7714 (mail-order), or fax 800-781-4050
Web site: www.dean-deluca.com
Catalog available: $3 charge refundable on first purchase. Carries imported

baking chocolates (Valrhona), specialty flours, and vanillas.

Economy Candy Market

108 Rivington Street (between Ludlow & Essex streets)
New York, NY 10002
phone 212-254-1531 or 800-352-4544 (toll-free outside NY state)
Free catalog available upon request. Limited selection of specialty ingredients includes cocoa, baking chocolate (Lindt, Tobler, American Baking Chocolate), spices, glazed fruits, assorted dried fruits, and nuts. Purchases of chocolate and spices are by the pound.

La Maison 8 Du Chocolat

25 East 73rd Street
New York, NY 10021
phone 212-744-7117
Free catalog available upon request. Carries primarily fine au couture eating chocolates, but cocoa powder and baking chocolate are made in-house (imported from Paris).

Maison Glass Delicacies

P.O. Box 317H
Scarsdale, NY 10583-8817
phone 914-725-1662 or 800-822-5564, fax 914-725-1663
Catalog available: $5 charge. Specialty ingredients include nuts, dried fruits, glacé fruits, praline paste, baking chocolate, chestnut flour, spices, extracts, syrups, honeys, and preserves.

The Sweet Life

63 Hester Street
New York, NY 10002
phone 212-598-0092
No catalog available. Wide range of hard-to-find specialty ingredients available including assorted dried fruits and nuts, Belgian baking chocolate (Callebaut), candied fruits, crystallized flowers (roses, violets), flavor extracts, nut pastes (almond and hazelnut), apricot and prune lekvar (for pastry fillings), syrups, honeys, ground poppy seed and sesame seed, homemade caramel, and battons (filling for pain du chocolate).

Zabar's

2245 Broadway
New York, NY 10024
phone 212-787-2000/2003 or 800-697-6301 (mail-order), fax 212-580-4477
Free catalog available upon request. *Note:* Everything in the store is available by mail order. Specialty ingredients include an assortment of baking chocolates, flavor extracts, assorted nuts, and dried fruits.

Vermont

King Arthur Flour
The Baker's Catalogue
P.O. Box 1010 Route 5 South
Norwich, VT 05055
phone 800-827-6836, fax 800-343-3002
E-mail: info@kingarthurflour.com
Web site: www.kingarthurflour.com
Catalog is available. Carries ingredients such as specialty flours, a wide range of sweeteners, decorative sugars, leavening agents, baking chocolate, extracts, flavored oils, dried nuts, and spices. Equipment includes hard-to-find baking utensils and pans.

Virginia

La Cuisine – The Cook's Resource
323 Cameron Street
Alexandria, VA 22314
phone 703-836-4435 or 800-521-1176 (toll-free in Canada and U.S.),
fax 703-836-8925
E-mail: lacuisine@vmcs.com
Web site: www.vmcs.com/lacuisine
Free catalog available. Specialty ingredients such as baking chocolate, flavor extracts, flours, and dried and candied fruits and nuts are available.

Wisconsin

Penzey's Spice House, Ltd.
1912 S. West Avenue
Waukesha, WI 53186
phone 414-574-0277, fax 414-574-0278
Free catalog available. Carries a whole range of spices for baking, such as nutmeg, cloves, vanilla beans, ginger, and cocoa. Also has flavored extracts such as almond, orange, and vanilla.

International

Chocvic
phone: 1-888-IFC-CHOC, fax 770-343-8458
E-mail: IFC@mindspring.com
Web site: www.chocovic.es
New chocolate couvertures from Barcelona, Spain. For use in recipes such as mousses, cakes, truffles, and icings. Includes varietal line (three chocolates made with three different types of cocoa beans from specific regions of Venezuela, Grenada, and Ecuador), blended chocolates, compound coating, chocolate flakes, frozen truffles, hollow truffle shells, and other specialties.

If you want to make a gingerbread house, cut out these stencils. Or, if you don't want to cut up your book, place wax paper over the stencils, trace them, and cut out. See Chapter 16 for the recipe and detailed instructions.

front door

cut 2

front
and
back

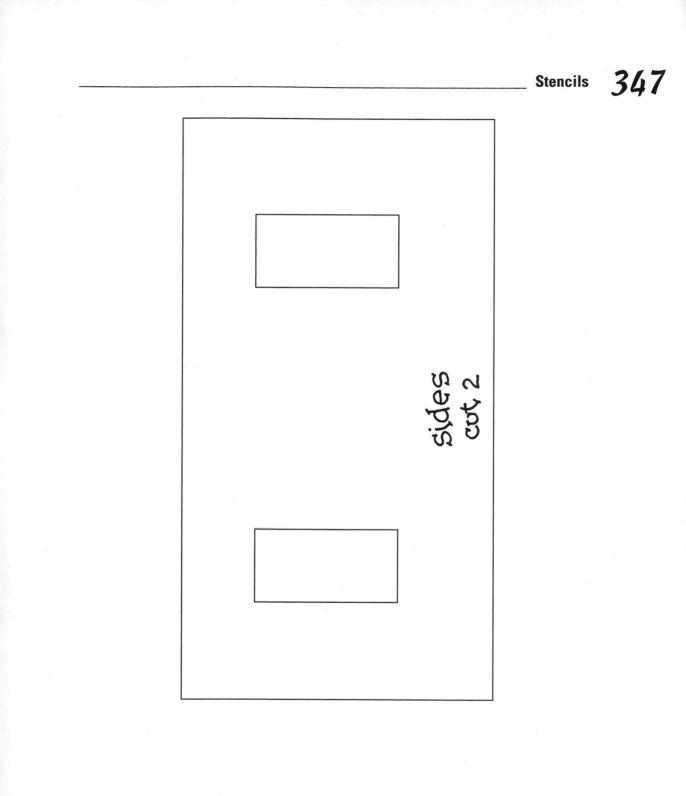

sides
cut 2

roof
cut 2

Index

●●●

(continued)

(continued)

(continued)

Notes

Notes

Notes

Notes

IDG BOOKS WORLDWIDE BOOK REGISTRATION